COMING OUT LIKE A PORN STAR

ESSAYS ON PORNOGRAPHY, PROTECTION, AND PRIVACY

Edited by Jiz Lee

Foreword by Dr. Mireille Miller-Young

ThreeL Media | Berkeley

Published by
ThreeL Media | Stone Bridge Press
P. O. Box 8208, Berkeley, CA 94707
www.threelmedia.com

Cover design by Jamee Baiser. Illustration based on photography credited to: Courtney Trouble, Jiz Lee, Karma Pervs.

Book design and layout by Linda Ronan.

Copy Edited by Lauren Manoy.

Republishing permissions: Some stories in this collection were previously published and are reprinted with permission. "Liabilities and My Mother" by Ashley Blue appeared in GIRL-VERT *(Rare Birds Press). Jesse Jackman's "Hi Mom, I'm a Porn Star" originally appeared in* Huffington Post. *Jackman's essay "Job Security" originally appeared on his blog at JessieJackmanXX.com. "How They React" by Zak Sabbath appeared in* We Did Porn *(Tin House Books).*

CONTENTS

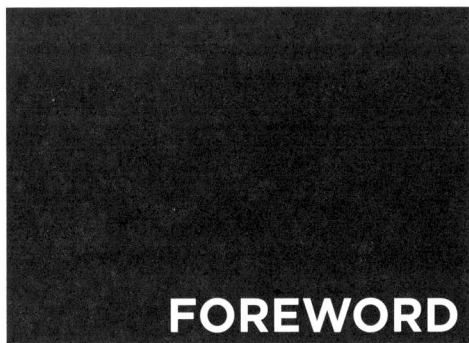

FOREWORD

Dr. Mireille Miller-Young

Dr. Mireille Miller-Young is associate professor of feminist studies at the University of California, Santa Barbara. She is the coeditor of The Feminist Porn Book: The Politics of Producing Pleasure, *and the author of* A Taste for Brown Sugar: Black Women in Pornography.

What does it mean to come out? Where do we come from, and at what place do we arrive? Coming out has been one of the central issues for the gay rights movement. The idea of "coming out of the shadows" became a rallying point for gays, lesbians, transvestites, and transgender folks in the 1960s who were fed up with the oppression of silence, denial, police raids, violence, and discriminatory laws that shaped their everyday lives. The famous Stonewall Riots of 1969, and other lesser known uprisings like the one at Compton Cafeteria 1966 in San Francisco's Tenderloin, marked the mounting awareness and activism of a new generation of queer people who did not wish or were not able to keep their sexual and gender identities and expressions "in the closet." They bravely defied abuse by eschewing the tactics previous generations of queer people employed to survive harassment. They became radical, outspoken advocates for the right to be "out and proud," and used their visibility—whether chosen or forced—to build a movement that would change the face of the nation.

Nowadays, in the age of colorblindness that refuses to acknowledge the abuse of our racial caste system, we also face the unwillingness to see sexual hierarchies and sexualized violence, which are endemic to our society. Here, I do not intend to draw an equivalency between racism, sexism, and homophobic repression, or the movements to end them, but to say that these oppressive forces overlap and intersect in important ways. We do not see the absolutely vital ways that sexual difference matters, the abiding injustice of sexual criminalization, or the everyday struggles of sexual minorities, and how all of these function alongside and through race, gender, ability, age, and citizenship status. But some of us are pulling back the blinders and claiming visibility as a tactic for gaining freedom. That is the story of *Coming Out Like a Porn Star*. The authors in this volume are, like their brave foreparents, coming out about their participation in one of the most vilified industries on the planet: porn.

In some ways the porn industry is viewed as more evil than Big Oil, Big Tobacco, or Big Pharma. The porn industry is not simply seen as an agent of rapacious greed that destroys our health and our environment. Porn is perceived as the cause of our modern cultural decline, the trafficker of thousands of innocent women and girls, and the purveyor of a rampant and misogynist prurience that is infecting the minds our youth. The sex panic around porn is, of course, convenient. It distracts from the more complex questions of what kind of sexual morality should be embraced in today's democratic nations, why so many people choose to work in the sex industry instead of more acceptable arenas for labor, and how exactly youth come to gain an education about sex and sexuality in the age of abstinence-only instruction and the repeal of legal and monetary support for comprehensive sexual health resources and information.

This book is so valuable, right here and right now, precisely because of these large-scale battles over sexual access and rights taking place. It intervenes in the sex panic about porn by giving voice to the industry's workers. Carving through the problematic misrepresentations of porn workers as dupes complicit in their own exploitation, these voices expose how the heavy stigma of porn affects the performers' everyday lives, choices, and aspirations. The disgust and debasement lobbied at porn filters down to its workers. These voices sound off about the painful ways that porn performance can lead to estrangement from one's family and friends. Porn actors find that negotiating the potential disappointment and dismissal of loved ones is one of the most difficult aspects of the job. Facing the wrath or dismissal of employers and colleagues in the "straight" employment sector, outside of the sex industry, porn workers who come out put at risk current and future careers. They constantly face the question: to come out or not to come out?

Coming out as a porn star has critical consequences for one's relationships, one's sense of self and integrity, and one's livelihood and social mobility. Coming out means risking everything. Coming out is hard. I applaud the authors in this volume for speaking so honestly and eloquently about their decisions to come out or not to come out. They are both aware of the *privilege* of being able to come out—as opposed to street-based sex workers who we might say do not have that option—and the profound *injustice* of needing to decide whether to come out when this is not something that workers in other industries have to face. Lawyers do not have to come out, nor do tax agents, or those in any other reviled professions. Sex work is one of the only professions where workers must choose whether to admit their status, and if they do, are potentially subject to merciless harassment and stalking, the release of their personal data online, the loss of custody of their children, and the foreclosure of opportunities for other kinds of work.

Given these stakes, most porn workers choose discretion in their work. Some find power in their anonymity and invisibility, while others feel that their race or embodiment already mark them in ways that put them at risk of violence, hostility, and misrepresentation. Still others believe that we must transform larger ideological and social structures that present porn as shameful and dirty before we can ask its most vulnerable workers to subject themselves to harm by coming out. Yet a growing number find that coming out is a kind of rebellion, an extension of the insurgent attitudes many sex workers already hold towards conservative sexual norms, expectations, and regulations. They challenge the notion that porn labor is bad and should be hidden, and instead insist on openness, pride, and vocal resistance to the status quo.

Grappling with these choices and consequences, the authors of this book show the courage and resilience of porn's stars, and their deep political awareness. We must listen to their voices and learn from the experts. So, here for your reading pleasure, *Coming Out Like a Porn Star*, which is to say, with audacity, artfulness, wit, and warmth.

Mireille Miller-Young
Santa Barbara, June 2015

HOW TO COME OUT LIKE A PORN STAR: AN INTRODUCTION

Jiz Lee

Jiz Lee has worked in porn for over ten years, in more than 200 projects from six countries spanning independent, queer, and hardcore gonzo pornography. They are the recipient of multiple AVN and XBiz Award industry nominations and Feminist Porn Awards, and were featured as one of the inaugural honorees of The Trans 100. Jiz presented most recently at Princeton University, the American Studies Association Conference, and Wonderlust Helsinki (awarded by the Finnish Association for Sexology). They've been on MSNBC, Fox News, and proudly, Lifehacker. Jiz works behind the scenes at Pink & White Productions (CrashPadSeries.com, PinkLabel.tv) and fundraises for LGBTQ and sex worker-focused organizations through their erotic philanthropic art project, Karma Pervs. Their writing appears at JizLee.com and in the pages of The Feminist Porn Book, Genderqueer, *and* Best Sex Writing, *among others. They are also the coeditor of the* Porn Studies Journal Special Issue: Porn and Labour. *When not working in porn, Jiz is training for an IRONMAN 70.3.*

It all started with one ignored phone call from my dad.

You see, I'm a terrible liar and answering his phone call meant having to explain why I was across the world in Berlin. (Porn. I was there doing porn.) I let his call go to voicemail and slumped down on the ground. This wasn't one of those moments where I avoided a phone call because I was either too busy or just not in the mood to talk; that one, single act represented something much more profound and problematic. Jetlagged and defeated, I sat there on the floor, haunted with the realization that I was going to have to finally come out to my family about my other life in porn. How does one even begin to do that?

Coming Out Like a Porn Star started from the personal questions I asked fellow porn performers as I struggled with the reality of telling my family about my increasing involvement in the adult industry. Were others out to their parents? How did they talk about it to their siblings? What could I learn from their experiences? In asking the questions, I'd hit a nerve. *Everyone* had a story to tell. Some were heartbreaking, others casual. Some surprised and inspired me. Stories ranged from funny to fucked up. They taught me about stigma. They revealed privilege. Gave me relief. Made me furious. They encouraged my own process of coming out. Through their examples, I found myself more prepared.

I realized this topic was bigger than just myself. Sharing our coming out stories might not only help other performers like myself, but may also help people outside the industry relate to us, humanizing our experiences. What these stories have in common is their honesty. I saw them each as truths that existed far beyond the narrow moralistic debate of whether or not porn could be feminist or ethical, good or bad. The stories ran the gamut, embodying the very essence of the grey area we all exist within. The details varied differently, but each story revealed what I had long suspected: although society may think of porn performers as some sort of "damaged enemy against the moralistic good," it is actually the stigma from having performed that proves to do the greatest harm and is our largest obstacle. If we are to overcome these cultural roadblocks and gain rights for sex workers, it is precedent that we create a dialogue that stands firmly on the fact that people who chose to perform in porn are no different than anyone else. If all people are to achieve universal sexual, gender, and reproductive freedoms, it will be through the undoing of the very same stigmas, the sex shaming and victimization, that is found in porn and sex work at large. Hearing the stories from people I admired and respected gave me the strength to begin talking to my family and trying to undo stigmas of my own.

I had been performing in adult videos since 2005, but being in a "niche" queer porn genre, I'd dabbled through the early years in relative obscurity without feeling like I particularly needed to tell my family anything. Unless they actively sought it or a friend let something slip on Facebook, their chance of coming across me was virtually nil. As my career grew, so were the chances of them stumbling across my photo in a news article. This hobby of mine was getting serious, and so was the very real possibility of being outed to my family.

I was traveling for gigs. I had begun performing in Los Angeles, and I'd been featured on box covers. I was invited to speak at schools and was given awards in other countries! I was regularly contacted for interviews by mainstream press. Years later, when my stepmother would open her laptop to find me on the homepage of MSNBC, I'd exhaled the biggest sigh of relief that she already knew, was proud, and had my back. At the time, I'd been keeping all my porn adventures a secret. I'd been hiding all the excitement from some of the closest people in my life. I was keeping it from them almost as if I were ashamed of what I was doing, when in reality I was very proud. What was the real reason I was keeping this part of my life from my family? Why hadn't I kept them in the loop? When I received that phone call from my dad, I suddenly realized how far off the map I had drifted away from my family. This distance made me feel as if I had been living a double life. But if I didn't tell them soon, they would find out on their own. I made a sincere vow to tell my dad the next time we were together, in person.

It wasn't easy.

I love pornography. Porn is an extension of my own sexual expression, a blend of art and documentation. My first sex scene was with a lover. I cherish it, and although we've long since broken up, the video remains one of my favorite performances. I learn a lot about myself when I do porn. It provided a space for me to explore BDSM through bondage and electricity. Porn has become part of how I practice being poly; shoots are a clearly defined container offering distinct boundaries where I can have sex with close friends on preestablished terms. Porn is part of my exhibitionism and a place I can literally own my sexuality. Performative sex is thrilling, and with sober sets, regular STI testing, and a crew of professionals, I've had the opportunity to explore the vast edges of my sexuality, gender, and fantasy. Some of the safest and most satisfying sex I've had has happened on camera.

I've had so many positive experiences in porn that I'm convinced it's one of the best decisions I've ever made. How can something that has so profoundly impacted my life be bad? Sure, there were some not-so-awesome times, but even those moments taught me how to better articulate my boundaries. Porn taught me to be emphatic about giving consent. Each shoot comes with new challenges and rewards, and if the many messages I've received from viewers are any indication, I'm humbled that my very existence in porn brings visibility to the simple fact that queer and gender-variant people are deserving of a happy and healthy sexuality, and capable of being loved. I'm working with friends and lovers to create images of intimacy, trust, and pleasure. And we're having fun! This is what porn means to me.

Not everyone understands my view.

Please forgive me as I skip the difficult details of coming out to my brother, father, stepmother, mother, and grandma. I don't want to speak on their behalf, and I am edging on what I feel comfortable disclosing. The past few years have been challenging, but well worth it. What I will say is that I am still moved by their various forms of acceptance, as expressed in my brother's curiosity; my father's efforts to empathize; my stepmother's supportive role as an ally in standing up for me when dealing with the reactions of less open-minded family members; and to my surprise, my religious mother and grandma's display of unconditional love. ("A good Christian doesn't judge.") It wasn't—and still isn't—easy, but I'm grateful for their attempts to better understand who I am. Coming out to them has made me feel closer to my family than ever before and my heart swells with the knowledge that they love and are proud of me.

I don't consider my process of coming out as over. On the contrary, I still have a very long way to go. It's still an uncompleted project in the back of my head that I am constantly fine-tuning.

As I continued engaging in conversations with my peers, a few familiar threads became clear. For one, there's what I'll call the "outing snowball effect": the potential that disclosing one's work in porn can result in the further outing of themselves and others. (For example, working in BDSM porn might also reveal a performer's personal kinks.) There's also the matter that when we out ourselves as porn performers to our family, they take on the responsibility of this knowledge. If someone asks my father what I'm up to these days, he must decide whether or not to talk about the porn career that is now one of my primary activities, or he can choose to focus on my triathlon training, a topic that has become convenient at large family gatherings. Some performers are outed by accident, others vindictively. Coming out on our own terms is a luxury; if we talk to family members when we're ready, we can create a better environment for the conversation to take place. We can control the privacy, even plan aftercare to unwind from a stressful talk. I also saw another big observation: Coming out about porn sometimes isn't too different than coming out as queer and/or trans. Parents can have strong reactions out of fear. They are concerned for our safety; they accuse us of drug use or assume that something must have happened when we were younger to make us this way. The misconception that we are victims incapable of sexual agency mirrors that of coming out as nonnormative gender expression and sexual orientations.

I've made mistakes in the process of coming out, many of which I'm glad to see detailed by other stories in this book. When I first came out to my family about working in porn, I tried to play up what I understood as more socially acceptable performances, describing my feature films as comparable to recognized films that include explicit sex, such as *Shortbus*. However, the logic that sex within a narrative plot would somehow be more respectable backfired when my hardcore BDSM scenes were discovered. Although I never said, "At least I'm not doing XYZ," I was too insistent on making comparisons to independent film. We're all affected by whorephobia spectrums of sex worker stigmas; when coming out like a porn star, it doesn't help to throw other kinds of porn or sex work under the bus.

My checklist of family members whom I want to tell is far from complete. At the time of this writing, I've yet to find the courage to talk to my little brother and sister, now in their late teens. We've grown closer as they've become young adults, and the possibility of losing them shakes me to my core. I tell myself I shouldn't place such steep fear on their reaction. It's entirely possible that they already know. They are children of the Internet, after all. But being a sex-positive sibling is easier said than done. When they were going through puberty, I tested the waters by giving them each, separately, their own copy of Heather Corinna's *S.E.X.: The All-You-Need-to-Know Progressive Sexuality Guide to Get You through High School and College*. It wasn't long ago that I'd been in their shoes. I told them I wanted to be a resource for them, especially if they didn't want to talk to Mom or Dad. That was the last and only time my siblings and I talked about sex, a brief exchange of "Uh-huh" and "Okay."

Years have passed, and I still want to talk to them about porn at the appropriate time and place. Yes, I know I've been stalling. The truth is, I'm scared. I sought out peers who have children or younger siblings. How did they talk about porn in an age-appropriate way? Former porn star (and new grandmother!) Sinnamon Love cautioned hiding information from youth in the event that they find out on their own. She likened it to kids finding out there's no such thing as Santa Claus or the Tooth Fairy. I certainly don't want to jeopardize my siblings' trust, but am I delaying the inevitable? Surely, it will be easier to talk about this when they're older. Maybe when they're dating? I'll tell them after they have turned eighteen, I've reasoned with myself. The countdown hangs over my head and looms like a prediction for the end of days.

The hardest part of loving someone is the fear of losing them. The thought that I might even *disgust* them absolutely silences me. Maybe this whole situation is better left unspoken, I tell myself. My other younger brother found out casually, years before anyone else. Being only a few years older than him, I felt comforted by our closeness. We used to keep secrets from our parents so I knew I could trust him. Perhaps his nonchalance about my doing porn means my younger siblings will feel the same? I run circles in my brain to avoid the hard part. How deeply have I internalized this sexual shame? I want to get to a point where the idea of it turning out well is more readily available than the worst-case scenario replaying in my head.

Maybe it will be easier when *I* get over it.

I realized early on in the process of creating this book that these stories not only served my own needs but could also help others navigate the process as well. Having found my voice while writing for *The Feminist Porn Book*, I was inspired to put these stories to paper. Books have been written about coming out as queer, as transgender, as poly, and even as kinky. However, *Coming Out Like a Porn Star* is the first of its kind to address coming out about sex work in pornography.

Where this book fails in scope (writers are primarily American, English speaking, and their eras tilt toward the most recent decade), it succeeds in being one of the more inclusive anthologies to represent a range of marginalized voices from commercial porn. Contributors span people of color, trans and nonbinary performers, people with disabilities, niche genres, and varying professional experience—from Nina Hartley, a legendary performer with more than thirty years under her belt, to the porn hopeful Verta, who had the door slam in her face before she had a chance. As an advocate for diverse expressions of human sexuality, it was vital to me that the less-heard voices of my peers ring loud and clear. I'm equally grateful to popular "mainstream" performers whose experiences show that we're more alike than one would think. Combined, the collection features honest and often emotional accounts from over fifty adult professionals, placing it among the ranks of other big porn anthologies. It may hardly scratch the surface, but it will spark a conversation.

Working on this book has not been easy. Dozens of performers who initially wanted to submit a story later retracted. This might be typical of publishing collections from various authors and limited budgets; however, in the case of *Coming Out Like a Porn Star*, contributors have much more at stake. Writing this piece proved to be an intensely personal process. Even *I* wanted to recant my own submission. For many peers, the danger of being exposed is simply not worth the risk. I understand that. Coming out is hard enough, but to do so publicly has dangerous implications.

Regardless of the outcome, all the experiences shared in this book reflect the social stigmas of a culture whose sexual maturity is still in an awkward phase of adolescence. Where media outlets and public opinion continue to portray a negative, one-sided view of porn and its participants, our stories reveal a more honest depiction. We write at a time when sexual knowledge is typically buried in shame, fear, and ignorance. Where hate crimes against people whose gender and sexual expression differ from a strictly defined template are alarming statistics; the suicide and murder of trans women of color in particular are screaming indicators that something in our understanding of sex and gender is clearly amiss. If our experiences of sexual stigma and its intersections are any indicator of the social inequity of our time, may our words be steppingstones for increased sexual awareness and nuances to come. And may we come out on top.

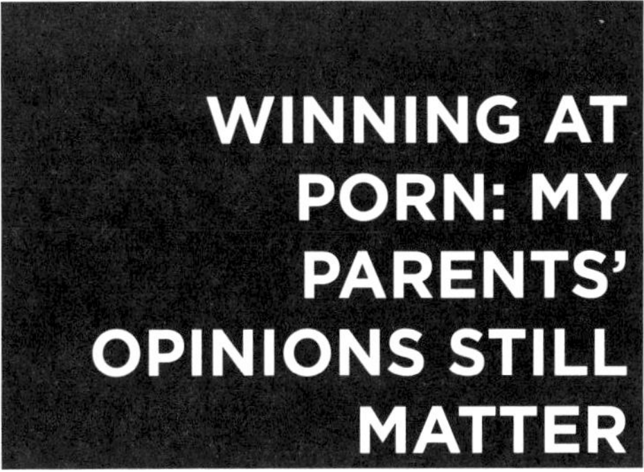

WINNING AT PORN: MY PARENTS' OPINIONS STILL MATTER

AliceInBondageLand

After a near-life experience in a plane crash, Alice set out to live her dreams and bring her mad visions to life in moving pictures on both sides of the lens. Now, Mistress AliceInBondageLand is on a mission to put the fun back into femdom, one movie at a time. Her videos feature female-dominant-lifestyle couples in all combinations. Winner of the Best Bondage Paysite award in 2014, her movies shine with innovative bondage, genuine orgasms, and real kinksters really enjoying themselves, with a surprising sense of humor mixed in.

All my parents really wanted was for me to win the Olympics. Instead, I produce pornography with every method of artistic creation ever made available to me.

That makes more sense with a little context. Both of my parents were Olympic competitors and, like most parents, they hoped their children would succeed where they had failed. They got a porn star instead of a normal athlete, one born with the same intense drive that pushed them to Batman-like lengths of willpower and sacrifice in pursuit of a possibly impossible goal: to be the "best in the world" at something most people have never heard of. They sacrificed their lives and didn't win. My sister and I were raised in the fallout of their dreams.

My early artwork was soundly denounced as pornography by my hysterical mother one day after I quit yet another Olympic sport at an athletic camp. I was copying the classics from photo books and had started sketching from Victoria's Secret catalogs. My mother was unnerved at the level of explicitness her eleven-year-old was extrapolating from the world of advertising, even though I was just redrawing what I saw all around me.

At thirteen, I remember looking at my own vagina with a mirror. I was trying to figure out how to draw a fully nude woman without ever having seen one. It was also a little obvious from an early age that I liked girls. My mother destroyed all of my vagina art when she found it. She didn't have words for why girls shouldn't draw that kind of stuff, just rage, fear, and fire. The rule was that we would never speak of it again, but her control tightened when she discovered that the money paid to send her talented daughter to art classes instead of sports camps was churning out smut.

I got a Polaroid camera for my sixteenth birthday. I immediately used up all my film photographing stuffed animal bondage and nude mirror selfies of my changing body. No more camera for me when they were discovered in my art stash beneath my bed. I got caught masturbating with a carrot. I was kicked out of the house a few days later. I moved out with whatever I could fit in the trunk of a Nissan.

A few weeks after my eighteenth birthday, we shot roll after roll of film at an older friend's house using my new 35mm camera. We tied each other to his pinball machine and posed provocatively with bananas. I was devastated when the photo developer exposed the film, destroying it all. He told us to never come back, even though there were no actual sex acts portrayed in any of the photos. We were all of legal age and could prove it, but that didn't matter. It was his religious imperative to destroy our young, queer photographic obscenities.

Yet every time I looked at the world, I saw it in porn-o-vision. Every piece of architecture was a potential attachment point for bondage. I cast every passerby in my lurid fantasies. I kept a notebook of video ideas with me where I constantly sketched, scribbled, and took notes.

I traded nude modeling to my landlord for an early digital camera while I attended college, insistent that I never wanted to risk my creations to a moralistic interloper again. I use my cultural anthropology degree in every movie, but probably not in the way my school intended it. I sold my motorcycle for a video camera. I traded yard work for dungeon rentals and bribed my friends with favors to join me, with or without masks. We showed it to our lovers but not anyone else.

I lied for years about other gigs while I secretly spent every penny I earned at "normal" jobs producing lewd fetish material for my personal wank bank. Part compulsion and part creativity, it consumed me. I watched other people's pornography, but nothing spoke to me. Where was the laughter in the bondage? Where were the smiles? Where was the female pleasure? Where was sex that looked like what I did in my bedroom? I kept making movies because I couldn't find my kind of movies anywhere else.

Many years later, while collaborating with friends that owned a website, I let slip that my secret stash now numbered in the hundreds of scenes and thousands of photos. They wanted to see what I had been up to.

The website happened fast, faster then I was expecting. I had not counted on finding an audience; my focus had only been on pleasing myself. In a rush I'd gone from "weird girl with a video camera" to "Internet famous" (whatever that means).

I hesitated to tell strangers. "I make moooooovies," I would say, drawing out the o as long as possible. They always ask if I have made any theatrical releases they might have seen. Everyone is eager to think they might be meeting someone famous. "Probably not," I would answer and let them assume I made obscure documentaries and very boring corporate training videos.

I kept a once-a-week day job for years, just so I could point to it and have something to talk about when someone asked me what I did. It wasn't until I won awards for my porn that I tried to tell my parents again what it was that I had spent my whole life doing.

I think they knew all along. My mom knew from the very beginning. She called it porn the moment she saw it. She grew up weird in a small town and was tormented by peers for being perceived as a lesbian. She married my dad in part to get away from the gay bashing. They found common cause in the Olympic Games and their shared sport.

My mother told me years later that she was so hard on me because she didn't want me to grow up too weird. In her twisted small-town logic, if you are too different, then no one will like you, and if no one likes you, you will never be happy.

I pointed at my crowded Thanksgiving, my Burning Man camp, my band of merry mischief-makers, all full of happy pornographers and performers. San Francisco is not small-town Wyoming and "weird" is an ethos embraced by the West Coast. I am not a lonely weirdo.

Mom is in a healthier relationship after her divorce and all she will tell me is "I am a lot more open-minded now," with the phrase pronounced in a lilting voice with extra-long vowels. I can only wonder. She is now dating a guy that *did* win the Olympic gold a few years after she retired. I hope she dances around naked except for it nestled between her breasts. I've never asked, but I hope.

My father still struggles with his kinky side, according to my stepmother. She wishes he would watch some kinky porn with her and get over his guilt about sex in general so they can move on to the fun stuff. We both agree that my films are the right attitude but the wrong cast.

Being the visibly odd one that couldn't stop drawing naked chicks made me the lightning rod of the family. They've all had time to grow and change; getting sober helped. Telling the truth to them helped more than I realized. It cleared the air. Gave us a chance to start anew with real honesty instead of pretty fabrications. Their acceptance has been a landslide for my acceptance, too.

Now when strangers ask me what I do, I still tell them, "I make movies," but I don't dread their follow-up question about if it is something they might have seen. I smile my most mischievous smile and tell them, "Only if you watch naughty movies!" I still don't use the word "porn" with strangers. It is easier for them to laugh off the word "naughty" as being cute and fun instead of scary. People spit out the word "porn" like it is a cussword or slur, followed by awkward sexual advances, as if being naked on the Internet obligates me to sleep with strangers. "Naughty" is cute, mostly harmless, and gets fewer propositions in response.

The after-school rule used to be "any sport as long as it is in the Olympics," but instead I host the CBT Olympics and the

Strap-On Olympics. I couldn't shake my parent's competitive nature, so I carved out a place for my own sexy challenges.

Ultimately, it was the trophy that cinched their acceptance. I finally won first place at something. Even though they don't understand how their daughter turned out this way, they do understand winning.

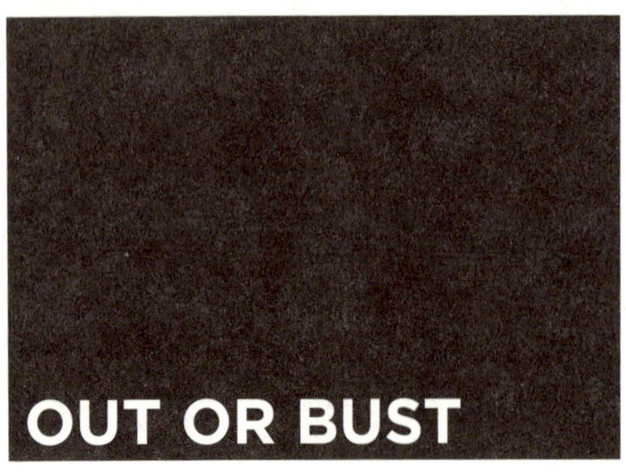

OUT OR BUST

Andre Shakti

Andre Shakti is a queer polyamorous educator, producer, activist, and professional slut living in the San Francisco Bay Area. She is committed to normalizing alternative desires, destigmatizing sex workers and their clients, and not taking herself too seriously. Follow her on Twitter @andreshakti and visit AndreShaktiXXX.com.

I live the vast majority of my life balanced on the outskirts of "traditional" society, and as such I'm often asked how the people in my life feel about the work I do. When the question is posed respectfully (as opposed to invasively), I give my rote, honest answer: "I'm completely out." As a stripper, as a professional dominatrix, as a live webcam model, and as a porn performer. Each time, I'm met with a mixture of wonder and disappointment: turns out, folks want to hear a story. Not just any story, either—they want to hear about secrecy, about living a double life, about navigating awkward situations. They want to know how my parents reconciled themselves with it, how I was ever able to find conventional employment, and how many partners I've lost as a result. They make their own assumptions about how condemned my life must be. In doing so, no matter how sincere their intentions, they set the sex-worker rights movement back exponentially.

The thing is, I don't really have any coming-out narratives of my own. I never felt as though anyone was entitled to a red-carpet presentation of who I am and how I identify. When I initially found myself attracted to women in college, for example, I simply showed up at the next family function with my first girlfriend in tow and introduced her as such. I didn't call each family member ahead of time and instruct them to brace themselves, nor did I write lengthy letters detailing the intricacies of my new desires. Likewise, when I'm meeting people for the first time at parties or other social engagements and they pose the inevitable, "So what do you do?" I respond as routinely as possible: "Oh, I work in the sex industry. You?"

I'm not trying to be provocative; rather, I've always believed that being "out" is the most powerful tool of activism available to disadvantaged minority communities, sex workers included. I find that when you approach a supposedly radical issue (queerness, nonmonogamy, atheism, gender nonconformity) with the same nonchalance as you would a less controversial topic (accounting, marriage, cooking, the weather), you give the other party permission to treat it with the same accepting ambivalence. We're pack animals, and we're constantly comparing ourselves to one another. We look for approval from our peers, and in many cases we use their reactions and opinions to help guide our own. I often observe people, who I've just disclosed to, pause to shift their eyes and gauge the receptiveness of those around them before responding. It'd be a fascinating study if it weren't so disheartening.

Additionally, putting a familiar, nonthreatening face to something perceived as alien can make it seem much less so. Let's continue with the party scenario. Say I'm introduced to an individual whose only context for sex work is an HBO special on sex trafficking, an industry that deals in the underage, nonconsensual selling of sex but is often disastrously conflated with legally-aged, consensual sex work. We immediately hit it off, talking and laughing and connecting for a few hours before I disclose what I do for a living. Assuming this person thinks highly of me, they now have to reconcile what they think they know about the kind of people who do sex work (coerced, substance addicted, disempowered) with who I am. All of a sudden, an unexpected hairline fracture appears in their presumptions. That's all I ever aim to do: present people with sound reason to doubt their prejudice. Give them complexity and nuance to sharpen their naïveté. Nonjudgmentally help to normalize the foreign.

An unforeseeable benefit of being radically out is that it acts as a near-perfect filter for potential friends and lovers. Because I work in the entertainment industry (I produce nightclub events and go-go dance in addition to doing sex work), and as a result of the overlapping nature of San Francisco Bay Area communities, I'm constantly meeting new people with similar interests through work and play. Many of these people have either seen at least one of my social media profiles, watched an erotic film I've been in, attended a sexuality-related class I've taught, or shared a friend or partner with me before we even meet. Whatever the case, it's very rare that I have to "explain myself" to people who are interested in my companionship, and that's a luxury that I am incredibly grateful for.

Of course, this approach isn't perfect. First of all, being out is not accessible to everyone. Young people still dependent on their family's resources for survival may opt to stay quiet about their proclivities for fear that they'd be disowned. Citizens of some foreign countries may also elect to remain closeted lest they face violence or death at the hands of their own government. Even in certain states in North America, there's a real risk of same-sex couples losing custody of the children they co-parent if their sexual orientations become public knowledge. I recognize my own privilege in never having to worry about any of the above. The whiteness of my skin, the conformity of my gender presentation to traditional expectations of femininity, and my upper-middle-class upbringing provide me opportunity and dramatically decrease the chances I'll be discriminated against on a daily basis.

There's also a hierarchy within the sex work industry. Although dividing and insulting our community makes it that much easier for people to denigrate us for working, there's a tremendous amount of classism rampant in the industry. Workers judge other workers on the services they provide and what they charge for those services, as though one person's preferences and boundaries should naturally extend to everyone. The fact that I am a sex worker who operates in niches of the industry where I can charge more for my services (which are always performed indoors in safe, controlled environments) and receive a certain level of notoriety for those services gives me privilege even within my marginalized community. I do believe that it is the responsibility of those in a privileged position, such as myself, to be out when others cannot. To speak out when others cannot. To use their privilege to steer the public opinion and legislation in favor of all sex workers. We need to hear from a diverse array of voices—workers of size, workers of color, street workers, transgender workers—but those who are more readily given a mouthpiece (like porn performers who have inflated social media presences) have no excuse not to use their power for good.

Second of all, not everyone responds to my flavor of enthusiastic, unabashed transparency. I still have one or two elder relatives who blame and resent me for never rolling out that red carpet and "formally" coming out to them. In my early twenties, I applied to and was courted by two graduate programs that I was exceptionally qualified for, only to be abruptly denied admission without explanation after I told them what I did for a living. And I'll never forget the time I chatted up a svelte Russian femme at a Los Angeles lesbian bar. She'd bought me a drink and sidled up next to me, batting her long lashes, when she asked me why I was in town. When I casually responded that I'd been shooting a pornographic film, she immediately recoiled, shaking her head and saying, "You're beautiful and everything, but I'm pretty conservative. I can't get down with that."

All that being said, I love my life. Being as open as I am has afforded me far more intimacy, support, community, and fortuity than I would have had otherwise. Because most everyone—from my childhood neighbors to my high school teachers—know what I do, I'm constantly fielding questions about my work, and I never let a question go unanswered, even when I'm feeling tired, overwhelmed, or disenchanted. I'm honored to act as an advocate for the sex industry, and I don't begrudge any of my fellow workers who choose other, more private levels of "outness." I just don't know any other way to be.

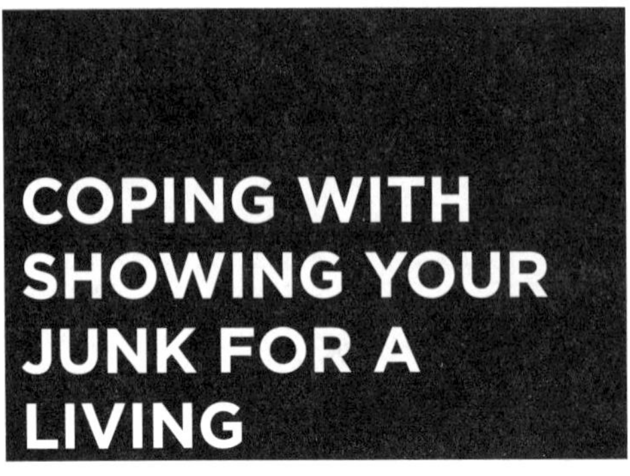

COPING WITH SHOWING YOUR JUNK FOR A LIVING

Anna Cherry

The three best things in life are laughing, thinking, and orgasms. I want to make you do all three A LOT. Professional Naked Girl.

First thing they always tell you: Once it's on the Internet, it's there forever. I remember being not exactly sure what that meant while also feeling the palpable fear that sentence always carried. Now I can tell you with confidence that I have discovered what it meant and gone beyond; and I have returned bearing gifts of how to emotionally handle adult industry public opinion job hazard.

I have been doing webcam live sex and filming adult videos for at least four to five years. Keeping it a secret from my family and public at large, 90 percent of that time was spent under that elusive but omnipresent, heavy weight. In fact, even after everyone in the city I lived in at the time (as well as people in at least three to four other states and *millions* more online) knew that I was an adult entertainer, my parents did not. Even after moving to a new city entirely to pursue further flourishing of my adult entertainment career, my mother still had no idea of how exactly I earned my living.

Truth is, we all have the equivalents of AI implants of the people closest to us in our brains—for instance, you can quote to me exactly what your mom would say in a particular situation. That means you hear the echoes of negative and hurtful attitudes in the back of your head if you have any unresolved cognitive dissonance. And trust me, you do. We all do. No matter how open I was with both strangers and immediate friends, and although I was eager for my parents to find out what I do so we can be over the whole issue, I still could not actually take that step myself.

Until a few months ago.

You may successfully assure yourself in the strength of your slutty convictions, but as long as there continues to be a feeling of need for privacy there is also that unbearable weight in the background that will endure to erode away your soul and mental peace until you come out and confront it yourself. Wage war on it. I dub us the Lipstick Warriors.

Truth is, you have to set them free. Everyone you have ever loved, you have to give them the opportunity to reject you and show the true colors of what kind of human being they are.

Then, you have to get mad.

Privacy is a tool we use to protect ourselves from the weapon of social judgment. Think of the Belle Knox backlash as a microcosm of the slut shaming we all feel every day in countless imperceptible ways. The same slut shaming we hear in the back of our heads, quoting our sensible mothers and prim grandmothers and all of their nice, clean, wholesome friends.

Truth is, clean is a lie. Nothing is clean.

Any true expression of freedom is by definition an expression of rebellion. No matter what you do in life or what path you take, if you continue to follow your one true path, there will be those who will try to enslave you, to bring you back into the fold of doing what *they* think you should. Stripping away all need for privacy, armored in righteous indignation, and armed with proven fact—you must make them pay for putting that pain of social exclusion inside you. Social opinion is mimetic warfare, and judgment is the first act of aggression.

You have to bring up that righteous indignation to defend your right to your own life and strike down anyone daring to impose their limits on your life. You need to refuse to be swept down and swallowed by their bitter fountain of feelings of inadequacy. You have to refuse to be limited by the fears of others.

Telling my mom what I do for a living was one of the best things I have ever done in my life. That invisible suffocating leash of fear of revealing the truth (see: fear of social rejection; see: ostracism;

see: death) has been snapped, and I have never felt freer, happier, and more unstoppable in my career—because now there truly is nothing holding me back. No limits. Although I was not perfectly fortunate to have a 100-percent supportive mother, I am rewarded with discovering that I am still loved and no less valuable to my parents as a result of my career choice. Fully keeping in mind that they have no right to make a value judgment on that in the first place, it is still a nice feeling, and one not many adult industry performers are fortunate to feel. Still, even those who have been severely hurt by social exclusion from their families as a result of their adult work will tell you that total exposure is a must and you will be better for it. As cliché as my favorite analogy is, this really is like ripping off the Band-Aid, except it's a little more like breaking through a cocoon. You are limited and in pain in the darkness, but you have to welcome that pain and rush toward it, expand toward that bright light you see and crave so badly, push through no matter how much it hurts because you have made the decision to follow this path, and *bam*! You're a butterfly.

Deal with it by knowing that they have no right to dictate the terms of your existence. Deal with it by knowing that you are perfectly allowed to erect a billboard showing you naked outside and inside, and anyone raising even an eyebrow to that needs to go through some heavy self-acceptance. Deal with it by knowing that it is already too late to do anything about it anyway. You can hope nobody close to you will find out—and they might not. After all, there are plenty of ways to cover your ass if parents suddenly announce, "Uncle Joe from Muskogee said he saw you naked on the Internet!" But beware that you are sacrificing a lifetime of true freedom, knowledge of who truly loves you, and true realization of your dreams in exchange for the immediate gratification of not rocking the boat. In the end, it is all about whether you chose what price to pay or if you let the price choose you.

I hope this helps.

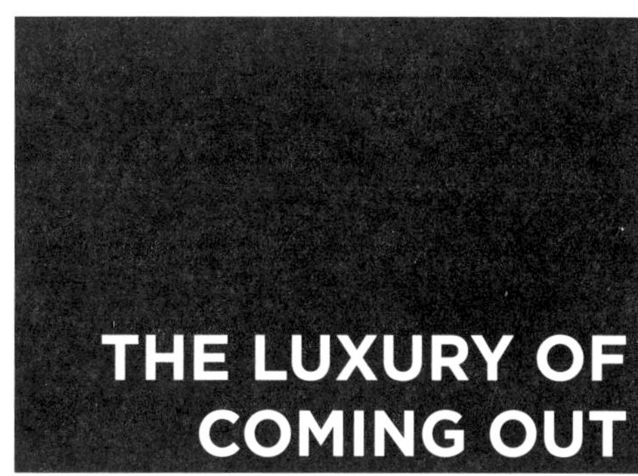

THE LUXURY OF COMING OUT

Annie Sprinkle

Annie Sprinkle has worked in sex for forty-two years. In the '70s, she was a porn star, pinup model, and prostitute. In the '80s she was a sex-worker-rights activist, writer and photographer for sex magazines, and directed her own post-porn films. She was a pivotal player in the sex positive feminist movement and put herself through college doing burlesque. In the '90s, Sprinkle branched out into the art world, toured theater pieces about her life in sex, and became a sex educator. In 2002, Sprinkle got a PhD and fell in love with artist Beth Stephens. Currently, they're pioneering the ecosex movement.

Hell, I didn't come out just once. I came out again and again, and again—multiple times. After I came out as a porn star, I came out as being into BDSM and fetish sex. Then I came out as being spiritual and into sacred sex. Then I came out as having transsexual lovers. Then I came out as a lesbian separatist, albeit briefly. Then when I came out as being heterosexual—again—some queer friends were horrified. When I came out as being celibate, that was probably the most shocking news of all. Then I came out as bisexual. Then I came out as monogamous! That was very radical in my world. Then most recently I came out as an ecosexual! Every time I came out as something new and different, I faced people's shock, judgments, and rejections.

When I was seventeen, my neighbor, who was like a mother to me, was on her deathbed, and she gave me the most important words of wisdom. She said, "Above all, to thine own self be true." I took it to heart, although I could never have imagined how many different selves I would end up having to be true to. When we follow our muses, our dreams, our desires, and we stay in the truth of the moment, we can end up in some pretty unexpected situations. However, for the sake of this book, I'll focus on my coming out as a porn star.

In 1973, forty-two years ago, when I went from being Ellen Steinberg, a shy, insecure eighteen-year-old ugly duckling to Annie Sprinkle, a sexually adventurous, glamorous porn starlet, no one was more surprised than I was! First I had to come out to myself. I had to admit to myself that I had a porn star inside me that wanted to bust out into the world. I shocked myself! However, as I was interested in filmmaking, and interested in sex, porn was something I was simply destined to do.

As a child, whenever I lied, I got caught. Plus, I noticed that lying didn't feel good. So after just two months in the sex biz, I knew that telling the truth was my only way forward. My two brothers took it the hardest. They were protective, concerned, upset. Dad tried to be supportive but was visibly shaken. Mom got pretty emotional and was "disappointed" in me. At first, my parents were worried maybe I was addicted to drugs or that someone might be coercing me. But that was never the case. In time, they grew to trust that I had made my own choices, and for good reasons. In some cases, it can take a lot of time for family members and friends to come around to accepting who we are, or choose to be. It took a good two decades for my family to come to accept the fact that my career in sex wasn't just a passing phase. Time can do wonders. Time is on our side.

When I came out to old friends, they were totally perplexed. They didn't understand why I would choose to do porn when I had so many opportunities. No one shunned me, at least that I was aware of. I did have one friend of years who one day told me we could no longer be friends because of my work. That experience was deeply painful; however, that wound was eventually healed by time.

Generally, I didn't tell strangers what I did. I lived in Manhattan. Most days, I took a taxi or two. Inevitably, the driver would ask, "So what do you do?" Rarely (if ever) did I say, "I'm a porn star." That would simply be TMI (too much information) for casual encounters. However, I didn't outright lie. Sometimes I said I was a filmmaker or an actress, or that I was in public relations. I'd tell the truth, but not the entire truth. People have so many stereotypes and expectations about porn star's lives that it takes a whole lot of energy to educate people.

When Jiz Lee asked me to write something about coming out like a porn star, these seven thoughts came to mind.

1. It's what we think of ourselves that matters most. When we tell people what we do, it's not what we do, it's how we say what we do that will radiate out and reflect back to us in the response we get. If we tell someone apologetically with shame and embarrassment, "I make porn," then people will feel shame and embarrassment too and worry about us. If we are clear that this is who we are, and this is what we want to do at this time in our lives, if we have worked through our own issues about it and feel empowered, then people will feel and see that too. Feeling at peace with who and what we are can be a process. Working on ourselves and how we feel about what we do can take some time. Coming out is an ongoing process, not a singular event.
2. What other people think of us is really none of our business. There will likely be some people who just won't accept who and what we are—ever. For the few friends I may have lost coming out, it was well worth all the fabulous new ones I made.
3. People don't expect much from people who make porn, which can work to your benefit. So anytime you do something of note, it surprises and impresses people. For example, in 1989, when I did my first one-woman theater piece, it got a lot of attention because people were simply amazed that a porn star could do a good theater performance. Then in 2001 when I became the first porn star to get a PhD, I got extra pats on the back and attention because people don't expect porn stars to be very smart.
4. People might think that being a porn star can make us targets for violence, but in my experience being a porn star has been a cloak of protection that has at times kept me safe. For example, late one night I was walking alone on a dark Manhattan street,

praying for a taxi. The neighborhood was known to be dangerous. A man came out of nowhere, with a scary vibe, and was walking straight toward me. I fully expected to be harassed, if not robbed, or worse. My heart raced. I wondered if I should cross the street or look down or be friendly and say hello. If I had to run away in my high heels, I would certainly not get far. I decided to stay my course and when I came shoulder to shoulder with the man, he squealed, "Oh my god, you're Annie Sprinkle!" I was stunned. He explained, "When I was in prison, I saw all your magazine spreads, and I read all your columns." (Note: Before there were blogs, porn stars had sex magazine columns, and they used to let sex magazines into many prisons.) He was over the moon to have run into me. He was not only respectful, he was worshipful. He offered to walk me to get a cab. Suddenly, I felt totally safe with him. His name was Sweets, and he told me that he had been in prison for several years for pimping. He said my photos and stories helped him through some tough times. I had a magazine column coming due, so I asked him if I could interview and photograph him a few days later. We did the shoot in my apartment. I hired porn star Sharon Kane to pose with him; we all had a great day, and I got a great story. Porn had given little ol' me street cred. Sweets and I stayed in touch by phone for several years. The last time I heard from him, he was back in jail for selling a VCR from the back of a car that was actually an empty VCR box he filled with rocks.

5. Coming out gets easier and easier the more you do it. Eventually, you will tell people you're a porn star (or whatever you are) with such ease that whatever negative responses might come at you will just roll off your back and won't even faze you. Your buttons will only be pushed if part of you believes the critiques.
6. Coming out as a porn star can get weirder and weirder the older you get. Although I haven't been in a porn movie for about twenty years, many of my old movies that came and went were rediscovered with the advent of the Internet. These days, once a porn star, always a porn star. If you are lucky enough to turn sixty, like me, you will be an "old" porn star. Try being sixty and

telling someone you are a porn star. It's a bit odd, and the responses can be amusing.

7. Coming out is a luxury and a privilege. Seriously, coming out as anything that isn't "the social norm" can be very traumatic for all involved. One must weigh the risks and benefits. In some places and in some circumstances, coming out can mean you will lose your job, have your children taken from you, be put in jail for years, get you shunned from your entire community, and can even get you stoned to death. Coming out can have its challenges and be scary, but if you are able to do it, be ever so grateful for the privilege. Being out is being free.

Well, I hope something here was helpful or a little food for thought. Remember too, if we expect others to love and accept us for who we are and what we do, we have to extend the same love and acceptance to others. Next time someone comes out to you as something that you don't approve of, be gentle, be kind, and try to not judge but to understand.

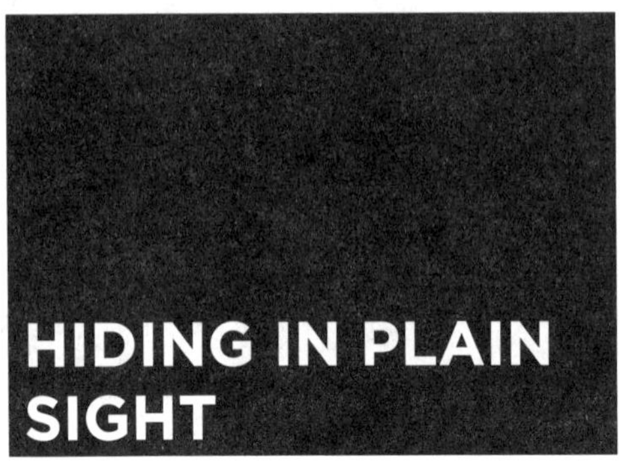

HIDING IN PLAIN SIGHT

Anonymous

This writer wishes she didn't have to be anonymous and usually is quite open about her involvement in porn and sex work, but she needed to be anonymous in this book to limit the risk her stalkers could discover that she has another name and use that to find and harass her employer. When not championing feminism and sex worker rights online, she enjoys a cozy home with a loving family and several pets, including an elderly cat that was on her lap for much of the writing of this essay.

Before I was performing in porn, I was blogging. It started just as a desire to participate in budding options for social media networks. LiveJournal led to WordPress, WordPress led to guest posts. Soon I was writing regularly for several blogs and building quite a reputation for myself. I wrote about racism and sexism; I wrote from my own perspective, shared my experiences, talked about the sex I had, about my friends' experiences with sex work, and I did most of it under my actual name because everything I said was something I felt was important and I was willing to stand behind my own words.

When I began doing porn, I couldn't imagine not blogging about it. I wanted my followers and readers to know about the work I was doing. I wanted some of the fans of my writing to have the chance to become fans of my performances. It was natural and only made sense. That's when I realized that names were going to become a dilemma. If I came up with a new porn name, I'd be losing out on the reputation I'd worked so hard to build. But if I used my actual name, did I really want to be that public about being in porn? I considered using a new name for porn and blogging that name and links to my work, but that just seemed like the worst of both options. I'd lose out on some of the value of using the name people knew me by, as inevitably some fans would miss the connection and not realize who I was. At the same time, I'd leave a large enough trail for anyone to make the connection if they were to Google me, including employers, family, and so on.

I had grown up without having to worry about my Google footprint, but as I was considering it for the first time, I realized it was too late. I had already left quite a trail of information I wouldn't want a potential employer to look up. If I'm applying for a job somewhere, I don't need them reading about my experiences with fisting or group sex any more than I'd want them finding out I do porn. That's when I realized I needed to come up with another option, another name that I could give potential employers.

I came up with the idea of doing porn under my actual name, the name I was known by through blogging, through activism, and with friends, but change my legal name to something entirely different that I would use with employers, banks, taxes, and anything else that requires a legal name. Kind of like a pseudonym in reverse. Of course, it meant my family would eventually find out, but I actually didn't really care about that.

It turned out to be quite necessary in the end, and not even for the reasons I had been thinking about. As is unfortunately too common these days for opinionated women on the Internet, I found myself the target of a harassment campaign. It started just by writing about how something was sexist. As people argued with me, I tried to further explain my position, but soon it was clear this was a coordinated attempt to overwhelm me and they really had no desire to listen to what I had to say. I was swamped with harassing email messages; at first, I blocked anyone who said anything inappropriate. Then I had to set up comment moderation so I had to approve every single comment. Eventually, I turned the comments off. That was about when they escalated it.

They tried to look up my information, harassed my friends and family, and they even discussed having a call-in campaign to my work to let them know what a dirty slut I was. One of the harassers had a reputation as a hacker who could find that kind of information. But they never did find my employment records because they never knew the right name to look under. They never even tried looking for my legal name because they assumed they already knew it. And for that, I was grateful.

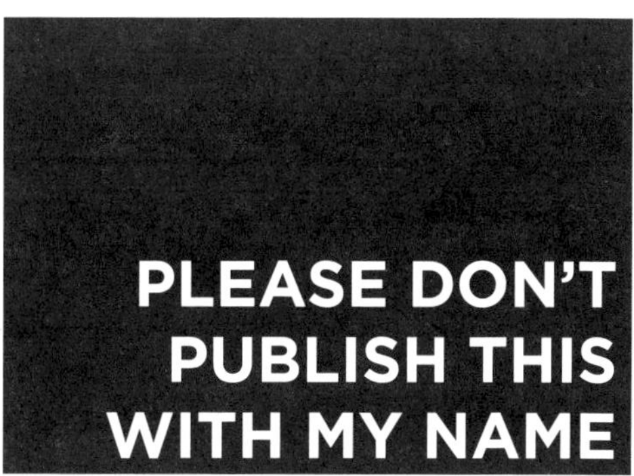

PLEASE DON'T PUBLISH THIS WITH MY NAME

Anonymous

The author's name has been withheld at their request.

I'm a photographer who has worked in the adult industry for several years now. I began photographing people in the sex work industry early on in college, beginning with my friends who were dancers, pro-dommes, and escorts, as well as the various subcultures around San Francisco. A few years ago, I was hired for a full-time job with a local porn studio and decided that I needed to explain to my family that I'd now be shooting this "unusual stuff"—their words, not mine—for a living. I always felt that photography was my true life's work, but I had to work day jobs to support myself in the meantime. This provided my parents with the usual cover story—that I was an administrative assistant, a marketing person, a server in a restaurant, and so on. I sat them down and explained that I got this new job that came with health benefits and a 401K, and that I'd spend all day, every day, on a porn set or in a darkroom editing what we'd shot. There went that cover story.

They weren't thrilled about the content I was helping to produce, but I'd lived for several years without health insurance and it was hard to argue that the practical aspects of the job weren't positive. I showed them the website I'd be working on, explained the rules of shooting, that we did our best to treat our performers with respect and consideration, that it was a positive workplace and that although outwardly the women might seem to be mistreated, it was all smoke and mirrors: We were creating a fantasy.

My father dislikes porn. He sees it as the objectification of women, and the rough sex and treatment of performers depicted is abhorrent to him. He's feminist enough to acknowledge that a woman has a right to choose her path, but on some level, I think he's horrified to see women treated poorly, even giving their full consent. He knows about BDSM and doesn't think it's unhealthy, but he expressed concern that it would be difficult for me to watch even staged sexual violence on a day-to-day basis. My mother feels similarly but is vehement in her insistence that women be allowed to make their own choices, even if those are choices she does not understand. Mostly, I suspect they are baffled by porn.

As much as I hate to admit it, he was right. When I left that job, it was an enormous relief.

I remain pro-pornography and will always stand up with my sex industry friends for the rights of performers to do what they do and to do it safely. I'd spent some time making porn full time while witnessing both the good and the bad sides of the industry. I went in with sex-positive blinders on, not wanting to admit that some of the detractors of the industry were right about problematic aspects. I witnessed some extremely bad behavior on the part of directors, and occasionally, performers. I overheard misogynistic and dehumanizing comments coming from other crew members and producers. I experienced instances where the need to get a shot or deliver a shoot overcame the physical and emotional safety of the models. I was removed from one particular shoot when I felt the performer was in danger of passing out and pointed this out to the director. These instances contributed to the burnout and exhaustion I was feeling, being so immersed in the visceral process of production in the adult industry.

I'd say about half of my family members know what I do for a living. I still shoot porn, but part time and not for mainstream studios. I do field a lot of questions about what it's like on set, how the performers are treated, and occasionally get asked how someone can get into the industry as a producer. I do my best to give a fair and balanced view of the industry. I've met some incredible people working in porn—some of the strongest, most intelligent and articulate women I've ever met in my life. It's only fair to them that my family hears about the human side of the industry. I can't deny the very real problems inherent in such a male-dominated and commercial industry, but I've witnessed similar issues in the advertising and fashion industries. I do my best to speak out to support the performers, who are literally putting their bodies on the line.

I've never come out to my partner's family about working in porn. They're religious, and it wouldn't be appropriate to tell some of them. As far as they know, I make "corporate training films," which sounds so boring that no one ever asks for details. My older cousins know and are supportive, but as I move into shooting more nonpornographic work, they're clearly relieved. There is a stigma to working in porn, for both performers and production people. I once took a video editing course in Final Cut Pro, and when the other people in the class found out where I worked, they all fell silent and stopped treating me as an equal. I still think porn is more valid than spending $50,000 on a thirty-second car commercial, but working on one gets you respect and the other does not.

I maintain a photography business completely separate from my adult work, and never the two shall meet. Not because I'm not proud of my on-set work, but because I work in a competitive and cutthroat industry where people are still biased against porn and the people who make it.

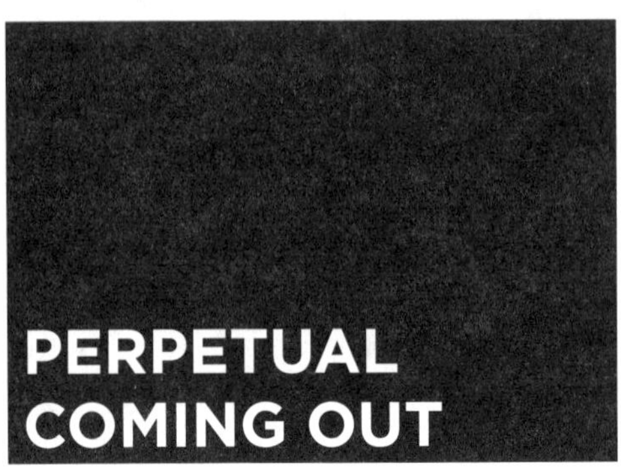

PERPETUAL COMING OUT

Bella Vendetta

Bella Vendetta is a classically trained professional and lifestyle dominatrix. She trained at the world's oldest BDSM training chateau as a submissive before taking the reins as a pro-domme. Since then, she has worked in prestigious dungeons all over the country, is a leader in the New England kink community, and has opened her own dungeon and community space. In addition to being passionate about the BDSM lifestyle, she is also a founding member of Rites of Passage suspension group, which has allowed her to reign with the best riggers and piercers from all over the country. Bella is passionate about doing dangerous things as safely as possible and frequently lectures at colleges and universities about cross-contamination, disinfection, and blood-borne pathogens. When she is not doing all of this, she is filming weird art porn, clown porn, and fetish content for her own company, Beautiful Revenge Productions. And when she is not doing that, she is writing about her experiences in the adult industry, as well as metal and rock interviews.

I have written and rewritten this so many times. I have so many stories about coming out as a porn star and sex worker in such a variety of situations, I couldn't quite decide which one to tell, and I kept putting this off to write and send. Over the course of about a year, this piece has changed so many times, and I think it's a testament to how varied your experiences will be when you are a sex worker and you come out to someone. It will be different when you tell your parents versus when you tell your kids, or your doctor or boyfriend or nail technician or banker. It changes constantly, and it will keep changing for the rest of your life. It's going to happen a lot of times, and each time will be different depending on the person and situation. I've been doing it for fourteen years and I don't think it's ever really gotten easier. Because when you do porn and are involved as a performer or sex worker and people find out, it will change their perception of you. Every single one of them. It changes the way everyone looks at you; it changes the way people treat you. Sometimes for the better, sometimes for the worse, sometimes for the most awkward.

I am out in My life in every imaginable way. I am a heavily modified woman. I wear glasses, have a lot of tattoos, huge breasts, and scarification. There's not really any toning it down for Me. I can put on jeans and a T-shirt, but I still look like, well, a tattooed freak with huge tits in jeans and T-shirt. It's sort of hard for Me to fly under the radar. I don't clean up real easy. I don't take out My flashy gold and diamond facial piercings, and I don't cover up My tattoos. What you see is what you get. I am simply Me all the time, Bella Vendetta, 24/7.

I have the extreme privilege of being out about My sex work. I've been doing this for a long time, and if you know Me, you know that I do porn, and I work as a pro-domme, and I am queer. You know that I am a sex worker and you deal with it; otherwise, I do not deal with you. I have enough awesome and supportive and open-minded people in My life, so I don't have the desire to fight for acceptance and friendship from folks who judge Me in negative ways or treat Me as less than a human being because I am a sex worker. I do not have a cover story that I tell people, to hide the fact that I am a sex worker. In some situations, I just say that I am an artist, and that's certainly not a lie!

Everyone in My life calls Me Bella, or My nicknames Bumble or Bee. A select few call me Mistress. Out loud, in public in restaurants, clubs, at vet visits with My dogs, everywhere. There's only a small handful of people who know what I refer to as My government name, and an even smaller percentage whom I allow to actually use it. It boils down to My sister, My father, and My grandmother. It isn't too difficult for people to look Me up and find out My legal name, but I ask people not to use it out of respect for Me. "Bella" is how I prefer to be addressed. I came leaping out of the closet as Bella Vendetta so long ago. I do not want to go running and hiding back again.

I have been out as a sex worker for so long that I didn't actually remember how I had told My father about it. I didn't recall some big, huge conversation with tears or hugs or throwing things or anything. So I called My dad to ask him. Since then, it's become a favorite story for him to tell.

My father and I ran a restaurant in upstate New York for a few years, which was nearby the world's oldest BDSM training chateau, La Domaine Esemar. Master R and Madame Sang, who both ran the chateau at the time, came into the restaurant. The food was so mind-blowing that they came into the kitchen and asked to be introduced to the chef, My father. Master R, who doesn't always tell people right off the bat that he runs a lifestyle dungeon household, immediately felt comfortable and told My father what he did and that they had this dungeon so close by.

Apparently, as the story goes, during their conversation I blew in through the kitchen, yelling at My father about something, slamming stuff around and barking orders. After I came and went like a storm, My father looked at Master R and said, "Please, train my daughter." And that's pretty much what ended up happening. I got to know the leather family at La D, and it wasn't long before I asked Myself if I could go and train to become a professional dominatrix. I told My father I was going over and was excited about it. I never hid it. I was pretty matter-of-fact about it when I would tell him I couldn't work at the restaurant because I was making more money as a pro-domme. I was having so much fun and such a positive experience. I felt like I had finally found My people. I didn't really give a fuck what My friends thought or what My family thought, and didn't listen to shit-talkers and haters. For Me, it was clear that sex work wasn't just a passing phase or for survival or to get Me through until the next thing. It was what I wanted to do. So, quite simply, I need to have people around Me who support Me and don't judge Me because I am a pornographer.

I've been coming out for fourteen years and it has not gotten any easier. I think I just have less and less fucks to give each year that goes by.

It does not always go My way. When My grandmother found out I was doing porn, she stopped talking to Me. I grew apart from most of My extended family. I had to rebuild Myself a new family. Thankfully, the adult industry is filled with open, loving folks who also want a chosen family, and that is what I have. I went almost ten years without speaking to My grandmother. So after I started writing this, I wrote her a letter. Enough time had passed, and I miss her and love her and want her in My life, so I told her as much and hoped that her love for Me was stronger than her opposition to something she didn't agree with or didn't understand. Well, guess what? It worked. I went and spent a day with her. She asked if I was still doing porn and the conversation lasted all of five minutes. In true Italian style, we just didn't talk about it after that, dropped it and moved on.

Sex work does not have to be your defining feature. You get to decide how much or how little information about your job to disclose to family and friends. But you should always have a plan and worst-case scenario of what will happen if, say, your grandma finds out you do porn.

EN SOMEONE
LIKE ME: HOW I
CAME OUT AS A
SMUT STARLET

Betty Blac

Writer, artist, porn performer, and lovable weirdo, Betty Blac is a Bay Area native. She is passionate about social justice, positive sexuality, art, and shiny things. Despite being known for her onscreen jigglegasms, Blac has a slightly nerdy side. She boasts both a BA in media studies from Mills and an MA in creative writing from the University of Sydney. She writes about everything from pop culture, art, sex toys, and porn, to oppression and injustice.

I thought the moment my first porn scene premiered that skywriters automatically would splash the news across the sky, that an old-timey newsboy would run through the streets shouting the news, and doves would be released, each bearing the message, "Betty's naked ass is on the Internet!" Okay, not really.

It's not like I thought that the moment I did a porn scene a gold limo would pull up at my apartment and sweep me away to a *Boogie Nights* fantasy world. However, I can't pretend I wasn't at least a little delusional about what kind of exposure the scenes would have. To be honest, I was a little delusional about what the porn world would be like in general.

I have long been a connoisseur of Bay Area–based indie and queer porn. I remember when I first saw the website No Fauxxx, now called Indie Porn Revolution. It was almost a little startling to see porn stars that weren't airbrushed to unattainable perfection. I saw brown folks, fat folks, queer folks and it was refreshing. The motley crew of queers sucking and fucking with wild abandon were all from "around the way," and many even run in the same circles. Seeing indie stars who were relatable and having real orgasms intrigued me. I too wanted to express myself on film and explore the erotic world. I realized I didn't have to be white or skinny or any of the stereotypes I had of what a porn star was in order to be in adult films. After a few false starts in previous years, I finally decided in 2012, at age thirty, to give performing in porn a try.

I didn't want to go into the porn world uninformed so I met with Jiz Lee, a porn star I knew whose perspective I trusted. I was feeling lucky they were willing to meet up with me and share their experiences in porn and their coming-out story. It wasn't without challenges, but their overall experience in porn seemed positive.

That same night I also met Shar Rednour, and it was all sort of surreal. Shar had been my femme idol when I was coming out as a baby queer, and the first porn I ever owned was *Sugar High Glitter City*, which starred Shar and her wife, Jackie Strano. They were local folks, but I was still star struck. That night with Jiz and Shar made me feel excited about becoming part of the world of the grown and sexy.

Because of my introduction to porn, I saw performing in porn as being revolutionary. Here was an opportunity for me to step outside of my shell, express myself sexually, be a bit of an exhibitionist. I knew porn could be feminist and creative, but that few people have been exposed to that kind of porn. In mainstream porn, I didn't see a lot of people like me. Not just women of color or fat women, but also nerdy, quirky types. I wasn't seeing a lot of people with my uniqueness. The black women I saw in porn often were boxed into tired stereotypes of black womanhood. Black women weren't portrayed as beautiful, sexy goddesses the way their white counterparts were.

Unfortunately, a lot of mainstream porn relies on stereotypes for all people of color. I wasn't sure whom I'd tell about being a performer. I definitely didn't want to tell them that I worked for the type of site that would refer to me as a ghetto gagger or, even worse, end up on one of those sites where the black section of the site was called something like "the watermelon patch." I definitely didn't want my career to be about reinforcing negative stereotypes. I guess, in a way, I wanted to be a porn role model, as peculiar as that sounds.

I would love to say I performed exclusively in the über-progressive world of Bay Area queer porn, but that wasn't practical. Performing in porn that aligns with my politics, although emotionally satisfying, isn't exactly lucrative. The majority of the mainstream companies I shot for didn't regurgitate tired racist themes, but that isn't to say they weren't racist to some degree. It is still a reality that women of color will have less opportunity and will be paid less in a lot of contexts, especially big beautiful women (BBW). Our scenes will get less exposure and be promoted less, and more often than not, if a black woman is on the cover, it's an all-black DVD intended only for a black audience. We often don't get crossover exposure; rather, we are boxed into genres and subgenres.

I didn't plan to tell my parents. My family is ridiculously crazy. I know everyone says this about their family, but it's actually true in my case. I grew up with an overeducated, pretentious and proper Trinidadian father and a hot-tempered Greek stepmother. I lived full time with my stepsiblings, and my half-sister would visit during the summers.

Both my parents, being immigrants, were peculiar in a way that is hard for me to explain to people who don't have foreign parents. Their way of processing the world and their expressions for things were always so comically odd. My mom had recovered from a Greek Orthodox upbringing and my dad is a recovered Catholic. We weren't religious per se, just an ambiguous form of hippy spiritual. They were whatever you call people who read the *Celestine Prophecy* and refer to God as "the Universe," with a dash of old-world Paganism thrown in.

Because of this, I wasn't raised with religious guilt or shame. My dad, being in the medical field, had informed us kids all about the ins and outs of sex and reproduction in the most clinical way possible, mostly as a means to tell me and my sister to never, ever, ever get pregnant; his biggest fear was us becoming teenage mothers. My sister was the rebellious one who did what she wanted, and I was the irritating goody two-shoes. I never dated in high school, and I didn't have sex until I was in college at twenty-one. I didn't have sex with a man until I was twenty-eight and in grad school. Maybe because it was taboo for so long, I was a late bloomer. But once I became active, I really loved sex. Part of what is great about porn is getting paid to do something I love.

I was really close to my family growing up, but grew estranged from both my parents in my later adulthood (see previous explanation about them being crazy). So when it came time to come out about being a porn star, I didn't feel the need to tell them because I wasn't speaking to them, anyway.

Later, my dad tried to start speaking to me again and I was having none of it. In my distancing email, I let it slip that I was a fat porn star. I knew it would burn him that not only was I in porn (oh, the West Indian shame he must have felt) but also that I was fat. My dad hates fat people. He was the type of man who would sidle up to me any time that I was making a sandwich with "too much mayo" on it and tell me that it would make me fat, before confiscating it and taking the type of bite that looked like he must have had to unhinge his jaw to get that much sandwich in his mouth. Being comfortable in my body has been a process, but I liked that women would tell me they felt more confident because they saw plus-sized women like me being portrayed as proud and sexy.

I didn't come out to my stepmother. We lived together when I was going to grad school in Australia, and that is when I learned it is a mistake to live with parents as an adult. I am lucky I escaped Sydney without there being a murder-suicide. I'm not really sure how she would respond if she knew.

In recent years, I have come to know my biological mother. I was separated from her when I was three, when my dad one day packed up all our stuff and kidnapped me. We drove cross-country from Virginia to California and she never saw me again. Even now, although we talk on the phone, I have not met her in person. When I told her I was in porn, she thought it was cool. She was like, "at one point I considered doing it myself." I don't know if that's true, but I think she's so happy I am in her life that she doesn't care what I do. When I sent her a picture of me on the cover of the local weekly, *The East Bay Express*, she was so proud she shared it with all my cousins, much to my embarrassment.

I came out to everyone else on Facebook, a nonchalant status update casually alerting a hodgepodge of my friends, family, and former lovers. I didn't care who knew. I figured I could just unfriend anyone who had negative things to say. None of the responses were negative, thankfully. Many of the people in my life are sex positive and progressive. My closest friends already knew, and the family I get along with, my siblings and uncle, were cool with it. Some of my exes tried to put the sexy moves on me, but other than that, my coming out was a ripple more than a wave. My bestie was a little awkward about it at first, but has been overwhelmingly supportive of me throughout my career.

Coming out to people I'm interested in dating is a lot harder than coming out to people I have known for years. For a while, I announced it on my OkCupid.com profile, thinking that it would be a good filter, but then I just got a bunch of sexual energy coming my way. My inbox was filled with badly written amateur porn. People wanted to date me as a conquest or add me to a harem. I had many short relationships where I felt more like a Fleshlight than a romantic interest. Then there were the other brand of dates, people completely freaked out and scared off by "porn me." One guy, upon finding out through Google stalking that I did porn, cancelled our date five minutes before it was meant to happen. This type of person tends to worry that I am an amoral, insatiable nymphomaniac, riddled with disease. Of course, this isn't everyone, but the amorous world has felt challenging to navigate and be open about being a sex worker.

In recent years, I have removed the porn part from my dating profile. I don't wait until weeks in to come out about it, but it is not something that people will know before meeting me. I want people to have the opportunity to meet me so I can shatter all their stereotypes first.

Things are a little different now because I am leaving the porn world. I wish I could say porn has always been rewarding and that I feel better for being in it, but that is not the case. My career was short, just three years. I had dreams of starting my own porn company, but there were so many false starts and setbacks that it became impossible to get things off the ground. I was sad to have to finally give up on that dream, or at least put it on extended pause.

I was inspired to be a different type of porn star than people were used to. Nothing really prepared me for being a pseudo celebrity. Nothing prepared me for both the adoration and the judgment of strangers. Putting your body on display on film leaves you up for scrutiny. I got weight loss emails and posts on my social networks critiquing my appearance. Sometimes I would feel on top of the world with all the admiration, and at other times discouraged by my critics. My Facebook was a shitstorm of unsolicited dick pics and sleazy come-ons from strangers.

I felt pressure to lose weight to gain more access to roles, but I also felt pressure to stay fat because I didn't want to let my progressive, fat-positive fans down. I wanted to be there for all the fat and brown girls who felt sexier and more confident because they saw someone like me. When I finally made the decision to lose weight recently, I stopped performing entirely.

I was the first fat girl who cammed for Kink.com, I was in the first BBW release by Evil Angel, and I was the only black talent nominated for BBW of the Year two years in a row for AVN. In my short career, I have made some strides I am proud of. I enjoyed performing. Sometimes it was awkward, but often it was fun and really hot.

There were parts of my career that involved hustling and strife, and I am not that great a hustler. It was challenging for me to try to be a porn star, a cam model, and work my demanding customer service job at a bougie adult boutique. Something had to give, so I decided to give up sex work.

I don't regret being in porn. I learned a lot about myself, the porn world, and about racism, to be honest. I was a little naïve about racism. I have been in the progressive Bay Area so long that it takes me by surprise sometimes.

Fans love to ask me if I had a child who wanted to enter sex work, would I let them. The short answer is yes, I would let them. With me as their mother, they would have a ton of support, and I would also be able to share some of my experiences in the industry. However, allowing it is not the same as encouraging it. I wouldn't encourage it, not because of any shame around sex or sexuality. I think there are many happy, healthy porn stars, and I am not anxious to portray the seedy side of porn that people are so fascinated with. Not every porn director is unscrupulous and not every porn starlet is a drug-addicted partier, or whatever the popular stereotypes are now.

My concerns for my child would be about them dealing with the stigma around porn and sex work in general. My child, like me, would come into the world already part of an oppressed group. Depending on their gender and ability, they might experience multiple oppressions. And while adding diversity to representation is a positive thing, it's not easy being that representation. It is not easy being the token or the different one. I wouldn't want the way the world sees them to have any negative impact on their self-esteem or self-worth, the way it has on mine. I would want them to have each and every opportunity to shine. I would want them to pursue their passion rather than enter sex work. I would want them to be able to be public with their brilliance and have their exploration of sex be private.

You never know how something will go for you until you do it. When I started out, I thought I was totally ready to be a porn star. I thought it would be a nonstop joy ride, and it wasn't. That doesn't mean it was all bad. I have cherished my opportunities to connect with fans. And admittedly, it's nice to have fans.

When I did webcam shows, I often was putting on my "sex educator" hat. It felt good that people would come to my cam shows thinking that they would just get off, and instead left learning better ways to please themselves and their partners. That is the direction I see my life heading, helping people to have better sex and better relationships.

Sex should be pleasurable, fun, and at times healing and transformative, and I want to be a part of helping people experience that. That is where you will see Betty Blac next. I continue to be the person I have always been: a writer, an activist, a social critic, and an informal relationship/sexuality advisor. I suppose one day I will have to have a grand coming out for that. Or maybe this is it.

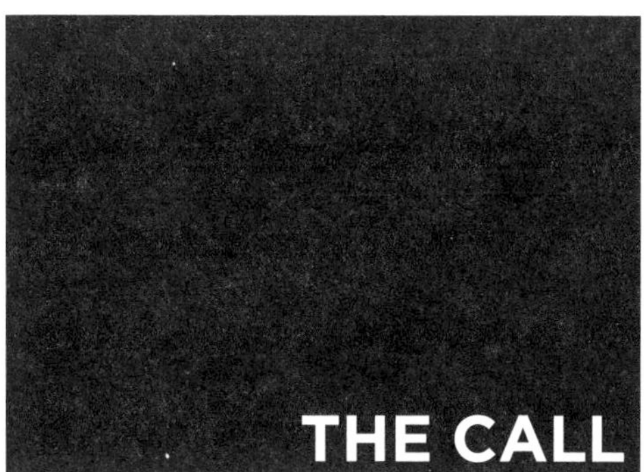

Candida Royalle

In 1984, Candida Royalle stepped behind the camera, from porn star to director, creating Femme Productions in order to produce adult films from a woman's perspective. Royalle gained international acclaim as a pioneer in female sexual empowerment and expression, and she became a sought-after speaker, lecturing extensively at such venues as the Smithsonian Institute, the World Congress on Sexology, and several universities and professional conferences. She has been a guest on countless TV talk shows and written up everywhere from the New York Times *to the* Times of London. *Royalle was invited to become a member of the American Association of Sex Educators, Counselors, and Therapists (AASECT); in 2014 she received a doctorate in human sexuality from the Institute for the Advanced Study of Human Sexuality for her life's work. She is currently working on a documentary about the search for her birth mother with award-winning filmmaker Sheona McDonald. You can find her at CandidaRoyalle.com*

I can't remember what kind of day it was or what I was doing when the phone rang, but I was definitely at the home of my close friend, Joe Morocco, with whom I was staying, and this was before the age of cell phones, if you can imagine such a time.

It was August of 1979, and I was on the cusp of some major life changes, both personal and professional. I had just spent the last eight years in the wildly colorful gender-bending counterculture of San Francisco where, along with Joe, I performed in outrageously unconventional theater productions with many of the original Cockettes and other infamous glitterati born of the gay rights movement. Contrary to what many presume, this is where I became known as Candida Royalle. We were all coming up with aliases to perform under, and here was my opportunity to use the name a beloved uncle had always called me: Candida, the Latin derivative of my birth-given name, Candice, and which in Latin means "pure." This uncle, whom I loved dearly, passed away when I was just thirteen. Having people call me by his special name brought me great comfort.

Although this uncle might have been somewhat amused had he been aware of how I eventually came to be known as Candida, I can't imagine he would have been pleased by how I next came to use the name he had lovingly bestowed upon me. Looking for a way to supplement the income I brought in from doing free theater, singing in jazz clubs, selling the occasional art piece, and modeling for artists, I answered an ad for nude erotic modeling and ended up in a porn movie. It was, after all, the days of the so-called sexual revolution, and defying social conventions and breaking rules was all the rage. Daring as I may have been, however, I still wasn't comfortable with the idea of my Italian Catholic family finding out, so once again it was time to come up with an alias. Assuming my foray into porn was to be brief and unremarkable, I initially left the producers with the task of naming me and found myself being credited with ridiculous noms de porn such as Candice Ball and Candice Chambers. It was time to come up with something quick. Unable to top Candida Royalle, I said five Hail Marys and a Lord's Prayer for good measure and began signing the model releases as Candida Royalle.

Contrary to what I assumed would be a few quick film roles to help pay the rent, I became a sought-after performer thanks to my ability to learn lines and carry a role. Performers nowadays might appear in hundreds of roles throughout the course of their career; I appeared in about twenty-five films during my five-year career, not counting the handful of "loops" I made, plotless quickies found in slot machines in Times Square and other red light districts. Don't be fooled by those lengthy lists of features credited to me; most of them were created by pulling scenes from one movie to create another. Naturally, the performers were never paid for those additional "features."

Manhattan in '79 was alive with the hottest discos and sex clubs and, unaware of the scourge that was about to overtake the gay community and put the adult industry on alert, things were about to get even hotter in the '80s, with lots more clubs like Area and Danceteria opening up. The porn industry, looking the threat right in the eye and refusing to take heed, was to explode in size and popularity, at least for a while. But for now, unaware of how I was about to have the ground shaken under me, I had plenty of reasons to feel happier than I had in some time.

One of the first things I did was have Joe Morocco take me to Studio 54. Joe was the perfect escort; he was a brilliant artist and performer who turned heads wherever he went. Using himself as a canvas, his outfits were as original as they were bizarre, and together we stole shows and took over dance floors. He had since moved back to our native New York City and into the Ansonia, an elegant old landmark building on the Upper West Side where he landed a fabulous three-bedroom apartment, one of the few grand old living quarters that hadn't yet been divided up into smaller apartments and gradually sold off as co-ops. (A noteworthy aside: the original notorious Plato's Retreat was located on the ground floor of the Ansonia when Plato's was at its prime, a convenience wasted on me as I wasn't particularly into swinging; but always curious, I occasionally ventured down there for a private party or a film shoot, managing to avoid the indoor pool.)

I hadn't yet moved back to New York myself, but having just fallen in love with the hot and highly popular Per Sjöstedt, who had recently moved to New York from his native Sweden and who would ultimately become my husband and business partner, it would be just a few months before I moved back to the East Coast.

In the meantime, you could say I was floating on a cloud. I had been flown to New York City to work for some of the top producers and directors when New York City was still putting out some of the best adult features. My close friend Leslie Bovee, one of the sexiest and most in-demand porn stars at the time, had me cast in a supporting role to her lead in a feature being directed by Kamal. These were the days when you had to audition and read for a part, and landing a lead or a supporting role often meant working for a week at a substantial day rate, rather than being paid per sex act which, I'm sorry, just feels to me like being paid like a hooker. I understand the need for the change in how performers were paid: Once they started shooting one- and two-day "wonders," thanks to the low cost of shooting on video, performers were suddenly expected to be in sometimes as many as three sex scenes a day for that same day rate. Something had to change.

Back then, you could still feel like you were in a "real" movie, negotiating daily and weekly rates based on your box office appeal. I understand that nowadays some of the talent resent being asked to act. They'll charge extra for having to memorize lines whereas we delighted in the notion of being talented enough to be asked to carry a role.

Having decided this would be my last year in porn, I purposely targeted New York City, where I began getting juicy roles for some of the top adult-film directors, like Henri Pachard and Chuck Vincent. The unexpected bonus was falling in love with Per, who was working for Chuck as a promising young producer—until that phone call burst my bubble, and I was seriously outed.

It wasn't unusual to get a phone call from my sister. The product of not one but two broken and loveless marriages, she and I had always had a close but difficult relationship. While we clung to each other for safety and support, our parents played us off of one another, as parents often do, setting us up for a lifetime of rivalry and misunderstanding. I was coming out of what I would describe as the lowest point in my life, having taken too many recreational drugs that sometimes led to bad behavior. About a year prior to this, I had done something to my sister that I would classify as a terrible betrayal, the sort of thing that feels like a nightmare, only worse because it's real. You really did it and there's no way to undo it and you live in fear of being found out. No, I'm not going to disclose what I did; let's just say it involved a man—*her* man—and a dangerous brew of party drugs, and I think you can get a pretty good idea of the nature of my shameful betrayal.

I can't recall how the phone call began, whether she took her time leading up to it or she simply and immediately dropped the bomb. I imagine she had to have first informed me that she had learned about my terrible secret. Then: "I told Dad that you've been making porno movies, and if you don't call Mom and tell her yourself, I'm going to call her and tell her too." Then she gave me a set amount of time to do the deed, or else.

I don't remember anything else about that phone call. I can only conjure up the look of utter shock and horror that came over me. Lips slightly parted but speechless. Eyes wide open but staring at nothing. Just complete, utter disbelief.

Five years before that, I had no intention of going into porn. Perhaps the greatest irony as I think back to that fateful day in 1975 when I decided to give it a try was this little bit of reasoning on my part: Who's gonna see it? One day, all these film reels will be left in some dark, forgotten storage room to collect dust and fade away, and no one will even be able to recognize who's on screen.

Now, five years later, I was about to take my final bow, to leave behind my swan song when fate interfered with my best-laid plans. I was about to get away with it, my secret safely tucked away and buried. If only my damned sister didn't have such a monstrous temper, a frightening level of rage, and an ability to come up with the most hideous and vengeful ways of getting someone back. If only I hadn't screwed up in the most, shall we say, *Royalle* way imaginable.

If only I hadn't betrayed her in the first place.

But there it was. It was all out in the open now. There were other juicy tidbits of information she had shared with my father. Just the usual sins of the young, drugs and partying, that sort of thing. Nothing else quite as shocking as porn, though. That would be hard to top.

Facing the prospect of calling my mother and telling her that I had been performing in porn movies for the last five years was not something I was looking forward to. In fact, I was dreading it. But it was better than having my sister tattle on me. And so I resolved to tell her myself.

It wasn't as if she were going to scream and haul off and slap me across the face like she did when I was a kid; besides, my parents were living in Florida by then, so there was little face-to-face contact. It was more the sense of shame I felt. I'd like to say I had a clear conscience and a strong sense of conviction about my porn career, but that came later, after going into therapy to make sure I was all right with what I had done.

It was also a different time back then. Not counting my friends from the counterculture whose reactions ran from mild amusement to wanting to know how they can get into porn and make a few extra bucks, people from the "straight world," as we referred to them back then, didn't know how to react. Although "porno chic" is a term that gets bandied about when describing the cultural response to films like *Deep Throat* and *The Devil in Miss Jones*, pornography was still something that was barely discussed then. I certainly didn't fit the image people had of girls who went into porn. I was neither a hooker nor a sad, strung-out loser with no other options or places to go. Something was terribly wrong with this picture.

I eventually came to terms with my choices and could honestly say there was nothing wrong with performing sexually for others to watch and enjoy. But I hadn't done that work on myself yet, and so it was with a sense of dread that I picked up the phone and dialed.

I am not exaggerating when I say this was probably the most difficult phone call I have ever made. I dreaded having to come clean to my mother, who had spent her hard-earned money on dance lessons and one of the best art colleges in the States for me. I knew she would think I threw all that away on something shameful, inexplicable.

Much to my amazement, my mother, who had grown up a moderately religious Irish Catholic, turned out to be far more accepting than I could have ever imagined. Here is what I remember she said:

> "I'm shocked to think of my little Candy doing that."
> "I envy you; you seem to have worked out your issues with men."
> "You're still my little Candy and I'll always love you."

Never could I have imagined that my mother would respond with such love and acceptance.

The comment about men was more of a projection on her part. I did work through my issues with men, but porn had little to do with it. Spending several years with a brilliant therapist is where I put the credit.

Later on, once I had formed my production company and began to receive an unprecedented amount of media coverage and financial success, my mother expressed even greater respect for what I'd accomplished. She occasionally made comments like, "I wish you had gone into a field that I could brag about to my friends," but she also expressed a sense of awe and admiration for what I had accomplished. Never one to manage her finances very well, I was living the life she had wanted: a successful, independent career woman living a glamorous life in Manhattan. Not that I always felt that way. I'm not sure she understood quite how hard I worked to be able to project that glamorous, successful image!

As for my father, we never did talk about the things my sister told him. But several years later, when I was at the peak of my media fame, my father, who had been living alone since my mother left him, caught me on one of the many TV talk shows I had appeared on. We spoke a bit about my work, which was unusual because my father and I never discussed anything to do with sex, and that included the work I did. Feeling a bit awkward, I told him, "I feel a little funny talking about this with you, Dad." To which he replied, "You have nothing to feel bad about. With all the things people do in this world—politicians lying to everyone, corporations cheating people, people hurting and killing each other—all you're doing is bringing pleasure to people's lives."

I can't tell you how much this meant to me, but I'm sure you can imagine.

A few years later, my father was diagnosed with Alzheimer's. That conversation would remain one of the greatest gifts my father left me with.

As for my sister, I knew I had hurt her and it was important that I make amends. Short of being able to undo what I had done, with the help of my brilliant therapist, I came to understand what had motivated my behavior and was able to ask for my sister's forgiveness. She saw how hard I worked to get to this point and it meant a lot to her.

My sister and I still have our ups and downs, but having gotten through this particularly traumatic event showed us that nothing is insurmountable. Our mutual love, born of the bond that formed out of years of clinging together when nothing felt safe in a home devoid of certainty, was solid.

Perhaps the greatest gift was that an act meant to punish me in the cruelest way possible turned out to be a blessing in disguise: I no longer had any secrets I had to keep locked away, living in fear of being found. And although I can never change what was—not the turmoil that filled our days growing up, nor the choices I made that seem to others to be inexplicable—in the end, the truth was our healing. I know I was loved and am still loved by the people who matter the most.

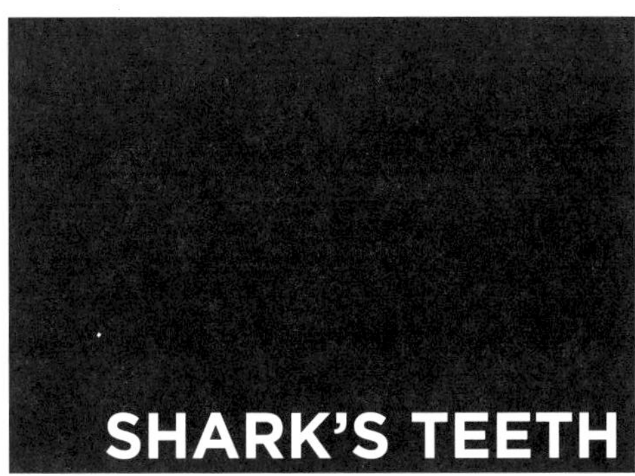

SHARK'S TEETH

Casey Calvert

Casey Calvert is an award-winning adult actress and naked model who spends her free time as a writer, rock climber, and expert level napper. She graduated magna cum laude from film school at the University of Florida and moved to Los Angeles at the end of 2012. She is also currently pursuing mainstream production as her secret real-world alter ego. If she is not at home with her cats, dog, and partner, she is probably at work . . . or sitting in traffic.

"Different people are into different things."

That's all she said. That's all I remember her saying. Sitting in the cold clutter of Miss Deborah's office, reading the diplomas on the wall for the thousandth time, chewing a hole through the straw of the Capri Sun she gave me, all I could really hear was the thunder of Absolutely Excruciating Embarrassment.

Miss Deborah was my brother's therapist. I had my own therapist, but I outright refused to see him. I didn't want to see anyone, but twelve-year-old me didn't get a choice, because twelve-year-old me's mom didn't know how to handle what she had just discovered.

Long before twelve, I knew I was different. I don't know how I knew. I guess it was just something I intuited as my friends talked about the boys they wanted to kiss, and I didn't understand.

I wanted to do things with boys, but it certainly wasn't kiss.

My fantasies were my Deep Dark Secret. Not a single soul knew.

It was the first day of band practice. It was also the last. We made it maybe an hour, but I guess that's how it goes in seventh grade.

"Do you want to see something cool?" Audrey said, sitting down at my computer. She told me I was lucky, having my own computer in my own room. She also wrote the lyrics to our song.

Three's better than two, and two's better than you.

I had absolutely no idea what that meant.

"Sure," I said.

The dialup tones played, and we were online. I looked over her shoulder, as she navigated her way past a screen that flashed "Adults Only."

"Ever seen porn before?"

"I . . . umm . . . of course," I mumbled, trying to be cool, actually having absolutely no idea what porn was.

Two naked, hard-bodied, harder-cocked men appeared on the screen. The blond one gave the other blond one a blowjob, and I had just watched my first porno.

I learned a lot of things that day. I learned what a hard cock looks like. I learned the word blowjob.

And I learned that you can find whatever you want on the Internet.

I guess you could say that the Internet landed me on Miss Deborah's sofa. But the Internet has also made me who I am today, so I don't blame Vint Cerf.

It was the Internet that led me to Spanking Teen Jessica.

That night, I masturbated, just like I did every night. But I didn't picture the pretty blond cocks from the computer screen. I went back to my favorite fantasy, a variation on a theme, a story of spanking. Just like I did every night.

Then I got an idea.

The next time my parents left me home alone, I went online. Typed eight simple letters into the search bar: spanking.

I chose the first link. I made it through all of three seconds of silent video before the explosion of arousal and shame. And orgasm.

So it became a game. Every time I was alone, I would log on. Each time, I lasted a little longer, watching more and more. But, mixed in with the arousal, there was always this underlying panic someone would catch me, an underlying shame. I knew what I was doing was Wrong.

I found SpankingTeenJessica.com pretty quickly. I started coming back because of all the previews, and as I got bolder, I started clicking around. I found a bio.

The bio was long, but I devoured every word. I was hungry, starving for someone like me. And I had finally found her.

I wasn't alone.

Jessica said she started making porn because she wanted to fulfill her fantasies.

I had another idea.

It was finals week, seventh grade. At my magnet school in the ghetto, during finals week, we weren't allowed to bring backpacks to school. They were worried about cheating, or guns, or something in between that I also didn't concern myself with.

I didn't care. I wasn't allowed backpacks in elementary school either, and carrying around my fifth-grade transparent purple folder was a way to cling to a part of my youth that I desperately missed.

In science, I sat next to my best friend, Erika. And Jessica had inspired me. In her story, she told her best friend about her deep dark secret, and her best friend spanked her. So I printed out the bio, and brought it to school with me in my purple transparent folder.

Erika laughed at me. And then told way too many people about my Deep Dark Secret.

The school year was over, and I brought the bio home in my purple transparent folder. I set it down on the kitchen counter, where I always put my school stuff.

And then I went away to summer camp.

"Mom wants to talk to you," Dad said, as I was sitting in my room. "She'll be up in a second."

As soon as she walked through the door, I saw the purple folder in her hand. And I knew.

My mom sat down on the bed next to me. I didn't stay long. The clouds of Absolutely Excruciating Embarrassment stormed in and became a Category 5 hurricane.

I spent the entire rest of the day hiding under my bed.

I learned a hard lesson about the necessity of clearing one's browser history that day.

So, off to therapy I went. My mother, my feminist, abused-as-a-child mother, couldn't fathom why her twelve-year-old daughter wanted to be hurt. In an act of I-don't-know-what-the-fuck-else-to-do, she drove me to Miss Deborah.

Miss Deborah wasn't wrong, you know. Different people are into different things. The thunder was just too loud for me to hear it.

Andrew and I were hunting for shark's teeth. That's what we called it: hunting. Like the fossils had to be chased down and killed before we could put them in our Tupperware.

I taught him how to do it. The shark's teeth creek was a sacred childhood place to me. Andrew was the only one I've ever taken there. He was a much better best friend than Erika ever was.

I was twenty. I hadn't had a boyfriend. I had my first awful kiss, but second base is as far as I'd gotten with a guy. I hadn't watched another single second of porn. My Deep Dark Secret had become my Deepest Darkest Secret.

Andrew thought that I lost my virginity at sixteen. And was vanilla.

We were horny college students. All we did at the creek is talk about sex.

"What's the one thing that turns you on the most?"

I froze as the clouds rolled in. Andrew noticed.

"What?" he playfully teased. "You've never blushed before. Now you have to tell me."

He was right. The lies usually came so easily.

"I . . . I like to be hit." It was barely audible.

"You mean, like spanking?"

"Yes. Like . . . spanking." It was almost impossible to say the word.

"Oh, that's not that crazy," he smiled. "Mine is that I want to have a threesome."

My Deepest Darkest Secret came out of its cave, and instead of the villagers seeing a fire-breathing dragon and running away in terror, they saw a harmless little lizard, like the kind that we used to catch in elementary school. Everything was about to change.

Professor Calvert brought DVDs to class with him today. He teaches First Amendment Law. I'm not even supposed to be in this class. I was supposed to be in Telecom Law, which was supposed to be absolutely awful, but it was full, and the college gave me credit for that, from this.

Thank you, College of Journalism and Communications. Thank you.

Professor Calvert passes the DVDs around. They are porn; but of course they are.

All we've learned about in this class was porn. That's what Professor Calvert studies. Free speech. Free expression. Porn.

This is the first porn I've seen since I was twelve.

It doesn't feel like shame anymore.

See, we've already learned that porn is a perfectly legal expression of one's First Amendment rights. Porn is not Wrong, as long as you're over eighteen.

I learned how much girls get paid for double penetration at Kink.com that day. I learned that I'm not exactly sure what double penetration is.

And I learned from Professor Calvert that there is absolutely nothing wrong with making porn.

The sunbeams started to break through the thunderheads.

I had this ritual. The same every night: Kink.com previews until I was really close, Niko's videos until I came.

Every night, Niko's video ended with a "for a good time, call" and an email address.

My twenty-first birthday was fast approaching. I wasn't having any of the oh-fuck-I'm-almost-twenty-one-and-I-haven't-had-a-boyfriend-yet, but at the same time, it was my twenty-first. It's the night that most kids get legally trashed for the first time. I wasn't interested in getting legally trashed, but I still wanted it to be special.

I had been thinking about it for a week or so. What can I give myself for my birthday? What's the one thing I want more than anything else in the entire world? Then one night, it came to me, post-self-coitus, 2:00 a.m., as Niko's lower third ran across the screen.

Oh. I know.

I composed a message that sat in my drafts folder for almost a week.

I hit send.

The next time we went hunting, I told Andrew about Niko and about my plan. In my excitement of just needing to tell someone, anyone, I accidently established a safe call with the only person I could tell.

I wasn't worried about safety. My deduction: Jessica made porn to explore her fantasies in a safe way; Niko makes porn; thus, Niko must be safe.

Andrew was genuinely supportive. For the first time, instead of the storm, the sky was blue.

I had to stop to pee three times during the half hour drive to the truck stop.

He was shorter than me, and his truck smelled like Axe.

I was there three hours longer than we had planned.

It was the first time I ever hugged someone without feeling awkward.

I thought I was gonna get it out of my system.

I was wrong.

I skipped school the next day, the day of my birthday. Actually, I drove in, dropped of my zoology homework, and drove back home.

My body didn't know how to process the trauma it had received, however sexual, however much I loved it. I dry-heaved in the parking lot of the blood bank, and a gardener asked me if I was alright.

Boy, was I alright.

I wrote in my journal that afternoon. I wrote down every little detail, so afraid to forget. At the end of my entry, I apologized to my mom. I apologized for staying out late. I apologized for enjoying it way more than I thought I would. The lightning flashed. Terrified. Of disgust, of hate.

The video was up a few days later. I wanted him to film it. I wanted the tape for me, as a way to remember the session. The time I got my spanking. It was so romantic.

I thought I was gonna get it out of my system, remember?

All you can see is my twenty-year-old, pale, not nearly as nice as it is now, ass. I made sure he didn't record my face or my tattoo. I figured it would be the only video of me ever, but just in case, I wanted to ensure no one would ever recognize me.

Still though, you could say, in a very loose sense of the phrase—it's my first porno.

"You should really be a model," Lew said.

Using my same "porn is safe" deduction, I'm at Lew Ruben's house, getting tied up for the first time. I'm lucky. A bondage porn god lives only two hours away, and he actually wants to tie me, of all people, up.

"But I can't. I'm not tall enough," I said.

Or pretty enough, I thought.

Lew disagreed with both opinions.

He set up a glamour shoot for me to start building a portfolio. I decided it would be okay to show my face if I wasn't naked.

Remember that other idea I had, that one that had been hiding in the back corner of the dungeon in my mind, behind the St. Andrew's cross, that one I got from Jessica. Well, it was still there.

Make porn, it whispered, every time a grown-up asked me what I wanted to do when I grew up.

Make porn, it screamed now. Make porn.

My mom was an absolute wreck. Holding my journal, the same way she held the purple folder eleven years ago, she wanted to talk.

I had been acting differently, going out more; moms always know when you're lying. She had read the last thing I had written, about my first time with Niko, the one I wrote on my birthday many months ago but didn't date.

She wanted to know why.

The sun was shining too bright now to let the clouds roll back in. I didn't hide under the bed.

I sat there and told my parents about my deep dark secret, no longer so darkest and deepest. I told her I knew I was unsafe when I met Niko. I told her about Lew, about how he was mentoring me. I told her about the shoots I had been doing. I told her about how I had just started to feel pretty for the first time in my life.

She sat there and listened. She didn't sweep me away to therapy. She tried her best to understand.

The art—that's easy.

The masochism—that one's a bit harder.

I'm graduating from college, magna cum laude; across the stage, smiling parents somewhere in the massive auditorium.

And in the past year, I've travelled all over the country, Canada, Costa Rica, as a fetish model. I have a spotless reputation, amazing new friends, and strangers on the Internet think I'm beautiful.

I'm happy.

I have no idea what to do with my degree.

My little idea, no longer whispering from the corner, but standing in the doorway . . . it started speaking again.

Porn. Make. Some. Goddamn. Porn.

And that's how I ended up on the phone with adult super-agent Mark Spiegler.

Sitting in the hot tub in our backyard, steam rising in the humid summer air, I'd just gotten back from a trip to Los Angeles.

This time, it was my turn to say I wanted to talk. There would be no finding out after the fact. My mom fidgeted in the hot water, nervous as I was when she said those words to me.

"I haven't done anything yet, I promise."

I had already met Mark Spiegler, already been wined and dined and wooed by Mark Spiegler, and I'd already almost made up my mind.

"But I'm thinking about it."

One flash of lightning, of fear. Not of hatred, not this time, but of being a terrible disappointment.

"I just want you to be safe," she said.

My parents paid my first three months' rent when I moved out to Los Angeles.

When my dad's side of the family found out what I do, my mom stood up for me.

My kink used to be my Deepest Darkest secret, and now it is an integrated part of my everyday life.

It's really nice not to have secrets.

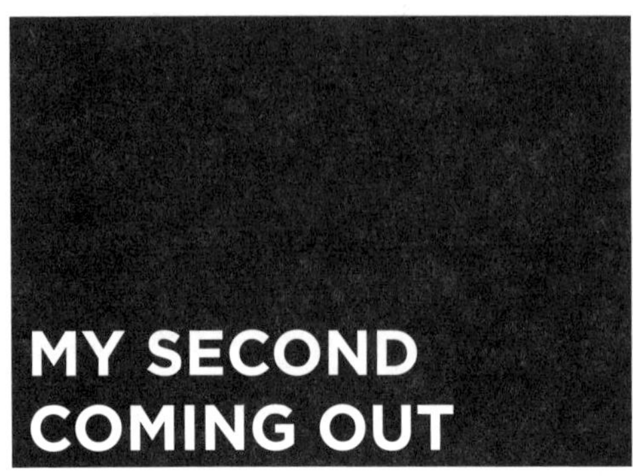

MY SECOND COMING OUT

Chelsea Poe

Chelsea Poe is a writer, director, porn performer, and trans activist from Grand Rapids, Michigan, currently residing in Oakland, California. She has been an outspoken advocate for better representation of trans women within pornography. In October of 2014, her first full-length feature, Fucking Mystic, *premiered at the Berlin Porn Film Festival and garnered her multiple AVN and Transgender Erotica Awards nominations. She launched a petition in November of 2014, calling for mainstream trans porn sites run by non-trans owners to stop the use of the term "shemale" within their marketing. The petition received over 1,600 signatures. Her website is ChelseaPoe.com.*

My story of coming out as a sex worker is a bit strange and a bit last minute. It was the night before I was flying out to California for the first time, and I was counting on my mom for a ride.

I came up with some really thinly veiled story of why I was going to San Francisco. My mom confronted me on it and asked, "What are you really doing in California?" So I decided to come clean and told her I was planning on doing feminist porn. Her response was, "Everyone who does porn is into drugs, and I don't want to see you go down that road. Why would you put yourself in such a dangerous position?"

I saw Jiz Lee speak at a college near where I grew up, and while watching their "Dirty 30 Orgy" scene, I knew queer porn was for me, and I knew this wouldn't be an easy thing to explain to my Midwestern family. I wanted to be able to show my sexuality and my story of being a queer trans woman. The next day, after I came out about doing porn, my mom drove me the long forty-five-minute drive to the airport with nearly no talking until she broke down in tears and made me promise her I would be safe. I made her that promise, but getting onto the airplane everything went through my mind: What if I get to the set and freeze up and can't do anything? What if all the stereotypes about porn are real and there are drugs everywhere? Are they going to force me to do something that I don't want to do?

My first shoot was a huge moment of my life. I never felt anything that so fulfilled everything I wanted out of it—showing my gender in a positive way, being able to perform, being able to live out my fantasies—and more importantly, it made me proud about being queer. I came home and my mom kind of backed off about it for a while. Then I told her I was planning on moving to the Bay Area within six months. After I moved, she commented on how I seemed happy and surrounded by a large group of close friends for the first time. She said, "I don't like the idea of you doing porn, but I can see it makes you extremely happy, so I support you."

The longer I was in porn, the more activism became a part of my life, and I was traveling all over the country. The activism had turned into writing and speaking gigs that were featured on mainstream media sites that my mom actually stumbled upon and saw that there was something more to this for me than just money or having sex.

In October 2014, I became the first-ever trans woman to be in God's Girls Purgatory, a popular alt-porn site where the community's network votes on which young woman will be the newest addition to the site's gallery. The morning of the first day, I got a phone call from my mom. She said something I never really had anyone express to me since I was over the age of ten: "I'm extremely proud of what you're doing, not only for you, but for what it can mean to your community. I miss you so much with you being across the country, but I am so happy to see you succeed to truly make a difference." I broke down in tears upon hearing this, because I never really thought she would understand what I do and why I do it.

My relationship with my mom isn't perfect and we still struggle at times, but the fact that she respects what I do is so important. Doing porn is one of the most important things in my life, and I know it will be for a very long time. I know I am very blessed to be in a place right now where I can talk openly about my job with my mom and to not have some secret part of my life. After feeling that way for so long before coming out as trans, queer, and a sex worker, I hope it goes to show that people can evolve after they have sex workers in their lives. Sex workers are some of the most highly stigmatized people, and I really think when people can relate real people to being sex workers, that stigma will slowly go away and create a more positive space for sex workers.

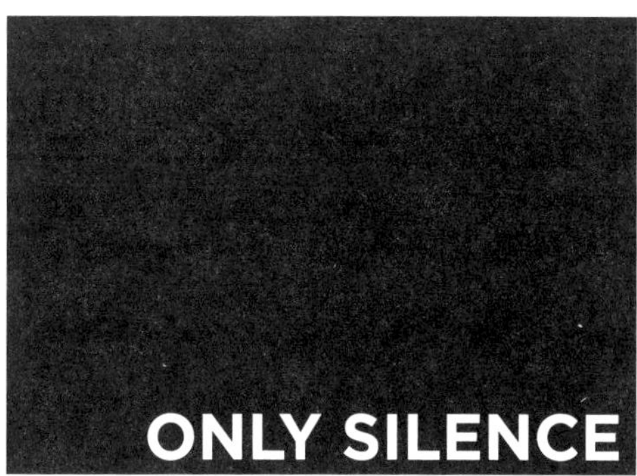

ONLY SILENCE

Chris Lowrance

As a freelance designer and web developer, Chris Lowrance has worked behind the scenes on numerous queer and feminist porn sites, including the original HeavenlySpire.com, PinkLabel.tv, and CrashPadSeries.com. Now web manager at veteran queer porn studio Pink & White Productions, Chris searches for practical solutions at the intersection of ethics, sex work, and technology.

The name I was given by my parents at birth, recognized by the government, and appearing next to a photo of my face on social media is also the name that appears in the opening credits of a long-running queer porn series. It's the name at the bottom of my company email there, as well as the name that appeared in the 2014 Feminist Porn Conference's schedule of speakers. I've made a career out of building and managing websites for pornographers and sex workers, and I've done it under my legal name.

It's an incredible privilege, being able to use a single name like this. It's one most of my friends in the industry do not have, especially not if they've performed in front of the camera.

A performer doesn't adopt a stage name out of shame for what they do. Rather, a stage name is a necessary defense against society's shaming of them, a shield not only against harassment, stalking, or loss of privacy but also the possibility of losing a job outside of porn, custody of their children, or even their life.

When I began working in this industry, I chose not to use a pseudonym because these dangers don't exist for me (at least not to the same degree). I wanted to use my "real" name out of respect for those who cannot, to show that I'm not ashamed of them or the work they do. I also don't shy from telling friends and strangers alike about my job. In this way, I hope I'm doing some small part to fight the stigma that affects others so greatly.

But shameless as I am, I cannot say I am "out." I have not told my parents.

It's actually one of many things I don't tell them—never hiding, just omitting. I never talked about when I realized my sexual attraction extended further along the gender spectrum than I once thought or when I began to identify as queer. They do not know my heterosexual-seeming marriage to my high-school sweetheart is actually a queer, partially open union of two pansexual people. They don't know about the faint question mark developing on the end of my gender identity.

If I am unashamed about these things—if I can write them here for the entire world to read—why haven't I told my family?

In some ways, I resent the idea of needing to coming out. I never came out as straight, monogamous, male, or any of the other things they assume I am, so why should I have to announce that I'm otherwise? I never sat them down to reveal all the mundane jobs I've worked, so why should I feel obligated to do so with porn? If these are lies of omission, it is only because of their problematic assumptions.

I would also have to educate them on what I'm coming out as. Not gay, or even bi, but queer? Not trans, but perhaps gender fluid? Sex work? Ethical porn? The truth is, I don't share a common terminology with them, and words shape thoughts. I would need to construct the scaffolding of language and ideas I only learned myself over many years.

Ultimately, I've been trying to protect them. While I began working for porn producers and making discoveries about my sexuality, my parents' lives became a chaos of chronic pain, poverty, depression, and substance abuse. I didn't want to introduce new sources of anxiety for people who are struggling to cope with what they already labor under. It seemed selfish and for little gain.

But only in retrospect can I see how these omissions add up. The things I hide from my parents are a huge part of who I am now. They are the source of so many of my wins and losses, my joys and anxieties, close friends, ideological battles. So much of what I've made my name mean is rooted in things I've kept from them.

Today, instead of the strained and uncomfortable relationship I was trying to spare them, we barely have one at all. What I've withheld isn't the only factor responsible, but it is a part. I may even be wrong, and they already know. Google would tell them everything. But even if so, it only means we've both contributed to the gulf of silence that, perversely, makes it even harder to come out now.

Not long after I started working as web manager, a customer told me the following:

> This site means so, so much to me because it was the first place I saw other trans men who didn't absolutely despise and hide their bodies.

I keep that email saved on my desktop, and I share it with anyone who would argue porn is a categorical evil. Because of it, and the many messages like it that my coworkers and I have received, I will never feel shame for the work I do.

But as valuable as it is to me, I've never told my parents about that email. Perhaps they would understand better than I realize, or perhaps they'd take things worse than I expect, but thus far I've never given them the chance.

For that, I do feel shame.

COMING OUT
TO MY PARENTS
ABOUT SEX
WORK

Christopher Zeischegg

Christopher Zeischegg spent eight years working in the adult film industry as performer Danny Wylde. He's been a contributor to The Feminist Porn Book, Best Sex Writing 2015, *and a variety of online publications, such as* Medium *and* Nerve. *He recently published his second novel,* The Wolves that Live in Skin and Space, *through Rare Bird Books.*

I was twenty years old the first time I approached my family regarding my work. At the time, it was as much a career as any superfluous labor one attends to in college. It was hardly what I'd call an identity. But I kept it secret for a time because I was nervous.

My mother was (and is) a fundamentalist Christian, and my father dabbled in various New Age philosophy/spirituality. I was influenced by both and knew that neither worldview thought highly of pornography, if it was considered much at all.

But there I was, fresh out of the house and making my first real income by having sex in front of a camera. It was an interesting bit of self-exploration and a quick way to earn some cash. Still, I had no long-term plans and zero thoughts of explaining it to my family. Only when I'd started dating another porn performer and planned to run away to Los Angeles did I find an explanation necessary. That, and my part-time job had become a bit more—explicitly—available on the World Wide Web.

I knew my family would eventually find out. I had to decide whether they'd hear it first from me.

"I remember that you called me and you said that you wanted to talk to me about something important," said my mother. "And you asked me to sit down. I thought, 'Wow. This is going to be something important.' Because you've never asked me to sit down."

Both my parents have agreed to an interview regarding my coming out process and how they currently feel about my participation in sex work. Given that I've just passed my seven-year anniversary in porn and I now consider it a career, it seems necessary to examine the ways my work has affected my family—with my family. Because I can offer only one perspective, and my journey with sex work in regards to my family has as much to do with them as it does with me.

For the sake of brevity, I've narrowed down the relationships to those with my mother and father, although this discussion could certainly extend to my siblings, grandparents, aunts, uncles, and even cousins.

I sat down with my mother first. The interview took place the day after Thanksgiving 2012.

"You said that you wanted to make sure that I knew this was not a personal affront against me in any way," she told me, recalling a phone conversation seven years prior. "Because you knew that it was not something within my value system. It was about your personal exploration of your own life. You wanted to make sure that if I had any questions or if there were any concerns, that you and I would discuss them personally. So that I wouldn't be surprised by it through external circumstances, which you said would probably happen at some point."

I asked my mother to recall the coming-out conversation so that we could begin on the same page. My memory is as faulty as any and I wanted to at least know that my mother and I remembered the same events. For the most part, we did.

I was nervous about telling my mother that I was involved in pornography, because I knew her point of view. She'd raised me with the idea that sexuality was something sacred to be shared between a man and a woman, and that the most fulfilling way to do so was within the boundaries of marriage.

We'd had debates in the past that proved our difference of opinion. By early high school, I'd come to believe that homosexuality was inherent to the natural variations in human sexuality. I also viewed marriage as a highly ineffective institution, based primarily on my parents' divorce and the single mothers and fathers who raised many of my close friends.

As far as sex was concerned, I wanted it just about as soon as I understood what it was. And I dreamed of it with as many partners as possible. Like many young boys, I was also scared shitless when it came down to the act. A few opportunities did arise in my youth, and I experienced my early joys and follies. But I didn't foresee myself with only one partner, I didn't much want to get married, and the only time I valued sexual monogamy was when I was hopelessly crushed out on a fellow schoolmate.

My mother at least knew my general point of view. She wouldn't have been shocked to hear that I had a girlfriend or boyfriend who I was having sex with. However, porn not only conflicted with her sexual values, it flaunted its opposition in a public space. Anyone with a computer could find out that I had become—quite literally—a whore. Even outside of Christian circles, I was aware this was not often looked upon with admiration.

I didn't want my mother, who raised me to the best of her abilities, to believe I had chosen pornography as a means to punish her. Or that it was a sign of her failure.

In terms of my own reservations, I had been told (I'm not sure by who in particular) that sex workers were often drawn to the profession because of a lack of education and a consequent lack of diverse financial opportunity. I did not want to be viewed as uneducated or unable. The fact that my mother had been so supportive in my pursuit of higher education made it all the more necessary to explain that porn was not something I was doing instead of school or in place of a long-term, real job.

My mother responded to this preface with appreciation, although as expected, she did not look upon my involvement in porn as a positive step in my life. When I asked my mother what her initial reaction was when I first told her, her eyes welled up with tears and she responded, "Sad."

Here, I must share a bit of my mother's opinion of me to show that her reaction did not necessarily come from the position of judgment or shaming.

"You're one of the most precious human beings. Not just because you've come out of my belly. Everybody, when they talk about you, they will say, 'Chris is very intelligent, talented, and gifted.' Beyond that, most super-intelligent, super-talented, super-gifted people are not as tenderhearted, kind, sensitive, feeling, sweet. And that's who you are. You have always been that since you've been a little kid. There's a purity in that, a sweetness in that."

Again, this is not shared with the purpose to gloat. I would certainly not say all of these things about myself. My point is that my mother loves me. I know that she loves me. And I know that she thinks very highly of me.

However, my mother also believes I was emotionally damaged (or that my purity/sweetness was "violated by certain individuals") as a child and that I make many of my decisions—in part—based on this damage. According to her, pornography is one such decision.

She continued, "Somebody who is a very pure, very beautiful human being who is nurtured into their full potential makes very good choices. Because they have that foundation of love, confidence, and security to explore who they are at a younger age within safe parameters that are not as dangerous—that are not as risky—they have a safety net of embracing arms, and hearts, and attitudes. I felt that when you told me [that you did porn], that my sweet, very sensitive, very beautiful, and very pure person didn't have that opportunity."

Without going into detail, my mother talked of "risks" and "dangers" inherent to the pornographic profession. I assumed from past conversations that she meant sexually transmitted diseases and performer exploitation (i.e., being coaxed to do things one's not comfortable with). She also reiterated that porn was against her values, with the addendum, "But I think you already know that."

I'm sure many parents show concern when their child picks up any interest that beckons physical harm. But my brother played club soccer all through school and broke his leg right around the time he would have earned a university scholarship. My mother supported him through years of intense training, when she knew full well the risks. In fact, during that time, a relative of ours sustained paralysis from a college sports injury. He died a year or two later.

For such reasons, I never fully bought the major concerns for physical safety when people talked about porn. Not even when they came from my mother. I'd never witnessed someone discouraged from sports based on the risks and dangers involved. And I couldn't imagine that construction workers or UPS deliverymen received lectures from parents on the dangers of their careers, despite the statistically high number of injuries.

Sex workers can, and do, contract sexually transmitted infections. But for those of us in mainstream porn, we're also regularly tested (which I've explained to my mother). Consequently, infectious outbreaks of the potentially fatal kind are rare and well contained. Performer exploitation is a more complicated issue, but I've argued (and continue to do so) that it's increasingly rare. In any case, it's something I'm unlikely to encounter at this point in my career.

On the subject of going against my mother's values, all I can say is that such transgressions extend into other facets of my life. My mother and I continue to have lively discussions over the differences in our ideological beliefs. Spirituality, including my lack thereof, seems to be a more interesting topic to the both of us than arguing the reasons behind our sexual proclivities. My mother even said, "There are other things that if you were involved in, I would look at you and maybe disrespect you. I don't disrespect you within [porn]."

My exposure to physical injury had never brought my mother to tears. Neither had engaging in sexual behavior that conflicted with her belief system. It's possible the combination of both impacted her emotional response, but I suspected something else. I think the following is an affirmation of that something.

"It perpetuates that thing that you would always fight," my mother told me. "Of not being totally accepted. It encourages some sort of rejection just by being in that profession. You are always going to be rejected by a certain segment of society. Tons of people use pornography. But the vast majority who use it are ashamed of it. It always has this stigma around it. To actually make that your profession has a certain stigma, a negativity, a shame to it. That's what you've dealt with through a lot of your life. To me, it perpetuates it. That's sad to me. You deserve not to be rejected."

This was the hardest for me to hear because it rang the most true. Even within my circle of closest childhood friends, it's taken the better part of a decade for my career to be viewed with some legitimacy, or at least without being assigned the notion that it must be an intermediary step on the way to something better.

Not to put all blame elsewhere. I've recycled the same thoughts about porn.

"It was okay for a time, because I'll get out of school and work my way into mainstream film behind the camera." If I didn't have that goal, then what was I doing? Certainly, wasting my time.

Porn was not a career goal of mine. It attained full-time status by the simple fact that by the time I graduated college, I had put in enough time to be known as a decent performer. It offered steady income. I could continue to pay my bills with porn, or I could take a gamble and start at the bottom of another profession with nothing but a liberal arts degree. For about two years, I tried both. Then I had an epiphany.

I realized that what I wanted to do with my life was not implicitly tied to making money. Like many starving artists, I wanted to create work regardless of its commercial appeal or success. The only thing is that I didn't want to starve.

Everyone I knew with similar artistic interests spent time on their personal projects and then went off to their jobs and earned money. Sometimes their art and financial income intersected. But even for those who made it in their chosen industry, most days were just like going to work.

Sticking with something I was good at no longer felt like failure. It just seemed like a decent way to make a living. Even better, because it allowed me enough time to pursue other interests. And because working in porn was basically still working in film, I often found opportunity to work on interesting projects and get paid. Once I stopped worrying about the legitimacy of porn, it became a lot more fun.

My personal acceptance was a process that spanned several years. So it was not something I could expect of someone whose only reference to pornography was that dirty thing to be enjoyed in private.

It may only be shameful because of cultural subjectivity (i.e., everyone thinks it's shameful). But that doesn't detract from my mother's concern.

Porn, as a career, is rarely taken seriously. It's often viewed as shameful. This is simply a truth. No matter what I accomplish along the way, if I tell people I'm a porn star, I'm likely to take on a degree of stigmatization. I mean, a talk show host recently told my girlfriend (also a performer) and I—on national television—that he looked at us "differently" as soon as he heard that we did porn. It wasn't viewed as a controversial thing to say. My girlfriend and I were the controversy.

With this understanding, I take on some of my own sadness when I listen to my mother speak of hers. Yes, she fears for my safety and all of this. But what I really hear from my mother is that she wants the best for me. She knows I've chosen a profession that almost guarantees I'll be looked down upon and sees it as her son facing a lifetime of rejection. From my mother's perspective, it's the knowledge that her son will be continually hurt.

By the power of empathy, I understand this perfectly. No more would I want to witness my mother face such rejection. However, I can honestly say that her fears have not been fully actualized. In part, this has to do with the role of community. I socialize with many of the people I work with. And if I extend that group to others, it's mostly to those who hold a fairly liberal stance when it comes to porn and sexuality.

Of course, I'm reminded of anti-porn sentiments every now and again. But it's not a part of my daily experience. Most of the time, I talk openly of my career. When I'm at work, I feel as if I'm held in high esteem by my peers. In actuality, it's around family that I'm most hesitant to talk about pornography. The fiercest criticisms I've received were from my uncle and grandfather.

Reactions like those from my extended family probably speak more to my mother's experience. Because my participation in porn does not only affect me. It extends to those around me. If there is a stigmatization of the pornographer, there is also a stigmatization of the parent who raised such a deviant. I may be relatively safe in my social environment, but my mother socializes with other mothers, other professionals, and other people with perhaps no ties to the adult film industry. It is this potential hurt that saddens me. Because my choice perhaps limits my mother's ability to partake in conversations with other parents about their children, lest she be put on the immediate defensive of having to explain her child's career. There is a social stigma in simply discussing my existence in more than superficial terms.

To be fair, my mother is one of the only family members who has regularly allowed me to speak openly about my professional experiences. Consequently, I believe she's been allowed to see some positive effects of my involvement in porn.

"You used to be extremely shy," she told me. "I feel like you can pretty much walk into any situation and say 'Hello,' and be who you are. If you've been in front of a camera for a long time without your clothes on, it gives you something on that level."

She continued, "And you do promote positivity within it. You bring out the best of whatever you're involved in. You bring out the most positive aspects of pornography."

To me, such examples are proof of my mother's love. Given her ideological stance, I can never expect complete approval for my career path thus far. It is only these hidden gems of congratulation. In some ways, it's extraordinary that a person who professes to hate (or at least strongly dislike) porn can tell me that it's changed me in positive ways, or that I'm doing some good within it.

It is also important to note that my mother never asked me to stop. Despite her claims to my "naïveté" in the beginning (which I totally agree with), there was no point at which she said, "I know better and this is bad for you." I believe that a parent who respects their adult child will undoubtedly share their own opinion, but will also allow that child a choice—without persuasive terms.

My mother never gave me an ultimatum. This conveys a level of trust. In terms of the relationship I want with my mother as I continue into adulthood, this is one of the only things I can ask for.

Love, respect, and trust: all of these are inherent to our familial bond. It is why I could approach my mother with the news that I was a burgeoning porn star. It also why I felt the need to. Because the feelings are mutual. I love, respect, and trust my mother. When a piece of my life becomes big enough to take on some importance to me, I want her to know about it. Even if she disagrees with the entire premise.

Going forward, I can only hope that my mother will understand that I am capable of flourishing as a human being within my current environment. Pornography may not be all of my life, but it makes up an important part of it. Because it is my job, I take it very seriously. I try to do the best that I can and promote the work that I feel is the most interesting. I can only imagine I'd do the same with anything else.

When it comes to my father and I, our history is a bit more complicated. I don't know if this made the coming-out process harder or not.

We were on decent terms around the time I told him I was doing porn. But a few years prior, things were different. I hadn't lived with my father since I was eleven. Around the age of thirteen, I refused to speak to him for an entire year.

I'm sure my story is similar to that of many who've been raised by an alcoholic. However, the tumultuous father-son relationship of my youth is not the topic at hand. The only relevance is that by the time I was twenty years old and an active sex worker, I was a bit ambivalent about whether I should tell my father, and equally ambivalent about whether or not he would care. In fact, it was during my interview with him that I first truly learned of his opinion.

I should note that I have a very good relationship with my father at the present time. At least, the best that I can remember. He's been sober for a while now, we talk about every other week, sometimes more frequently, and although I don't visit him often due to distance, I enjoy the time I get to spend with him.

But back to the coming-out conversation. To be honest, my memory is a bit of a blur. I more or less knew what I was getting into when it came to my mother. Prepping for the conversation was a pretty big deal, so it remains an important event in my personal history. When it came to my father, I had no idea what he thought about porn or sex. And because he didn't have the ability to really do anything to me if he disapproved, there wasn't much riding on his response. To put it simply, I had no qualms about telling him to fuck off (albeit in a more passive-aggressive manner) if he got upset.

"I have a vague memory of a conversation with you where I expressed that I don't understand why you do it," said my father. "Because it's so foreign to me. It's not part of my life experience to even consider this. I couldn't relate to it."

That sort of matches my memory of his initial response—meaning, there wasn't much of one. I have this image in my head of my father nodding and perhaps looking confused or unsure of what to say. Then a memory of something that caught me off guard.

"I remember one of the first things you said was; you asked me how I keep an erection for so long," I told him during our interview.

"Yeah, that certainly was a big question," he responded, laughing. "You know, how do you do that? Certainly, when you get older this becomes a big deal to get one at all or to maintain it for any length of time. I was just curious from a physiological point of view."

The physiological effects remain one of my father's primary concerns. "When I found out that you were using erectile enhancing drugs," he continued, "I was worried about what that might do to your physical apparatus. You know me. I'm always keenly aware that you pay a price for whatever you do."

For anyone familiar with the male performer side of the adult industry, it's no secret that a lot of guys use Viagra, Cialis, and many other erectile dysfunction drugs in order to maintain erections under pressure and for long periods of time. The pills aren't fail-safes, but they're better than nothing.

My father is a chiropractic neurologist. Much of his work deals with how one's environment affects brain function. "One of the simplest ways to assess brain function is through muscle-tone testing," he told me. "Muscle tone is not strength. It's the resistance to the stretch of muscle fibers. If you hold your arm up and I push down on your wrist, I stretch the fibers of your deltoid muscle."

He went on, comparing the muscle fibers to an instrument. "You have strings that have a certain tension so you have a certain tone—a note. The same thing holds true, that all muscle fibers have a certain base tension. They have to have one to function properly.

When you bring me medication that you use, if it decreases your muscle tone, that's not a good thing. It means it has a negative effect on your brain function."

This is one of the objective side effects of porn that I have no real argument against. I am a health nut in many aspects of my life, but I also consume a large number of pharmaceutical ED drugs. It can't be that good for me, but I mostly shrug it off. I figure I'm no worse off than many Americans. Luckily, my father is not only there to remind me of the consequences of such behavior. He's taught me ways to counter the negative effects.

However, physiological function was not the focus of our interview. "My main concern was AIDS," he told me. "There's an inherent danger in what you do that you have no control over. Ultimately, you can be preventative. But you can't say, 'I'm safe.' You can't."

I acknowledged his fear but reiterated, as I have with my mother, that it is statistically unlikely for men working in heterosexual porn to contract HIV. Still, I'm aware there is always a chance.

It was interesting, however, that halfway through the interview, my father showed no signs of being upset or even morally opposed to my participation in porn. He hadn't shared much about his stance in the past. But I was curious. Did my father really have no emotional or ideological response to my career in sex work? I had to ask.

"To have a partner and not share that partner, that's a sacred thing for me," he responded. "In terms of my basic stance, I'm totally monogamous. I was that way with your mother. It never occurred to me to cheat on her. That doesn't even enter. I can't imagine it any other way.

"It's also true that I've watched porn—especially when I didn't have a partner—to get some satisfaction," he said. "Ultimately, I felt my own response was actually worse afterward. I masturbate and I actually feel worse. Because there was nothing fulfilling. I wish you saw that my way. That was my debate.

"But then the real debate was, 'What do I do?'" he continued. "Looking at how I treated my mother? I mean, I disappointed her with everything I did because she had very strong wishes for me. I did everything the opposite. Not intentionally. But I had my own way. Who am I to judge what is appropriate? Especially given all the havoc I've wreaked in my own life. I knew that then. I'm even more keenly aware of that today. To run around, sit on a high horse, and dictate what the world should look like has never worked very well for me. It actually made things worse. From my limited capacity at that point, I wanted to at least let you know that I heard you, and that I appreciated that you were actually telling me."

I was a bit taken aback. When I first told my father that I was doing porn, I had no concept of his internal process. He listened, said some things about erections, and that was that. When I came to him with the request for an interview, I was mostly curious. But as a grown man, and also a son, I suppose I was looking for something more. I'm not sure exactly how to describe it. Approval, maybe.

There was something in me that wanted to know that my father not only respected me, but looked at me as an adult, and acknowledged that I'd done a good job. I guess when I listened to his response, I tried to decipher it in such a context.

He said that he appreciated that I was telling him. It was an obvious step forward in our relationship to share such things with honesty. Something on par with respect. But it wasn't exactly what I was looking for. Maybe because our relationship had more of a conflicted past. Or perhaps it was inherent to the father-son dynamic. Because I couldn't say I needed the same thing from my mother.

It's funny, but his approval, or my interpretation of it, came in the form of a question.

"Let me ask you something," said my father. "How do you feel if I tell friends about what you do? Is that okay? Or is that not okay?"

I wasn't sure why my father would want to tell someone. But I thought about it as if I were a doctor or lawyer, or some other universally accepted professional. In conversation, I might be brought up as a bragging right. As in, "Look, my son has had success."

"It's interesting to me that you would even ask that," I told my father. "No one else [in my family] has even thought about asking that. Because I don't feel like anyone is usually willing to tell other people what I do for a living. I feel like it's always masked."

My father told me that he often goes on walks with his friend. They've established a routine where one person talks for five minutes and the other listens. There are no interruptions and no responses.

"I actually told him that," said my father. "I said, you know, 'My son works in the porn industry.' He was going to react, and I said, 'Uh uh. It's not your turn.' That was pretty cool because I didn't have to defend or anything. I said to him afterward, 'This is something I wanted you to hear. But I don't want your comment.' I don't."

It may have not been a boastful act, but it made me happy to hear that my father wanted to share such a thing about me. It meant that he was at least not ashamed. In fact, I could interpret it to be quite the opposite.

I told my father that I didn't mind, that it was totally fine.

"Good," he responded. "Thank you. That clarifies that. I didn't think that would be an issue. But that's probably weird that nobody wants to say or speak what you do, right? I can't imagine. What a bummer. Walk around on tip-toes and come up with some bullshit story."

The following was my response. It may reiterate some of the things I've written in this piece. But it is meant as a most sincere explanation to my parents, and any of my family, as to why I've chosen porn:

> I feel like I live in a bubble. I surround myself with people who essentially agree with my politics, which involve fairly radical sexual politics. Or I surround myself with people who are in the sex industry. We have a little community. Within that community, I think I am well respected. Especially within the past two years, a lot of the work I've done is very important to me. Prior to that, it was a very interesting journey within my own self that involved figuring out how I felt about this career.
>
> Starting out, I didn't intend for it to be a career. I intended for it to be some sort of sexual exploration. A way to make a little extra money while I was in school. In my

head, it was like, "Well, I'm going to get out of school and go off and do something else." The more I was exposed to the mainstream film industry—which is what I thought I wanted to be involved in—it became really upsetting to me. I don't really want to have a lot to do with that, except on the fringes. To work within things that I think have some artistic integrity.

So I think that porn allows me to make, not an incredible amount of money, but I live a middle-class lifestyle like I always have growing up. I'm able to do a lot of things that I'm very proud of. It also allows me the time to create art in other contexts. That's incredibly important to me.

I think most people who go to school with the intentions of being an artist have to make a decision at some point to either make money or fulfill their artistic pursuits. A lot of times one of those has to kind of drop off. Unless you're incredibly lucky and make some big hit, or something. But for most of us, that's never going to happen.

A lot of the things I'm interested in live on the fringes of people's interests in general. Especially when it comes to things, that are monetarily successful. Like the music and film I want to create. I know it doesn't make a tremendous amount of money.

Porn is both a way to fund those things and keep creating those things, because I don't have to work twelve hours a day, every single day.

I have also become a part of a community of people who I really respect, and I think respect me as well. And we're able to do some really interesting things. I have people who write me on a regular basis now, thanking me for my work. I don't know that in any other profession if you received the same response, you could say that you're doing something wrong or go, "I don't want to be here."

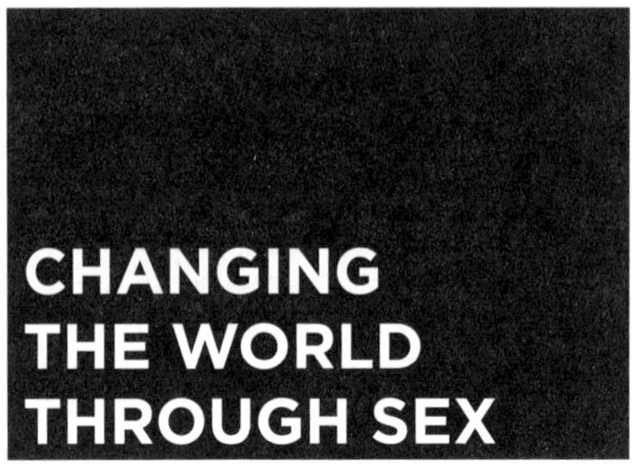

CHANGING THE WORLD THROUGH SEX

Cindy Gallop

Cindy Gallop started up Bartle Bogle Hegarty New York in 1998, and in 2003 was named Advertising Woman of the Year. She is the founder of IfWeRanTheWorld.com, a marketing coaction software (and Harvard Business School case study) that enables brands to do good and make money simultaneously, by implementing the business model of the future: Shared Values + Shared Action = Shared Profit (financial and social). She founded MakeLoveNotPorn.com in 2009—the subject of a notorious TED Talk—and in 2013 with cofounders Oonie Chase and Corey Innis launched MakeLoveNotPorn.tv in beta: "Pro-sex. Pro-porn. Pro-knowing the difference." She speaks at conferences around the world and consults, describing her consultancy approach as 'I like to blow shit up. I am the Michael Bay of business.' Follow her on Twitter @cindygallop.

I date younger men—usually in their twenties. Which is how I began encountering, seven or eight years ago, an issue that would never have crossed my mind if I had not encountered it personally, directly, and intimately: what happens when total freedom of access to hardcore porn online meets our society's equally total reluctance to talk openly and honestly about sex, and results in porn becoming, by default, the sex education of today. In not a good way.

The average age today at which a child first views hardcore porn online is eight—not because eight-year-olds go looking for porn, but as a function of what is inevitable in our digital world today: they stumble across it. That's why, as I discovered for myself in my own dating life, young men and women who grow up today watching hardcore porn online for years before they ever have their own first romantic or sexual experience assume that is what sex is and that is how you do it for real.

When I realized what I was encountering, I decided to do something about it. Six years ago, I launched MakeLoveNotPorn.com, which posts the myths of hardcore porn and balances them with reality—"porn world" versus "real world"—in a straightforward, nonjudgmental, humorous way.

MakeLoveNotPorn is not anti-porn. Our tagline is "Pro-sex. Pro-porn. Pro-knowing the difference." The issue we're tackling isn't porn, but the complete lack in our society of an open, healthy, honest dialogue around sex in the real world, which would, among many other benefits, enable people to bring a real-world mindset to the viewing of porn as artificial entertainment. Our message is simply "Talk about sex"—openly and publicly, and privately and intimately with your partner. Great sex is born out of great communication all around.

I launched MakeLoveNotPorn at the TED Conference in 2009, and the response was extraordinary. It resonated with huge numbers of people globally—young and old, male and female, straight and gay, from every country in the world. They wrote and poured their hearts out to me. They told me things about their sex lives and their porn-watching habits they had never told anyone else. Receiving those emails, day after day, made me feel I had a personal responsibility to take MakeLoveNotPorn forward in a way that would make it more far-reaching, helpful, and effective.

I decided to pursue our mission of "Talk about it" by deploying the dynamics of social media to socialize sex, to build a platform to act as sexual social currency, with the aim of making discussion around real-world sex more socially acceptable and socially shareable.

Two years ago, I and cofounders Oonie Chase and Corey Innis launched MakeLoveNotPorn.tv (MLNP.tv)—a user-generated, crowdsourced video-sharing site that celebrates real-world sex, catalogued via #realworldsex. Anyone, from anywhere in the world, can submit videos of themselves having #realworldsex. What we mean by that is simply not performative sex. MLNP.tv is not about performing for the camera, but simply about capturing what goes on in the real world, in all its funny, messy, wonderful, ridiculous, beautiful humanness. We're not porn, we're not "amateur," and we're not competing with porn; our competition is Facebook and YouTube; or rather, it would be, if Facebook and YouTube allowed sexual self-identification and self-expression. If they did that, MLNP wouldn't need to exist.

We view every video submitted to MLNP.tv and operate a revenue-sharing business model; our members pay to rent and stream #realworldsex videos, and half of that revenue goes to our MakeLoveNotPornstars, a number of whom are real-world porn star friends. MLNP.tv is honored to be the place online where porn stars share the sex they have in their real-world relationships and talk about how different that is from how they perform on camera.

When my team and I embarked on this venture, we had no idea that we would fight a battle every day to build our business.

Every piece of business infrastructure any other startup can at least take for granted, we can't, because the small print always says "No adult content."

Finding funding is extraordinarily difficult. I can't find a bank anywhere in the world that will allow us to open a business bank account. We had to build our video-streaming/sharing platform from the ground up because streaming services and off-the-shelf solutions won't host adult content. Our biggest operational challenge has been payments: PayPal won't work with us, Amazon won't, no mainstream credit card processors will. I had to write an explanatory blog post for our members entitled, "Why We Make It So Hard For You to Give Us Your Money." Even something as apparently simple as finding an email partner to send our membership emails out with has been a nightmare; we were rejected by six or seven before we found one willing to work with us.

All of this was a revelation—which is why I am now fighting this battle very publicly, on behalf of all of us. Because the answer to everything that worries people about porn is not to shut down, censor, clamp down, block, repress. It's to open up—open up the dialogue around sex and porn. Open up to welcoming, supporting, and funding entrepreneurs who want to disrupt and change the world of sex and porn for the better. Open up to allowing us to do business on the same terms and conditions as everyone else.

On the challenging journey to build MLNP.tv, I regularly encounter well-meaning people who say to me, "Cindy, why don't you just change the name of your company? Take the word 'porn' out of it, create an innocuous holding-company name doing business as. It'll make your life so much easier." There are practical reasons why I refuse to do that, but the primary reason is principled. When you design a venture around societal bias and prejudice, all you do is reinforce it. I refuse to bow to bias and prejudice; I'm out to change it.

Our battle has connected me with other sextech entrepreneurs who ask for advice, and I find that I often have to say to them, "Take yourself out of the shadows." People working in sex unconsciously internalize society's disapproval in a way that negatively impacts their ability to do the business and achieve the vision they want. You have to change the world to fit your business, not the other way around.

In every industry, currently we see the syndrome I call "collaborative competition," where everybody in a sector competes with everybody else in that sector by doing exactly the same thing everybody else is doing. I believe the future is "competitive collaboration," when everybody in a sector comes together and collaborates to make things better for everyone on the premise that a rising tide floats all boats. That then enables everyone to be uniquely competitive, leveraging individual skills and talents.

Fast Company called me last year to say they'd like to do an article about the battles we face with MLNP.tv. My response was, "I'm happy to be interviewed, but here are six other sextech entrepreneurs I want you to interview as well." I don't care if MLNP.tv gets less column inches; I want the world to know there's an entire movement of all of us in sextech, to make people understand the Next Big Thing in tech is disrupting sex.

We all watch porn; we don't talk about it. Porn exists in a kind of parallel universe, a shadowy underground. When you force something—anything—into the shadows and underground, you make it easier for bad things to happen, and you make it a lot harder for good things to happen. I'd like to help good things happen, and that's why I'm so pleased to be here, in this book, in this company, working with everyone else to change the world through sex.

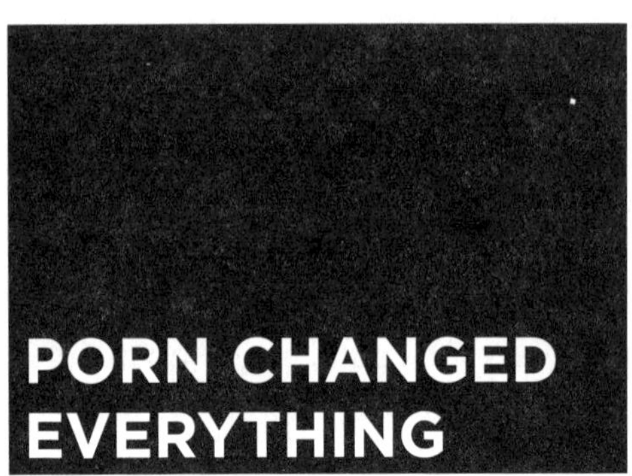

PORN CHANGED EVERYTHING

Cinnamon Maxxine

Cinnamon Maxxine is a San Francisco Bay Area original diva. They're a queer porno personality, stripper, and all-around fierce fat femme of color. They're on a mission to confront racism, race bias, fat phobia, and the generic femme bias in sex work and porn. These issues are real, not just in mainstream society, but in our cherished and loved alternative and subcultures as well. Cinnamon fights these issues every day and loves to educate people. You can find Cinnamon as CinnaMaxx on Facebook and Twitter, or email cinnamaxx@gmail.com.

I've been doing porn for eight years, as well as other sex work. And a wonderful eight years it's been! I am out about my porn to friends and my chosen family. I was not out to my biological family. I had no interest in being out to my family because it just didn't feel worth it to have them criticize me, judge me, and try to change me.

However, in July 2014, I got cellulitis in my breast. For those that don't know, cellulitis is a nasty, painful skin infection. My case of cellulitis got so bad that it reached the tissue and I started having scary flu-like symptoms. Due to being sick, I was out of work for several weeks. I was unable to pay bills and other living expenses. A dear friend of mine put together a crowdfund for me and helped me raise the money I needed to get by while I was sick and out of work.

During this time, I called my parents to check in and let them know how I was doing. They knew that I had been sick and they worried when I told them I was starting to have flu symptoms. I told them that a friend of mine had been kind enough to put together a crowdfund for me. My parents know I am a performance artist, burlesque performer, and stripper. I figured, why not share the link with them? There's nothing on there that would out me as a porn performer.

A month or so after the crowdfunding campaign ended, I'd been trying to reach my parents, but to no avail. I got a text message from my stepmom saying something to the effect of, "Not now. Busy." I started feeling like they were avoiding me and something was up. The next weekend I was able to reach my stepmother and she confirmed that yes, there was something up. She confessed that she'd snooped and Googled my name and found out that I do porn. In fact, she called it the elephant in the room.

Needless to say, I was frustrated, hurt, and even angry. I'd been doing porn for eight years at that point and I'd been able to keep quiet about it. In the early years, she hadn't really shown much interest or curiosity in my work. However, in the last couple of years she's gotten really nosey about my private life, even though I specifically told her I didn't want to share. I did everything from tell polite little lies—that I'm still just stripping, I'm doing some modeling, or even that I'm doing nude modeling—to outright telling her it's none of her business and she doesn't even want to know, so stop asking. But I avoided telling her about the porn at all cost.

My stepmother is one of those feminists that believe I'm doing a disservice to all women everywhere by "letting myself be objectified." She believes this is not what women fought for and that I'm only hurting myself. There's also, of course, the moral issues of it all. She thinks I'm inappropriately exploring my sexuality.

When I tried to explain to her that she violated my privacy by doing something I explicitly asked her not to do, she ignored me and, instead, told my father. She also tried to justify her behavior by arguing that because it's on the Internet for everyone else to see, it's fine. Obviously, this argument is weak; porn performers deserve privacy too. If you don't believe that, then you can stop reading right now and move on to another story. She told me she wasn't being nosey and that she was simply curious about my life. She even made me feel a little guilty for being upset with her. She made it my problem that she snooped and found out about my porn. She didn't take any responsibility for her behavior. Instead, because I do porn and it's on the Internet, I was culpable; I was the one to blame for this new family drama.

I tried to talk to my parents about it, but it wasn't a very productive conversation. They spent the whole time beating around the bush and being afraid to actually have a real conversation. There was one question they asked that immediately signaled their deep lack of understanding; in other words, after they asked this question, I knew that I would probably never get through to them. My dad asked, "I mean, why? What did I do? Did your stepfather ever touch you?" This is the stereotypical response. I was hurt. I thought my parents knew better than to stereotype in this way. Clearly, they didn't.

My dad hasn't spoken to me in months, and I think it has more to do with his inability to come up with anything productive to say to me. It's like my whole person has changed since he found out I do porn. He doesn't feel like I'm his daughter anymore. It's hurtful, but I get it. I'm the one who always tries to understand where someone is coming from and, in this case, I understand the logic that my parents are using to make sense of my work. That's what my parents taught me to do. They taught me to make a difference in people's lives when I can; and if people are unwilling to change, learn, or be touched, then you meet them where they're at, especially people you love. I don't understand why they can't do the same for me.

Why does my work in porn outshine who I am as a person, as their child?

Months have gone by and I'm actually starting to feel terribly relieved. I know that I made the right decision by trying to keep it to myself. I made the right decision by making my own chosen family that loves and supports me and thinks I'm awesome. I made the right decision by moving away from my close-minded biological family and discovering new things. I became my own person, and that's worth more than anything my parents can ever do for me. I feel relieved that I don't have to go to great lengths to lie, hide, pretend, and let my secrets weigh on me. I'm relieved and it's great. I can move on, knowing that I'm content in what I do and if what I do impacts who I am so greatly in the eyes of my parents that they won't talk to me anymore, then I am okay with letting that go.

Throughout this whole writing experience, I tried to keep it professional and classy, but I couldn't help but think that my adult performer persona would simply say, "Fuck that. Fuck them. Do you." And that is actually all I need to hear.

FROM OPERA CONDUCTOR TO PORN PRODUCER

Colin Rowntree

As the founder and CEO of Wasteland.com, the Internet's oldest and most popular BDSM and alternative sexuality site, Colin Rowntree is a true pioneer of the online adult entertainment industry. An eloquent, witty, and thought-provoking commentator, Colin is a frequent contributor to industry trade publications and websites, including Adult Video News, *XBIZ, and other media outlets. He has been interviewed by and featured on* International Business Times, *CNBC,* Rolling Stone Magazine, *BBC Television, the Fox Network, HBO, ABC Nightline, NewsCorp,* Time, Wired, *Cnet.com, and Bnet.com. Most recently, Colin was awarded the 2015 Progressive Leadership of the Year XBIZ Executive award.*

I've had a lot of vocations in my life. From music teacher and music therapist working with the elderly thirty years ago to a long career as a symphonic, choral, on-Broadway director and opera conductor and, as is the case with most working musicians, all kinds of side gigs ranging from wholesale accounts manager for an occult goods company and even a few stints as a late-night radio announcer. But little did I ever expect that I would eventually become a porn director and producer—one specializing in BDSM at that!

In 1994, my wife and I literally stumbled into online adult entertainment by launching an experiment—Wasteland—to see if people on this new "Internet thing" might like to request a mail order catalogue of our offerings of BDSM and kinky bondage gear and leather fetish apparel. Within a short period of time, it became obvious that no one was really interested in getting a mail order catalogue sent to them, but a lot of people were highly interested in seeing attractive models in kinky clothing in various stages of nudity. So we took a wild chance and started charging a whopping $10 for people to view the photos. Wasteland.com, one of the first Internet adult paysites, was born!

It quickly became apparent that we needed to get more kinky photos—lots of kinky photos to satisfy the surfers' lust for naughty fare. My wife, Angie, was a photojournalist and began showing me the tricks of the trade for shooting high-end fetish-glamour photos. Within a year, I became a full-fledged pornographer.

For the first five years, we kept it all very hush-hush as to the kind of Internet business we were running. Living in a very conservative, small New England town, it just made sense not to be too open about that little detail, especially as I was still working as a choir director in a local church and conductor of a well-known opera company. As luck would have it, by 1997 Wasteland was doing very well and we bought our first home with attached office space, but in a town just a bit too far for the twice-weekly drive to the church for rehearsals and services, so I left that position just in the nick of time.

Shortly after our move, I was contacted by a small regional newspaper that had heard of me from my speaking engagements at the AVN show. The reporter wanted to do a story about our porn business being operated in a tiny town in New Hampshire. Within days of that story being published, I got a call from the *Boston Globe* asking if they could come by our office for an interview and perhaps take a few photos. They came, interviewed us, took some pictures, and that following Sunday, there was a full-page upbeat and positive story about us in the *Globe*, complete with a large, full-color photo of my wife sitting at her desk, editing naughty pictures.

At that time, pretty much everyone in New England read the Sunday *Boston Globe* (it was, after all, before the newspaper industry moved over to the Internet). The following Tuesday, I headed down to my weekly opera rehearsal and was intercepted in the parking lot by the president of the board of directors and a couple of other board members. The board president was holding a copy of the paper, opened to the feature about us with my well-known wife's smiling face in the middle of it. I anticipated being fired on the spot, but an amazing thing happened: The board members all had nervous smiles on their faces and the only question they had was if it was legal. I assured them it was, and they all laughed and said they would cover my back from any backlash from members, which they did for the following eight years. I eventually got too busy to keep up with conducting and devoted 100 percent of my time to both Wasteland, and my wife's new porn site for women—Sssh.com—that went live in 1999.

In a similar unexpected reaction scenario, by 2000, we had outgrown our house and offices and bought a much larger house nearby, assisted by the same elderly female real estate agent that helped us into our first home. After the signing, the agent pulled us aside and said something to the effect of, "Just what is it you guys do for a living that you were able to upgrade real estate so quickly?" I took a deep breath and told her the truth—that we run Internet pornography sites—fully expecting disapproval from her. Her eyes widened a bit and the first thing out of her mouth was, "Oh, thank God! I thought you might be dealing drugs!"

As for friends and family, pretty much everyone knows what I do and most are very amused and accepting. In fact, my eighty-year-old mother-in-law, who speaks five languages, does the bulk of our customer service email translations!

I know we got off pretty lucky in light of some of the horror stories I hear from performers about being banished from their families, ending up in custody battles, and the like, and I thank our lucky stars for our friends, families, and community acceptance—and the endlessly entertaining dinner conversations!

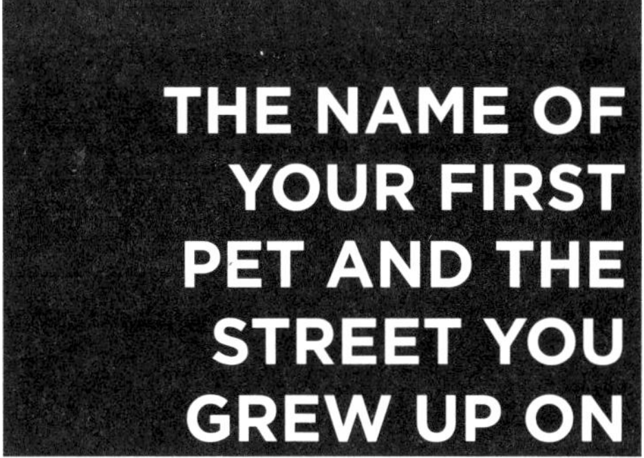
THE NAME OF YOUR FIRST PET AND THE STREET YOU GREW UP ON

Conner Habib

Conner Habib is an author, lecturer, porn performer, and vice president of the Adult Performer Advocacy Committee. His Twitter handle is @connerhabib and he lives in Los Angeles.

The email was from another Conner Habib, one who wasn't in porn.

"My grandmother searched for me on Google and nearly had a heart attack," he wrote. "So is Conner Habib your real name?"

I had just started appearing in scenes, and it was the first time I'd been asked what my real name was. The email ended there, but I imagined the sentence going on: "Because if it isn't, can you please, please, please change it to something else?"

"What's your real name?"

It's a question every porn performer is asked, and asked often. Answering isn't as easy as you'd think.

My birth name is Andre Khalil. The name I chose for porn is Conner Habib.

Conner: the name of one of two drunken Irish boys I saw dry humping each other at a pub in Killarney when I was fifteen. "Oh, Conner!" one jokingly yelped to the other, as they played at being gay. He was stocky and drunk and I watched them, electrified and silent, as my family sat close to me, talking about something I didn't hear.

Habib: the Arabic word for "sweetheart" or "beloved one."

I'm Syrian and Irish, and the name reflected my origins and

displayed my Middle Eastern heritage, which is all but unrepresented in porn. It also helped me avoid innuendo names like Dick Powers or Johnny Thrust. Conner Habib sounded like a real person's name (and it was!); it's slightly clumsy, easy enough to remember.

Is it real?

Which one should I use?

It seems like your name depends on context. But context turns out to be complicated.

It was cut-and-dry on set, where directors and crew called me by my porn name. And it was simple enough for anyone who knew me before I started porn. But sometimes, someone would recognized me at a bar and say, vaguely, and coyly, "I know you from somewhere." He might have seen my dick in his spam email and it blew past him, hanging around in his unconscious. Or maybe it was in person; maybe he met me at a party. Maybe he just didn't want to admit he watched my scenes, or maybe he really didn't recognize me at all. Maybe it was just a bullshit line.

Sometimes I would go to a coffee shop and know for a fact that fans were sitting in the café when the barista called my name. Sometimes a fan would ask me out on a date, or know one of my close friends.

If this all sounds like a little too much, let me explain: Porn performers pick their stage names for different reasons, but the most common idea is that if you create a name, you create an identity. That identity is a thin veil that's supposed to help you avoid job discrimination in the future, prevent your family from finding out, protect you from certain overzealous viewers who may think they have a relationship with you that oversteps the boundaries you're comfortable with, and more. You live out your porn life under a performance name and the rest of your life typically under the name you're born with.

Implicit in this is the old, now hopeless fantasy that when you're done with porn, you discard the name and identity and you're born again. Putting aside the fact that many of us don't want to be born again, choosing something "after" porn has become more difficult. The Internet has made birth names more searchable and created a permanence of visibility, not just for porn performers who have started recently, but also for ones who had, for a time, faded into obscurity on dissolving reels of VHS tape. Now their porn pasts have been resurrected.

There is no "after" porn.

Now what?

When I began to publish essays and appear more often in mainstream media, I had to decide what name to use. Initially, it seemed obvious: If I were writing about sex or pornography, I'd publish as Conner. But other essays seemed to call for Conner Habib as well. For example, I'd written an essay on the philosophy of time that I thought more people would read if it were published under Conner. I assumed—and was proven correct—that more people would be willing to engage with philosophical topics if they came from an unexpected source.

Then in late 2011, my friend and mentor, the renowned biologist Lynn Margulis, died. I had studied with her for three years at the University of Massachusetts and felt compelled to write an essay about her work. I knew many of Lynn's friends and colleagues, as well as some of her family. Lynn herself knew about my porn career ("Habibi!" she'd often call me happily), but not everyone else did. If I published under Conner, they might miss it. So the essay appeared in an anthology under my birth name, with a contributor's bio in the book that included both my names. It was a way to dispel any illusion that I could ever go back. There was no way to go but forward, carrying everything I'd done with me.

Increasingly, it seems as if there's no "after" anything for anyone. Our lives are recorded. Our days are categorized by statuses, filtered photos, and updates. The world has become a big Linnaean list of identities.

Compartmentalizing different aspects of our lives has become more and more of a problem for everyone, not just porn performers. Potential employers investigate drunken Facebook photos, and there's a pervading anxiety of making a public and YouTube-able misstep or off-colored comment.

Who are you? Let's check the record to see.

At best, it can be confusing and annoying to juggle both identities and to keep them separate. At worst, it's traumatic. As many porn performers know—particularly outed ones who went on to become, and be fired as, school teachers or cops or athletes—the costs of trying to cordon off certain parts of our lives can be high when someone forces our identities together for us.

There are other, subtler demands on porn performers' identities too.

"What's your real name?" is a demand for intimacy. Who are you really?

I'd go on dates with guys who would say things like, "I want Andre, not Conner," as if this were a request for closeness rather than a command to dismember my personality.

I wish I had understood all this more deeply when I started appearing in porn; I might not have chosen a porn name at all. Maybe I would have seen, instead, that porn performers, who have sex publicly, are in a unique position to consider and talk about integrating private and public aspects of life.

Perhaps it would help end discrimination against and misunderstanding of porn stars if more performers expressed both their names publicly—neither name is "real" and neither is hidden; or maybe new performers don't have to take second names at all. If there's no getting away from being in porn, why should one name be more important than the other?

So I introduce myself to everyone as Conner now. Who cares if it's my "legal" name; it's real. Instead of being reborn in my birth name "after" porn, I will be born into my porn name after my birth. My porn name, anyone's porn name, may now just be the name of a braver self, one that's not afraid to be open.

A few years into my career, I was asked to give an autograph as Conner, but I had no idea what that signature would look like.

I scrawled out "Conner Habib" quickly across the photo and saw that the frantic symbols tilted into the same gestures as Andre Khalil. They shared the same loops and the same dot on the "i" just before the end.

It was as if the name were there all along.

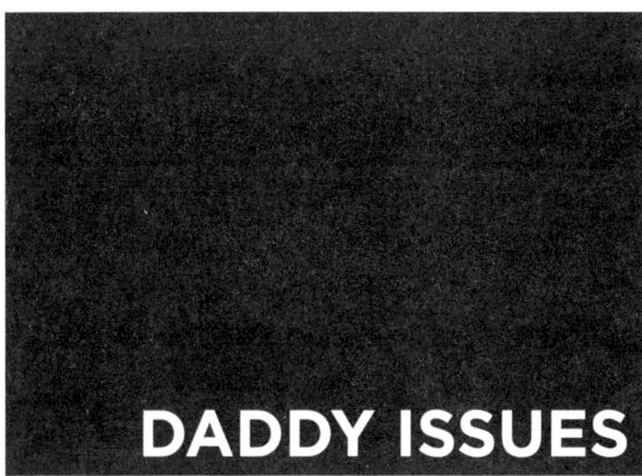

DADDY ISSUES

Courtney Trouble

Having spent their entire adult life in the adult industry, Courtney Trouble is currently in graduate studies at California College of the Arts and owns the film production company, TROUBLEfilms. Their company funds the films of trans, POC, and plus-sized queer sex workers, as well as their own art and short films, which range from experimental shorts, music videos, and of course: queer porn.

Mateo Griffin is Courtney Trouble's dad. He is a fifty-six-year-old stay-at-home dad in Seattle with his wife, Heather, and two four-year-old identical twins, Sky and Sparrow.

The funny thing about coming out is that it relies on the belief that the information you're keeping about yourself is shameful. If you were raised to be somewhat shameless, it's less of a one-time shock and more like a lifelong rumble. I feel like I have come out to my dad either 100 times or never at all.

Mateo: I've never been ashamed of your work. You're an amazing individual and a profoundly deep artist.

Courtney: I've also never been ashamed about what I do. For me, coming out to you has been more of a process of wanting you to be proud of me, your child, the porn star.

M: I always get a little twinge when you say you're a porn star because I don't personally think of what you do as porn the way most people think of it. It seems to me that "porn" is like the word "queer," that you are trying to change the perception of it a little. But I still have a little twinge, I guess. There's some kind of gravity to that word.

C: There's a world of stigma around the word "porn," for sure. But there's no way to deny that I'm doing porn, even if it does have artistic merit. Honestly, it makes things more complicated for a conversation about sex work and shame because when I talk about it to you, I can say, I'm making queer porn, I'm making ethical porn. I can show you articles in academic journals and *Bitch* magazine; I can show you the "ethical legitimacy" of my work, and that kinda gets me off the hook.

M: Off the hook?

C: I can say I'm a porn star, or a sex worker, and people can then say, "Oh, but you're *this* kind of—" as long as I say I'm an ethical, feminist, sex-positive female porn director with an education and social capital. A lot of the people I hire as performers do not have an attached "legitimacy" to their work. There's an imbalance of privilege there to say what I do is "good sex work" and what someone else might do is "bad sex work."

M: When I was single and living in Tacoma, I liked porn, and I didn't know any better. I enjoyed it and I never felt that it was wrong for me. Some sites I went to, I wouldn't go back to again because they seemed to be awful and degrading to women.

So, if you didn't include all those extra details . . . like if you said, "Dad, I'm a porn star and I'm making porn for Reality Kings," I'd be like, whoa, really? That's not uplifting of women, or even men. I would really have some concerns. I really think the context is important. I don't think of it as you making it easier for me, lightening up or sugarcoating it, I just think it's all in the details.

C: You're right, some of them do feel really degrading to women and men, also just because it's dumb, generic, and impersonal. I think that the real problem with that kind of porn is that it's created for the lowest common denominator, right? It's not the Sundance Channel, it's McDonalds.

M: Well, I don't like McDonalds, and I feel really sad and upset that people have to work at McDonalds in the conditions that they do.

C: I don't think there's going to be anything out there that I would ever do that would make you McDonalds-level sad. That's the reality of my privilege as a sex worker that I'm speaking to. I have made enough opportunities for myself now to manage my own sex work in the form of porn performance, so that I don't often have to work for other people to make ends meet. I get to make my own burger for my own burger company, and that's an important privilege that I have that also lets me be able to be out to my family.

Like, when I "came out" to you about working at the Lusty Lady, you were like, "Oh god, you're a stripper," and I was like, "But wait, it's a co-op!" I said, "Dad, I'm the madam, there's a union!" And you were like, "As long as you're the boss."

M: You were able to minimize your student loans and survive going to school doing sex work, and I just have always admired how self-sufficient you are and how businesslike you are about things.

C: If I were more of a survival sex worker, like I somehow hadn't been successful in starting my own productions and relied on taking random adult-industry jobs to make ends meet, I don't know if you would know about that.

M: All I've ever wanted for you is to be happy and do what you wanna do, and I guess make money or be successful. You dove deeply into those things that you're interested in, and found a way to make a living and make your life about it. From a parenting standpoint, that's a huge victory for me!

C: I learned it from you, honestly. When we were growing up in Tacoma, you went to school to try to make money to raise me. You raised me alone. You did all of these things to make money but at some point, you felt bored or desperate enough to quit your safe job, start your own business, and try to support your family and yourself on something you're more connected to creatively and spiritually. I was fifteen when you started your landscaping business, and that taught me more than anything I learned in high school. The corporate world wasn't going to do anything for me after watching you succeed in starting your own small business. I just kind of knew my life would be one big hustle. No bosses.

M:You know, when I did that, and I came home and told you I left, you looked at me like, oh my god how are we gonna eat, how are we gonna live? You were kind of mortified for a day or two and then, you know, it was kind of a process to find what I was gonna do next.

C: Sounds kind of like a coming-out story.

M: I think it was really nice for me to all of a sudden have all this time to hang out and pay attention to you because it was kind of a crucial age for you and you were getting harassed at high school, so it was kind of nice to just do projects and hang around you.

C:Were you worried about me being queer in high school?

M: I was worried about you being bullied. I was worried that teachers would misunderstand you. There was also another thing going on with you too, you had a resistance to authority; and in this case, I don't think you liked male authority. Not mine and definitely not male teachers.

C: No offense, but men just kind of always seem to pose a threat to my happiness and queerness, and my general feelings of freedom and safety.

I have a pretty low tolerance for jerks. As a teen, I worked in fast food, coffee shops, video rentals. In all of those situations, my bosses treated me like total crap. Expendable, disposable trash. I was always at school, always working, always doing something—so the thought of doing any kind of sex work seemed really appealing because I'd be able to make it to all of my classes and work on my own schedule, and finally get away from these pigheaded managers I suffered.

Honestly, doing phone sex seemed hilarious because I was totally talking to just about the same guys, paying me in cash and intimacy. I was totally gay, I just thought it would be funny and interesting and nobody would harass me. It was an incredibly viable option as a young person to make a living and be in school and make art. And it wasn't degrading, it was fun.

M: I guess I've always trusted that you would look out for yourself. It didn't take me long to figure out that what you were doing was fine. I've never called a sex line, but being a man and imaging that transaction kind of seemed to be, in terms of a power dynamic, fairly equal, and I just don't judge stuff like that. There are a lot of lonely people out there. It seems like a good service.

C: When you're talking about coming out, a lot of the pain around being "out" comes from parental disapproval. I honestly don't hold a lot of pain around being a sex worker. I've never been hurt at my job, I've never been taken advantage of. The pain I do have though, honestly, is the constant hum of my mother's disapproval. That's affected me for life, far more than any bad boss ever has.

Not having support when you reveal something secret or personal, like sex work or gender or sexual orientation, can be far more damaging than anything else that's gonna happen to you. Thank you for not making me fight for your approval. A lot of people I know have these life-long struggles with their parents.

M: I wouldn't want to lose you. We've been so close, you know. I felt like it was just you and me as a family, and I didn't even consider that that would be some kind of deal breaker or something that I would shun you for. It just kind of made me love you more.

C: Aw! Have you sought out any education about sex work or whatever in the past ten years? I remember the first time I saw you again after telling you I was working for the Lusty Lady, and you name-dropped Annie Sprinkle and Carol Queen.

M: I did. I mean, I'm very much kind of a research person and you had mentioned names and books in this growing field of feminist porn or queer porn. I already knew Annie Sprinkle from . . .

C: Your own research?

M: From our church!

C: She's a good gateway for all of us porn stars coming out to our parents!

M: Yeah. And I think I saw an early, late-'90s viral video of her performance art stuff.

C: The only way an adult performer can actually BE a sex educator is through porn or art performance. We can't actually go into a classroom and teach kids.

M: No.

C: Oh, don't say no like, no, of course not. Of course we should! I can't think of anyone more qualified to tell teenagers in high school about gay sex than myself. I can't! They would never let me do it because of my stigma as a sex worker.

M: Okay, I was imagining you going into a public school classroom and teaching kids about gay sex.

C: It would be brilliant!

M: Yeah. I think that there has to be an opt-in process from the parents.

C: Well, like with any sex education. But what would this opt-in be like? "Hey, do you want your child around this porn person?" Is that what you're saying?

M: I don't think that's the way you would approach it. When I did "Our Whole Lives" in the Unitarian Church, we sat down with the parents before we met with the teens, went through all the materials. When you do it that way, you get more participatory attitudes from the parents. But I think there's some work that could be done. You have to educate the parents first, then it will be easier for the children.

I agree with you that sexuality should be open, and I think that children are curious about it and then forced by society to stifle it. Many people rediscover sexuality as a teen, and it can be traumatic. If it's more of a continual flow throughout childhood, then I think it can be a lot less traumatic or explosive. When you get back to the important drama around coming out, wondering, "Will I still be loved if I reveal my true self to my parents and my friends," that's an incredible question to ask, and my hope is that most parents would give their kids enough space to never have to ask that question, to add to that trauma and explosiveness.

C: Are there trainings for the parents about things that they might have to hear, like things that kids come out about?

M: Our Whole Lives is a five-part series that spans kindergarten to young adult, exploring sexuality and society and spirituality and growth. It's facilitated by open-minded parents who have gone through training. I was a trainer for all of the age groups.

C: What inspired you to get into OWL?

M: Someone in the church approached me, I think because they liked the way I raised you. OWL instructors have to be able to speak of sexuality without shame or judgment, and be able to create a safe space for teens, especially to express themselves and be curious.

C: There are few things more beloved in the UU church than the parent of a gay child.

M: So there have been some times in your life when you've had to tell me things, and I'm just curious about your personal process. Did you have to muster courage? Did you feel a lot of fear? Did you mistrust what my reaction would ever be?

C: When I think about revealing things to you, I realize I was never afraid of telling you who I was. We've come to a point in our relationship as child and parent where nothing I say is going to shock you. Unless I told you I was pregnant.

M: The six months between when you came home from Michigan after being raped and when you decided to come out about that to me were such a struggle. I just didn't know what was going on. I know it took a lot for you to tell me about that, and I'm glad you finally did because I just didn't understand why you were being so angry and sad.

C: Revealing to you that I'm a rape survivor is absolutely the worst thing I've ever had to do.

M: It's the hardest thing I've ever had to—I still tear up just thinking about it, that you had to go through that without proper support. I just always wondered why you couldn't tell me sooner.

C: I couldn't tell anybody sooner. That's part of being a rape survivor—you don't want to tell people because the consequences can be incredibly mentally destructive. For example, I can tell you a little bit of the fallout. After my stepbrother molested me, I was in ninth grade at high school—I had a boyfriend, and I broke up with him because I couldn't imagine being anywhere near a guy anymore. Robby was very popular in our little '90s alt-rock corner of the high school, and all my friends were like, why did you break up with him? My solid group of friends that I had for years no longer trusted me because I couldn't tell them I was molested, and I couldn't come up with a good lie. They caught me lying, and they all turned their backs on me. It was violent. I got death threats. I got outcast from my friends. They never came back to me; they never apologized; I never got a chance to tell them what really happened. It literally destroyed my life. I couldn't trust anybody.

M: Yeah, and it made your subsequent time at that high school really impossible.

C: I talked about being a survivor at my keynote for the Feminist Porn Conference. How there's such a stigma around porn stars and their upbringings. Sex workers are always trying to prove to the world that they're not "damaged goods."

M: I don't think that you being a survivor turned you toward sex work. I always thought that it was some of the work that you did at Evergreen that got you curious about sex work. What you're doing now just kind of seems like a natural progression of everything you've been curious about since about the age of sixteen or seventeen. There has been trauma in your life and you've handled it well, and I don't think that the damage that you've experienced in your youth geared you toward sex work at all. It seems very natural to me.

C: A lot of things have changed for me since your twin daughters were born in 2011. I skipped the Feminist Porn Awards that year and spent that night with you, Heather, and the twins, and I read the Twitter feed for the awards show. I got to experience winning two film-making awards with my dad and my little sisters with me, and that is one of the times in our relationship as father and son that I have felt most loved by you. The pride of having a father that I could share that moment with, in the quiet peaceful darkness of this brand-new, gigantic family that we have. That was one of the most amazing nights of my life.

M: I'm so proud of the recognition that you're getting. It's good work that you do; it's adding love to the universe.

C: When I was eighteen, I did not have any queer porn resources out there. Now there's these eighteen-year-olds out there finding my work, images of queer sexuality that I didn't have when I was growing up. It's having quite an intense impact on queer youth.

M: Yes, I know! (Mateo has younger, queer friends who are total CT fangirls. It's awkward and awesome.)

C: I know, your lesbian friends love me. And some day, my sisters are gonna be grown-ups, they're gonna be women. If I can somehow make my art effective in making queer sexuality more acceptable, and making femaleness more acceptable, if I can somehow change people's perception about all the things that we have to come out about in the first place, maybe my little sisters can grow up and be queer or straight or kinky or poly or boys or girls or whatever the fuck they want, and maybe I can help make that a reality for them, that acceptance, through the work I do now.

I see part of my responsibility as an artist is to leave a legacy that will make it easier for folks like me to become happy and healthy adults—especially those who aren't as lucky to have had a queer-friendly family like mine.

M: You will, and Heather and I will be right there with you as well. We are going to try to avoid that shame curtain that adults seem to put on their kids. Children at age three have no shame. They're very much in love with their bodies and play imaginary games where they are boys or are girls. They play act the gender roles of men and women already. They play act like they might have a penis, and they aren't getting told not to do that.

I think, in my mind, ideally, they would go to seventh- and eighth-grade OWL, and they would come home and over dinner we would be talking about it and I would say, "Well, you know, by the way, Courtney's a sex worker. They make queer porn, and they're one of the tops in their genre. They make art and do important things that teach people and also make them happy." I think that would just be a pleasant, nonoppressive conversation. And hopefully, they would say, "Oh wow, that's cool," and maybe want to talk to you about it.

C: I imagine I should be there for that.

M: Oh, you could be there! You can't always plan it like that. The questions always come up when you are least expecting them.

C: I'll remember to be present around seventh or eighth grade!

M: Or they'll say, "Daddy says our sister's famous. Let's Google her!"

C: I clearly don't agree that any of my family members should *see* any of my work that I'm performing in, but I'm proud of my art and I guess it's comforting that I can share those feelings with my family.

Thank you so much for being open, and being a good dad, and really taking all of this very seriously. I think our story is an inspiration to parents because so much of the shame around sex comes from our parents, and the more that we can share with the grown-ups how to talk to the kids and how to educate the kids and remove that prejudice, not allow that prejudice to take form in children, it's so important.

M: Yeah. It is important.

C: One last question. Do you remember how I came out to you as gay?

M: I don't think you needed to come out. I kind of just noticed that you were starting to like girls, and I was like, oh, I know this!

C: I feel very lucky to have been raised in a queer-positive, sex-positive upbringing. There are a lot of people out there who grew up in a lot more repressed households, and I'm very thankful for the opportunities I was given growing up to be myself. You did a really good job. And thank you for loving me just as much as an adult.

M: That's so cool. Aw. I love you very much. I'm glad you're happy and doing what you love.

C: I love it. I'm so happy. You now know everything. I have nothing else to report, and I feel really trusted and loved. Thanks for letting me be shameless, Dad!

M: You're welcome!

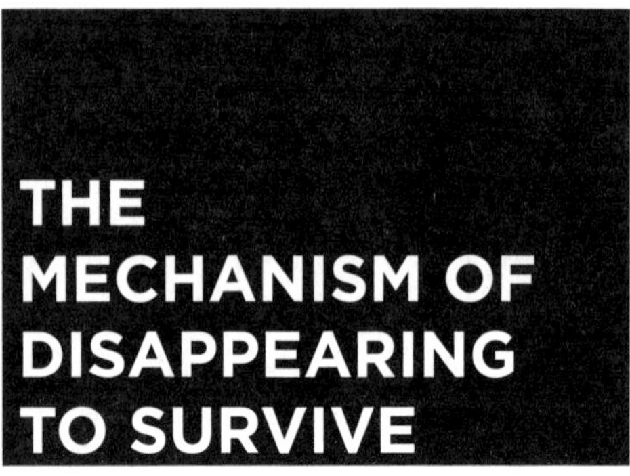

THE MECHANISM OF DISAPPEARING TO SURVIVE

Cyd Nova

Cyd Nova is a writer and community organizer living in Oakland, California. He works at St. James Infirmary, a peer-run clinic for sex workers, and is the director of gay FTM porn company Bonus Hole Boys. He has spent over a decade trying out every nook and cranny the sex industry has to offer. Cyd's writing has appeared in Tits and Sass, The Rumpus, Visual AIDS, Prose and Lore, *and* The Collection: The New Transgender Vanguard. *You can read more at CydNova.wordpress.com or email him at cyd.nova@gmail.com.*

On the day I came out to my dad as transgender, somebody jumped in front of the train before mine and we stayed stalled in between stations for twenty minutes. Neither my dad nor I had cell phones in 2009, so I couldn't tell him I was running late. The anxiety grabbing ahold of my guts made reading my book impossible, so I sat looking at the second hand tick on my watch, trying to breathe evenly.

Dad and I had been living in different countries for the last two years. I had seen him a week before, the first time he'd stopped in town on his way to find a new home in the Midwest for himself and my stepmother. That time, we'd gone to my sister's house, and I watched all of my nephews play baseball and all the women sip cocktails and all the men barbeque. My dad and I stood next to each other for a photograph, and he grabbed my arm and asked me why I looked so muscular. I told him I'd taken up boxing and tried to speak in a soft, feminine voice.

The train finally reached the airport. I paced through the terminal, looking for him, my head full of static. I saw him standing in front of a baggage counter. He's the same height as me, well-worn clothes, an old cowboy hat on—the same model he wore when I was a child. We started walking toward each other and then, when we were less than ten feet away, I knew. The set of his mouth told me that this would not be an idle chat. I was not prepared, although I'd done nothing to prevent this conversation from happening, and even planned on the possibility of bringing it up. Ultimately, my hope had been to let my body be and pray that people would continue to see what they wanted to see, and that maybe a switch in understanding would spontaneously happen without the use of words.

Instead, he led me to one of the seats next to the sliding glass doors that kept sweeping open and asked me, "Do you think you're a man? Is that why you are doing this to your body?" This referred to taking hormones. I was impressed that he even knew that taking testosterone was a thing; I didn't until a couple years ago. I looked at the ground. I did not know how to answer his questions in a rational way.

Why did I think I was a man? I had cut off all my hair and started the journey toward male as more of a compulsion, something I had to do to find some goddamn peace in my mind. Any answer I could give seemed nonsensical, and under his gaze, womanly. I didn't want to cry, and I also didn't know how to explain that within my queer sex-worker community, all this makes sense! I knew he couldn't understand my roadmap, but I promise, I have one.

To say that would have been to admit to more things that make me sound more messy and delusional. I felt like a liability, a problem, a freak. After a while, the conversation devolved into nothing. We talked about a hike he took that left him lost in the desert without water. He hadn't told anyone where he was going and it was over a hundred degrees; the rocks were hot and flat and went forever. Eventually, he ran into someone who led him to a road, otherwise he might have died. He's getting to be an old man, my dad. In 2009, he was sixty-nine. We drank milkshakes together and waited for his flight to arrive. We didn't talk much. Six years later, we still don't.

Emails at Christmas and birthdays. I talk about my dog, about nice walks I go on, not much else. My friend suggests that I send my parents a package of envelopes postmarked for the next twenty years, in each one a card that simply says, "I am alive and am behaving in an economically responsible fashion," and save myself the angst of figuring out what's acceptable three times a year.

This book isn't about coming out as trans; it's about coming out as a porn star, so let me back up—but they are not as disconnected as it might seem. Long before I came out as trans, I covered my tracks around sex work with a similar kind of gracelessness. I started turning the odd trick or two at seventeen, but got into it for real around the age of twenty.

My parents and I had never been very close. I'd stopped living with them full time around the age of fourteen, so they were never the first people I was going to tell when I started stripping. Especially since it became such a good thing. Through my job in a strip club, which challenged my previous concept of how unclean a place of business—especially nude business—could possibly be allowed to continue operating, I had found total happiness.

Growing up, I felt like a burden. Sex work made me feel powerful and independent. My body was a tool that gave me money and attention, and people were greedy for the chance to be near it. The people I met in the sex industry felt like a real family—messed-up girls who had drug problems and laughed too hard and spread menstrual blood on the peep-show booths when motherfuckers didn't pay. Working in the sex industry from a place of force and suffering would have been acceptable, perhaps; jobs to them are supposed to be hard. But how do you tell your semiconservative parents that faking lesbian sex for the camera makes you feel better than fucking anyone you've ever loved?

I needed to talk about it though, so I told everyone else. It was the best thing that had ever happened to me. From a punk background, I went about it the only way I knew how—organizing activist groups, leading workshops at festivals, writing zines about the surreal world that I had made my home. Eventually, sex work became almost everything about me, and if you didn't know I was a sex worker, there wasn't much to know. When my parents rejected me, yes, it was because I was transgender and weird and too much for them to handle, but also it was because they'd stopped knowing me a long time ago and they knew it. They probably know I am a sex worker too, but why bring it up?

In 2011, 15,000 porn performers' legal names were released on a website. Mine was among them, but that is hardly the point. As a minor player at that point in the porn industry, my biography simply labeled me a pornographic whore. Others had their home addresses, family members, and details of their health statuses published on the Internet. I heard of people being stalked. Of families who loved their children one week, the next week telling them they were the spawn of Satan. I heard of people getting fired from their straight jobs or just treated like foreign objects until they quit. I'm a counselor at a sex worker clinic, so all these stories came to me but weren't mine to tell. All these parents and employers and, more than anything, those douchebag men-children who decided to fuck with thousands of people to feel powerful—I want to take them over my knee and spank them. I want to shake them. Sometimes I cried, but it's not about any one experience. Just because it's so terrifying to hear that someone decides to no longer love another person because of the job that they do, or the people they love, or their decision to change their body because of something inside.

This is the real grip of the painful coming-out narrative. It interrupts the concept that certain types of love are unconditional. In our society, it is considered acceptable for someone's family to decide to take away their love for their child because of a choice they make. To make a lie that they will protect you, forgive your mistakes, watch you make your own choices, and try to mediate for you the cruelty of consequences. In my heart, I want to only believe that they might be angry, disappointed, or frustrated, but ultimately, family is family and should be each other's home. To learn this isn't true is one of the hardest lessons.

Here is the flipside of the resentment and betrayal: Not having my parents in my life provides me with definite, tangible benefits. Although I miss many types of support—grounding, life context, financial assistance—I do get freedom. I have no responsibility to make sure the boundaries of my life do not transgress past the limitations of acceptability to family, so I have been able to be as out and loud as I want. Recently, I started a porn company, one of the few in the world that have gay content of trans men and cis men fucking. I try to get my name and pictures in as many places as possible because I am the face of a business and that business includes me being naked, smiling, a cock in each hole. I do so, knowing the unlikelihood of our worlds intersecting, and if perchance they do—well, there isn't much to threaten me with at this point. I feel lucky, and even privileged, to have no leverage against being who I am. Because of this, I have been able to speak up about sex worker activism and say things that would have too many consequences for those with biological families.

Often, I don't think about my parents at all. But recently I've been dreaming about them. In these dreamscapes, we talk honestly. I tell them about what the last decade has been like for me—starting with the nude pictures I took on a whim for a trucker magazine and the resulting discomfort of hitchhiking to owning a porn company, struggling to figure out how to adjust the skills of an employee to a business owner. My dad is gruff, tells me that if I want to succeed I have to stop dicking around and focus, like he wanted me to do with school. My stepmother does not want to talk about it and continues chopping vegetables for the meal we are about to make, but there is a smile that seems to be playing at the corner of her mouth.

These dreams stay with me for a week, and after a while I can't stop myself from staying up till 3:00 a.m. looking at YouTube videos of my old hometown. Googling a street view of my old high school and cruising around the parking lot that I used to stand in, hot and dirty, waiting for the bus and thirty minutes of childhood social-order torment. After I look at every picture ever taken of my small rural town, I move to searching for traces of my stepmother on the Internet. I find pictures of her with a class of fourth graders. We have not seen each other for seven years, and I assumed that when saw her, she would look foreign to me. But she doesn't. Her face is preserved with the timelessness of farm women's bodies. Handsome. She looks like someone who gets up and rides horses at 6:00 a.m. and can throw a bale of hay ten feet. I feel proud of her, looking at that photo; my anger falls to the side and I remember what a badass she is. I allow myself to think of the possibility of reunion, something that has long since felt like an attainable future.

Here is my wish: that freedom/duplicity was not the choice I felt I had to take. Coming out as a sex worker, especially as an adult film worker—so available for dismemberment in the public eye—could be something else. Not an evidence of parental or personal failing. Not a source of enjoyment that feels it should be down-played as a source of shame. Not a conversation that can never happen between parent and child because to admit that a child has a sexual body is obscene. I wish I'd felt like I could have had them celebrate that I finally felt in control of myself as a sex worker, and then as a trans man that I finally felt whole as a human being. That the privilege to talk honestly about our lives should be assumed to be for those with nothing else to lose. To be a sex worker, an activist, a trans person, and a good child.

LITTLE DATA

Dale Cooper

Dale Cooper lives in Baltimore, Maryland, with his cat, CatJim. This is his first author's bio. He has a website, which is DaleDoesPorn.com.

A while ago, I received an email. I am terrible with email in general and email for my porn persona in particular, so I did not notice it until about a month after it was sent. I'm a bit of a slacker at heart, to be honest.

> Hey Dale, this is Kyle and I'm fifteen years old.* I was asking for advice because I've been struggling with sexuality. The thing is, I'm a Christian and I fear every day that I am just not good enough in life. My mother is very strict on things like that as well. My siblings and I are not even allowed to look at certain shows that support homosexuality. I am not really sure, but I saw some type of post about you online and I just decided to reach out. I am just so confused about everything in life. My mother is suspicious of me and says if I ever do that, I will go to hell, and keeps telling me that over and over. Also I just can't see myself "that" way. So tell me, what should I do,

* *Kyle is not named Kyle. I should mention, I suppose, that I don't condone minors contacting me, and on every public listing of my professional email address that I have control over, I mention that I and my social media representations are for those over the age of 18 only, in accordance with federal law. But this is the Internet, after all. If you are Kyle, go to the last page of my essay.*

> and how was that whole situation like for you growing up? It would really mean a lot to me. Thanks.

Nested in the same email thread, sent just over four hours after the first:

> I'm sorry. PLEASE DO NOT RESPOND.

Out of respect for those sentiments I did not respond, so I don't know what happened to Kyle. Even if I wanted to respond, I probably shouldn't, with the legality of an adult film actor communicating with a fifteen-year-old being something I don't think I would like to tussle with, regardless of how I may empathize with his situation.

I can only wonder at what may have happened in the intervening hours between those two emails. Had Kyle's mother found the email? Was he worried about leaving a trail that could lead to uncomfortable questions about his burgeoning sexuality? Had Christian guilt, standard-issue teenage apprehension, or straight-up fear become too great? Had he just thought better of it?

It is the day and age of, at one and the same time, the need to carefully guard your information and to disperse it as widely as possible via friends on Facebook, YouTube views, Twitter followers. For some, it's not just the "big data" concerns of an increasingly surveilled life that are important. On the other end of the data-size spectrum is a person's "little" data. The data that may coexist on your Internet-enabled devices that others use, the one most immediately linked to your physical presence. For some, such as Kyle, your ability to secure emotional, psychological, familial, financial, perhaps even physical stability can hinge on your ability to control the traces left on your computer.

I was outed by my parents finding porn traces on my computer. My mother found gay porn in the browser history. My dad, independently, found straight porn. They decided I must have been bisexual. I am not, at least not in the commonly understood sense, but I think that may have been some comfort to my parents, both fairly liberal Puerto Ricans living in suburban Texas. This happened despite my being a computer-savvy youngster. All of my life, my father had been a computer hobbyist (my mother was a probation officer), and I could fiddle with computers and circuitry as easily as I could play with LEGOs in my house. I still wasn't vigilant enough to impeccably scrub my browser history every time.

Although the early days of the Internet were redolent with the myth of "bodiless interaction," the opposite has proven more true: People share themselves and all the particulars about themselves, down to the naughty bits, on their devices. The Internet can be deeply personal with its selfies, information about your health, buying habits, likes, browser histories, your sex.

You must give in order to get online. This idea is central to the technical structure of the Internet—sharing (to be somewhat euphemistic) information, not just downloading. When you used to open a browser, the computer sent information such as IP addresses, browser type, language preference, user domain, and so on. This, despite the fact that your blank screen seems to suggest that your computer only reacts to your requests. Today, the list of transmitted data is far greater, including access to "nonidentifying" info, perhaps GPS location, links to your social media profiles. Internet users must take the time to agree to terms and conditions, to share cookies with some and not others, navigate through spam email and pop-ups on sites with nude pictures, tinker with purposefully arcane "controls" on how your private information is "shared" on social media, wait five seconds to dismiss a video advertisement.

I am a grown man, and I don't have to worry about the people I share my computers with finding my "little" data. I do not risk losing a roof over my head or the ability to continue to feed myself if my mother and father found, not just traces of porn, but straight-up participation. Yet ostensibly, the risk and concern has magnified. I could pop up on any computer in the world, whether I was searched for or not, and one of those could be in use by someone I would prefer not see it: a family member, potential employer, future love interest.

A connection of my pseudo-public persona to my private life could have far-reaching ramifications, for sure. People, frankly, love to out people, and the news it generates leads to plenty of clickbait and page views for hungry content providers. The antennae of public attention seem finely attuned to the freshness of every drama of (especially involuntary) sexual uncovering, and it is made more desirable, rather than staled, by the increasingly intense atmosphere of public discussion of a love that is famous for daring not speak its name. But when that love has the curtains of its boudoir pulled aside, you've got the makings of some decent ad revenue.

At a prestigious university, a student was outed by a peer after being in the industry for less than a year. A public school teacher left her job after being confronted with her porn past, over a decade gone cold, by a student. A porn gossip website outed a chef who appeared in a reality TV show as someone who also chose to participate in a grand total of four porn scenes a few years prior; if that sounds like a lot, imagine it as four days on the job. Health information is fair game. Patient databases at clinics that cater to the porn industry have been breached, exposing test results and private information on thousands of current and former adult film actors. And pocketbooks are just as susceptible; Chase Bank, one of the largest financial institutions in the nation, shut down an untold number (estimates range from a few dozen to a few hundred) of personal bank accounts for individuals involved in the adult entertainment industry.

Even people who aren't involved in the industry are fair game when it is outing season. There is revenge porn, where porn production is cruelly crowdsourced to vindictive exes. Today, if you're going to be naughty, even if it's just a sext, you must learn to balance, on the one hand, the implicit distinction between the supposedly protected and identifiable fact of your sexuality proper (provided it is legal), and on the other hand, the highly vulnerable management of information about it. "Outing" now verges on being an all-purpose phrase for the crossing of almost any politically charged line of representation, and anytime someone can be pushed over it, all the better for generating buzz.

I highly value my privacy. I really like having some semblance of control over where my porn name and given name overlap. I chose to be a porn actor, and I navigate the consequences of having videos of me fucking online. I should emphasize that my work is a choice because, as is often pointed out in discussion of this particular vice, for some it isn't, or the willingness of the participants is suspect—and that can be particularly fucked and vile when true, but it is not my case. You could say that a consequence of that choice is to live in a state of constant jeopardy of outing.

Well, yeah, sure. Do I want people to see these skin flicks? Yes, absolutely! Do I want everyone to see them? No, of course not. Do I want fifteen-year-olds to see them? No, but I know this is the Internet, after all. My porn is a big part of me, sure. It was also a big help paying off my student loan obligations in a shitty labor market. So were a few others jobs I've done, none of which are as salacious as porn. And while I'm proud of some of the work, regarding other parts of it I was just happy to get my paycheck and head out the door for a happy hour beer because sex work can be a lot of fucking work, and sometimes you don't want to be reminded of it after the fact.

That said, although I signed up for it, I wasn't familiar with the landscape of this kind of open secret. As a gay man, you'd think I would be used to that type of closet—of hiding what "everyone" knows, a blind trust in "out of sight, out of mind." Like any secretive structure, it is only by being somewhat shameless about risking the obvious that all the bullshit gets done with and out of the way.

I've been open about it to boyfriends, friends, fuck buddies, acquaintances—and during those times when I was relying on my porn income to pay all of my bills and people asked me what I do, I answered honestly.

The thing that gives me the most pause about my porn participation is that, while there is open and constructive dialogue (among other types of talk) about almost any other imaginable scenario that you can see people acting out on a screen—war, death, love, faith, consumerism, the environment, family—there is not around sex.

The thing I most want to be open and out about is that sex needs to be something that people are open and out about. I do porn and I act like I am supposed to act in it, but that ends when the camera is shut off. My number one desire is to be comfortable, honest, open, assured, and relaxed when I am asked about the sex industry and my participation in it. All of those adjectives are just about the opposite of my usual disposition: sarcastic, a bit of a loner, a bit moody, perhaps a bit of a dick unintentionally but kind of funny about it (I crack myself up constantly), and generally a good dude. Perversely, I have to perform as someone who is a better human being than I am when I am questioned about getting fucked on camera. I have someone openly talking to me about something that we are all told should be the most private part of us—sex—and I have to set them at ease. There are times I am better at that than others, but I try.

We live in a society where people like Kyle feel so threatened about something that feels natural, ingrained, and right to them that they reach out across cyberspace to an actor in a porno they saw for advice. Think about this.

> Dear Kyle,★★
>
> I am sorry I did not respond to your email in the four-hour span I had before you asked me not to respond. I hope you are okay and that you might read this some day.
>
> Get your own computer that you can use in a private space where you can lock the door. I understand that computers can be very expensive or that may otherwise be impossible. If you share computers with your family, try taking the following steps:
>
> - Download a browser that has a privacy mode. Many offer this now, and while I don't normally recommend Google products, Google Chrome has an excellent, if not foolproof, "incognito mode" that will not save your browser history.
> - Always have a second window on your screen open that is safe for mom, and practice pressing the Alt and Tab buttons simultaneously and quickly if interrupted. This will swap to the next open window on your computer. I must stress the importance of practicing this.

- When you are done reading or viewing whatever, open a command prompt (look up how to do that online if you need to), type ipconfig /flushdns and close the command prompt.
- Consider using a program like the excellent CCleaner, which has macros you can program to automatically wipe and delete potentially dangerous Internet history from your computer with the push of a button or even automatically.

I am sorry that you have to do all of this.

I have to be honest and say my parents were supportive, if saddened by it, despite their general openness. I should also add I did not come out officially to my parents until I was older and out of the house, which may be a strategy for you to consider. If you read any of the above you may understand why. My mother did admit to crying about it, but she was more concerned about what I could face in the wider world. I understand your mother may not react the same way.

The Christian Bible can say some scary things about homosexuality. I understand that this, as a believer, could make you feel conflicted about your sexual feelings and your faith. Know that the Bible was written in a certain time by certain people for their own reasons, but if you believe it is the word of God, I would seek out the books of Samuel for guidance. Samuel talks of the relationship between David and Jonathan. First Samuel 18:1: "And it came to pass, when he had made an end of speaking unto Saul, that the soul of Jonathan was knit with the soul of David, and Jonathan loved him as his own soul."

And 2 Samuel 1:26, where David says: "I am distressed for thee, my brother Jonathan: very pleasant hast though been unto me: thy love to me was wonderful, passing the love of women."

Find a friend or an adult that you trust who shares

your faith and, if you feel up to it, you could use these passages as a way to start a conversation with them.

This may be a very difficult part of your life where you will have to manage the expectations of your mom until you are capable of supporting yourself. I do not know entirely what your situation is, of course. As such, I must advise for a worst-case scenario. Find a job you can manage while still performing your other responsibilities and start saving money; this will also get you out of the house. Do your best in your classes. If you want to pursue college, that is a great place where you can find other people you can talk to about all manner of things, including sexuality. If college is not for you, consider what you want to do and where you would be most comfortable being who you are wherever you are doing it. A lot of young men who like men found living in the city a more open environment.

If you believe you are going to hell, so am I and I will see you there. Just please don't do anything that would cause you to get there before me. You must be brave. More importantly, you must be smart.

Take care of yourself,
Dale Cooper

[**] This is not your name.

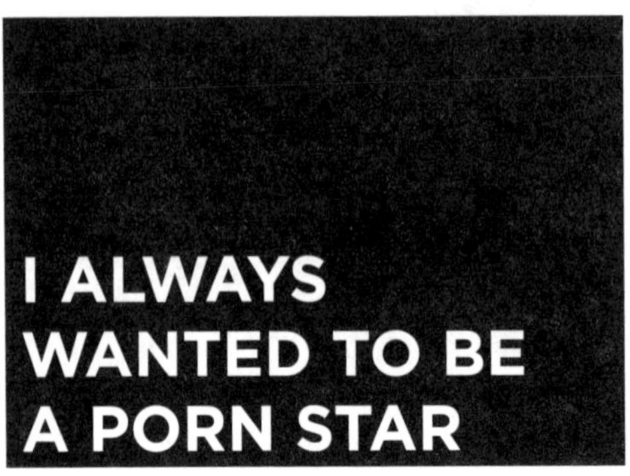

I ALWAYS WANTED TO BE A PORN STAR

Denali Winter

Denali Winter is a genderfluid dinosaur who lives on the Internet. They are also a hair stylist, drag queen, porn performer, and proud feminist. Their free time is spent working on their pet project, PetplayPalace.com, a queer fetish porn site focused on BDSM and animal role-play. They have one cat and a habit of making bad porn-related puns. They will probably never stop being naked in front of cameras.

My interest in BDSM and sex can probably be traced all the way back to the third grade. I was an avid reader as a child, the stereotypical nerd in school with the big glasses and big books. I was a ten-year-old with the reading level of a college student and there wasn't much my teachers could offer me that presented a challenge. My dad had just remarried, and my new older sister became my roommate. When she moved in with an entire bookshelf of young adult novels, I was incredibly excited. Suddenly, there was a whole new bookshelf in my room with a fresh supply of far-off lands and alternate realities that I couldn't wait to tear into.

Some of those books should probably not have been on a shelf low enough for me to reach. I think perhaps my sister had never read all of them, or it hadn't occurred to her that I'd want to read them. But I wanted to read everything. And so I started unwittingly reading books tinged with eroticism, clearly intended for young adults of the late teens/early twenties variety, and not overeager not-yet-preteen bookworms. Sexual attraction, power exchange, taboo love affairs, all of these mature concepts flew over my young head. I didn't know at the time what these things really meant, but

I had some kind of notion that they were the book equivalent of PG-13 movies, which I wasn't allowed to watch. But the books had big words and complex plots and long storylines, so I made myself a nest in my closet and would lay there for hours, silently reading and absorbing materials that I feared my parents would not approve of. The framework for my future sexuality was being unintentionally laid by fantasy romance novels.

Gradually, middle school and high school wore down my innocence, and I found a social safe haven with the geeky girls who traded manga books and vampire romance stories at lunch. They also read a ton of fan fiction. Fan fiction blew my mind. It had never occurred to me that people could write their own stories about characters that already existed, and suddenly I could find really long and involved tales about virtually any character I'd ever found attractive. The concepts I had once read and skimmed over were now bubbling and brewing in the back of my mind, and popping up again in the things I was reading on the Internet. I soon found myself swimming in a sea of "M for Mature" erotic stories, always a few clicks away from something new.

I was in my late teens when I finally made the jump to watching porn, and I dove in headfirst. I remember not really caring so much about watching heterosexual sex; I had read all about that and it sounded pretty straightforward. I was more turned on by role-play, bondage, and dominance. The first full porn video I saw was a hardcore lesbian BDSM scene starring the long-haired beauty Chanta Rose, from a website called Chanta's Bitches. It was a scene between her and another woman whom she had bound up and was forcing orgasms out of while the woman screamed through a gag. I learned to masturbate right there, that night at the computer.

It didn't take long at all before I was searching for hardcore porn sites and poring over their model applications, counting the days until my eighteenth birthday. Although I lived in a small Alaskan city, I dreamed of going to these dungeons and porn sets and having a sexy dominatrix or dom do to me what they were doing to so many other lucky models. It was sinful, I knew, but I had never met someone who could or would do these kinds of things with me, so watching was the next best thing. But I was confident that one day, I would be one of these characters, and I would get to live out my fantasies on film. I was barely sexually active, and I already knew I wanted to be a porn star.

In 2009, I was working at a popular local coffee shop and getting ready to move into the dorms for college. The shop's owner was a longtime friend of my mom's, such old friends that his daughters used to babysit me, and now one of them was my manager. I'd been working for them for a couple of years when news hit our conservative town: one of my boss's daughters was in porn, nominated for best new starlet, and was shooting for big-name hardcore companies. Her name was now Chanel Preston, and she was my new hero.

Of course, I was ecstatic. I (vaguely, through family) knew a porn star! Someone who used to give me her old Archie comics had hit it big in the adult industry! And most importantly, someone had escaped this cold, dark place and had awesome porn sex, and if she could do it, so could I!

My favorite reaction to Chanel's career choice was definitely her sister's. She was so excited that her sister was a porn star, and she bragged about it constantly. "She's in an Avatar porn parody!" she proudly told me one day. "It's even in 3D! I got a copy, I want to have her sign it!" She even entertained the idea of going back to school to be an accountant so she could help Chanel manage her newfound income.

My mom, ever the critic of other peoples' personal matters, mentioned the matter to me a few times. I dreaded talking to her about it because I knew her politics, and I knew that as a devout Christian, she completely disapproved. Sure enough, one day as I was standing in our living room, it happened: "I feel so sorry for [Chanel's father]," she told me bluntly, laptop across her legs. "He's having such a hard time coming to terms with this. It's so hard for him." She paused and looked me in the eyes. "I don't know what I would do if you ever did something like that."

Oh. Whoops.

I decided not to tell my family the real reason that I moved to San Francisco at the age of twenty. I had visited the Bay Area for a New Year's concert with a friend and gotten up to the kind of mischief you can only find in a big city. By the time I came back from my nine-day, parent-free vacation, I had gotten my first tattoo, had group sex, been to my first goth club, and had a Dom/sub couple waiting for me to move down and live with them as their partner. San Francisco had people making kinky and alternative porn all over it, and I was now really ready to join in.

My parents, knowing none of this for sure but assuming the worst, were completely against me moving away. They swore they'd only ever lend me money or send help if it was to help me move back to Alaska. I told them that I needed a change of scenery, that I'd get settled in and then maybe look at colleges. But mostly, I just wanted to run away and be kinky in an area that allowed people to do things like have a master or do porn or shave half their head without people making a huge fuss. Only my younger brother, four years my junior but the strongest and most supportive friend I've ever had, knew my true motives for leaving. I'd already chosen a stage name and put in modeling applications with every porn company in the Bay Area by the time I bought my one-way plane ticket.

During my initial visit to San Francisco, I had heard about FetLife, a social networking site for kinky folks. I used this to scope out the community I was soon to be a part of, and eventually also to find a place to crash when the couple I had met over New Year's and I inevitably broke up. I connected with a few people who offered to buy me coffee and show me the local dungeons if I managed to leave Alaska. One such person was Mistress Alice of AliceInBondageLand.com, a lifestyle dominatrix who made outrageously kinky porn with her friends with a "home video" feel to them. Of all of the studios and performers I'd contacted, she had been the most encouraging: "If you can make it to a shoot," she said, "and you're willing to sign a model release form, we can make movies together!"

And so we did. It was only a month or two after I had landed in Oakland when I did my first porn shoot. It was like nothing I'd ever done before. I didn't have sex with anyone, but I got to be tied up and spanked in front of a camera, among many other things. Fuck, it was fun! This was what I had been missing. I knew I'd made the right choice. I started connecting with fetish photographers and other newbie models and put my work out there as much as possible. I modeled, I cammed, I volunteered at play parties and took BDSM classes. I finally got to have the kind of experiences I had been fantasizing about since my LimeWire and fan fiction days, and I got to be a total exhibitionist while I was doing it. I was still a nobody, but that didn't matter. I felt amazing. I felt like I was finally who I was meant to be. My new Facebook profile, which I had made upon moving and only added a select group of people to, was covered in news of my wild exploits and bemused but encouraging comments from my friends back home.

But apparently I was too out there for some people, or rather, too out to some people. Depression hit me hard toward the end of my first year in the Bay, and after a series of disappointments in my personal life and my modeling career, I was feeling low. I had no reliable income, having just parted ways with a former client who had been paying me to do kinky Skype shows. Due to another job falling through, I had become dependent on the money I made from him. Having always been the type to wear my heart on my sleeve, and having gotten used to being able to say whatever I wanted, I caved and shared a bit too much about how unstable my living situation and mental health had become. I didn't realize when I asked my Facebook feed for advice and moral support that some people back home were interpreting everything in a different way. A girl I had worked with at the coffee shop was uncomfortable with my porn career and incorrectly surmised that it was the direct and only source of my depression. Out of what I can only assume were good intentions, she showed my profile and statuses to her mother, who worked with my mother.

Long, painful, how-could-you-do-this-to-yourself (and how-could-you-do-this-to-me) emails and phone conversations from my mom came first. She told me she would not support me in any way as long as I continued these degrading activities, and was absolutely outraged. I called my younger brother, crying, desperate for emotional support. He told me what I had been afraid of hearing: Mom already told Dad.

Before I could attempt any kind of damage control, my mom had confronted my father and told him everything. Well, sort of everything. She'd added a few dramatic twists in her retelling. "She's doing torture porn," she told him, in front of my seventeen-year-old brother. "She has a phone sex ad and she's a hooker or something, and there are naked pictures of her all over the Internet, and she's been lying about everything she does." My brother told me that our dad had looked upset, and uncomfortable, like he didn't really want to hear any of it. But my mom gave him an earful before he and my brother left.

The phone conversation with my dad was terse, short, and extremely uncomfortable for both of us. I called him, knowing sooner was better than later and wanting to set the record straight if at all possible. He told me that my mom had found "things" about me online and I admitted to doing "some nude modeling." He told me my mom had found a Craigslist ad where I was advertising some kind of sex for money deal, which was completely false. If I was going to put up any kind of ad, I told him indignantly, Craigslist stopped being the place for that years ago and was very unsafe. He told me he didn't approve of whatever I was doing, that I needed to realize that all future employers were going to find out about any adult industry work I did (to which I replied that I am neither an aspiring teacher nor government employee), and that my mom had every right to be angry with me. She would come around after a while, he reminded me, but I really should stop doing "that stuff." The offer still stood, however, for a free plane ticket home to Alaska, any time I needed it, no questions asked.

And then, sex workers came to my rescue. After posting a feeble, "Help, I'm depressed and starving, maybe I should just move away" online, I got an overwhelming amount of responses. We want you here, they said. San Francisco is tough, but you must keep going because you came here for a reason and you belong here. Friends checked in on me and helped me look for jobs. Alice, who had become like a big sister to me, got us a paid shoot and gave me her share, telling me that I was her "Kickstarter of the month." An eighteen-year-old escort I had only known through Tumblr sent me $100 for rent and invited me to come watch cartoons with her at her sugar daddy's apartment. Kitty Stryker drove to my house with a huge bowl of soup and a jug of orange juice. A friend I'd met in the scene and done photo shoots with asked her boyfriend to get me a job at my favorite night club. I also, with some prodding, went with one of my web-camming friends to audition as a dancer at a peep show called the Lusty Lady. By my one-year Bay-versary, I had two fun, quirky part-time jobs where I got to be with my kind of people and keep modeling. The people of the adult industry had saved me. I had never felt such love and support from a community like that before. I was so touched.

Eventually, my mom called me again, and our make-up talk was both frustrating and relieving.

"I hate to ask this, but are you still doing that stuff for money?"

"Do you really want to know?"

"No."

"Then no, I guess I'm not."

And then we were friends again.

Since that summer, there have been good times and bad in regards to my relationships with my family. We're still figuring each other out, I've realized, and while we share blood we have very little else in common. I'm polyamorous, I'm genderfluid, I'm a sex worker, and I'm kinky. They've never had to deal with any of that. It started as a "don't ask, don't tell" situation, but we're learning how to talk about my life without really talking about it. My mom even shocked me once recently, when she cracked a good-natured joke alluding to one of my fetish videos.

I'm not an AVN-award-nominated starlet, but I have had some incredible experiences thanks to the porn industry. One summer, Alice made me a human pride flag by duct-taping my entire body to the iconic Castro flagpole during Pride Week. That was the video my mom apparently found amusing. I've led naked men around Folsom Street Fair on cock leashes. I've had a clown nose pulled out of my vagina (we actually shoved it up there and then pulled it out on stage) for a live sex show performance. Once, I was paid $200 to shave a friend's eyebrows off. I was a booth babe for a cosplay pinup site with a couple of friends last summer; and at a charity poker tournament where all of the players were men in "sissy" outfits and chastity devices, I coined the term "punch-fucking" during the winner's on-camera dominatrix gangbang.

Last summer, I even launched my own porn site called Petplay Palace, which is based around my first and favorite fetish, pet play. (Side note: The name of my website is a play off the pet store my dad and stepmom ran when I was growing up. I couldn't resist the personal joke, and the name was too catchy to not use. I still haven't heard how they feel about it.) I crowdfunded the launch, and thanks to the collaborative efforts of basically every friend I've made since I moved, it was a success. I now have found my dream job, although I haven't reached a point where I'm getting paid for it. I'm told that most triple-X companies go under in less than a year, so if you're reading this after July 2015 and I still have a website, we've made it over the hump! The content is genuine and the experiences are real, and I'm making exactly the porn I always wanted to see. We won Best New Bondage Website in the Bondage Awards last year, which was based on a fan vote. *Fan* vote. I have *fans*. Three years into modeling and it still blows me away that people are watching and enjoying what I do. Getting feedback from people who believe in what I do and are happy to see ethical fetish porn being created reminds me of why I keep going on this weird, often uphill journey. I'm truly living my dream.

I tend to use my experience of being outed as a cautionary tale for people who are considering getting into the industry. I wasn't trying very hard to keep my persona a secret, it's true; but porn does get leaked, people do gossip, and as I always tell new models, if you don't out yourself, someone will do it for you. I don't recommend that people with a lot to lose get into the adult industry. If your family could be torn apart, if your spouse could lose their job, if you're doing it to pay for a childhood education degree, consider the long-term impact of your choices carefully. If you do out yourself, do it as safely as possible. I moved to California to find out who I was and to be able to wear it proudly. I have immense privilege in being able to do so now. Here, people respect my gender pronouns (they/them, folks, it isn't rocket science), I hang out in cafés where I can edit porn at my table without bothering anyone, and even my teachers at beauty school make jokes about my "double life" as a dominatrix porn director. I have a huge network of friends and supporters who have become my big, queer, scantily-clad family.

And my blood family, although far away, confused, and mostly unable to relate, are trying really, really hard to understand me. I live in a bubble where I am reasonably well-protected from mainstream society's stigma against sex work.

Even in the hardest of times, I've never regretted being a professional naked person, and I love and respect myself more than I ever had before. I have confidence now that I never knew was possible. I've learned a lot of valuable skills and made wonderful friends. There are so many beautiful, funny, sexy moments in this world that you would never experience anywhere else. My life is positively absurd, and I wouldn't have it any other way.

I ended up running into Chanel Preston again in the model's shower room at Kink.com's Armory Studios a while back. I had just finished a cam show and she'd just finished a shoot. We recognized each other, laughed, and chatted while we casually washed off lube and body fluids. Her dad heard from my mom that I was also doing porn now, she said. How crazy, we both ended up here! We dried off and said goodbye, then tweeted each other.

"I used to babysit @DenaliWinter and now we both have sex for a living. Weird? More like awesome."

Couldn't have said it better myself.

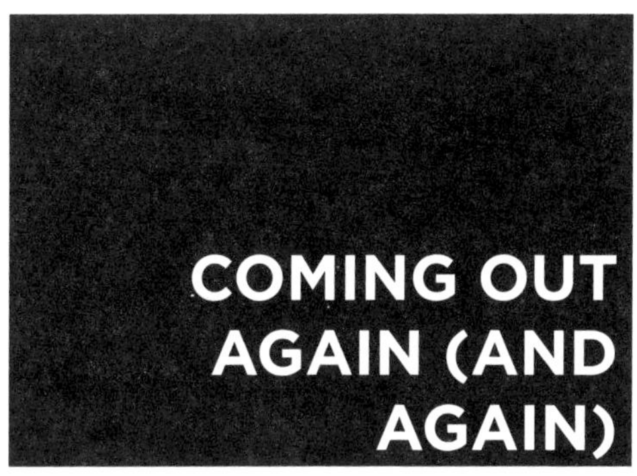

COMING OUT AGAIN (AND AGAIN)

Drew DeVeaux

Drew DeVeaux is a queer-identified trans woman who works as a part-time porn star/nurse/epidemiologist/educator and activist in Toronto, Ontario, Canada. She is recognized as a boundary breaker and game changer for trans women in the porn industry. Her films have been nominated for various awards, and she was a past winner of the Heartthrob of the Year at the Feminist Porn Awards. As a trans activist, Drew coined the terms "cisnormativity" and the "cotton ceiling" (the systemic exclusion of trans folks from everyone's spheres of desire, i.e., whom we find attractive). Drew is a sci-fi geek and has a dream to film the first-ever porn scene in space.

I could be in so many closets. A closet within a walk-in closet in a closet-sized apartment. Except I learned a long time ago that closets, instead of protecting us, are more likely to suffocate us and leave us vulnerable. As a trans woman (who is post-op), as a queer woman, as a porn star, as a disabled woman, there are a lot of parts of my identity that I've had to come out about, that I've had to make decisions about when to disclose, to whom, and how. When you have to come out as many times as I have, coming out as a porn star isn't as big a deal as you might think.

I'm a nurse. And I'm also an actress, including my work in erotic films—that is, porn. My life is full of seeming contradictions in this way. I also was a high school dropout and I also went to graduate school. I have not only one but three university degrees. I've been a modern dancer and I've been an exotic dancer. Being a nurse and a porn star have both been important work that I've enjoyed immensely. And while they seem completely opposed to one another, both are important and respond to important issues that I've identified in the social world we all live in. In both forms of work, I've had to make important decisions related to disclosure, not only of my previous work history but disclosure of my health, of being a queer woman, of being a trans woman. I know that I'm a skilled health professional and a talented performer. I'm damn good at both my jobs. I think that I'm good at what I do, not in spite of all that I've been through, but rather because of the strength and clarity of purpose I've fostered when deciding to transition, or deciding to make porn, or deciding to fulfill my dream of becoming a health professional.

So when I talk about "coming out," it's not a simple story of recounting a time when I told just one thing to someone. Coming out is an ongoing process. I come out about different things, at different times, to different people, and for different reasons. In writing these words I am, in essence, coming out to you, the reader, in a way that doesn't really happen in my everyday life. No one really knows everything about me. And even though I'm very open about things on social media, it is another thing to simply "truth dump" as I've done in the start of this chapter. It's rather a lot to handle, and generally, strategically speaking, it's not the best idea to just throw all that information out there at first encounter. The ideas that others have about women who work in porn, or about trans women (especially a trans woman who has worked in porn) make it potentially dangerous to come out without others first knowing me in my entirety, as an individual and not as a caricature or stereotype, and without knowing my reasons for making porn, in particular. That takes time, and that takes an open mind on the part of those to whom I'm coming out—open so they can question and tear down their ideas about what my being "queer," or "trans," or "disabled," or a "porn star" really means for those whom I perform my work as a nurse, how I will be a sibling, or friend, or lover.

Indeed, there are more stereotypes about all these parts of my identity than I can keep track of. Let's chuck out the stereotypes that all trans women are promiscuous or hypersexual, that we are all sex workers (although many of us proudly are), that we are all awkward, that we all stick out like a sore thumb. Here's a newsflash: You can't tell someone's a trans woman just by looking at them. I'd bet my savings that every reader has met a trans woman, spoken to them, perhaps even gone to bed with them and had no idea that the woman they were with wasn't cis (i.e., non-trans). Just in my circle of acquaintances, I know trans women who are doctors, lawyers, nurses, police officers, social workers, teachers, surgeons, firefighters, actors, and Olympic athletes. Why is this important? Well, for starters, by recognizing that porn stars or trans folks (or queer or disabled folks) are not only recipients of care or services but also providers flies in the face of conventional wisdom, which likes to place each and every one of us into discreet boxes that are simply, at best, mythological and, at their core, serve to reinforce the marginalization of these groups. And therein lies the transgressive and powerful nature of me coming out, of me saying that I am proudly a member of all these groups. And I would contest to the death that I am a better nurse, a better lover, and a better person because of this.

Just like how stereotypes about trans women drive me to distraction, so too do those thrust onto the real lives of the porn star. Let's ditch notions that porn stars and sex workers more broadly are all victims or need saving; that we feel shame or even ambivalence about our work; that we have no talent (or no other talent); that we lack intelligence; that we are not girlfriends, boyfriends, mothers and fathers, sons and daughters. The friends and lovers and amazing folks I've met shooting porn are truthfully the smartest, most driven, and most down-to-earth people I've ever met—the salt of the earth, as the old expression goes.

Many in porn are doing it as a step in their lives, a way to make money; for others it's more long-term, something that becomes a part of who one is, akin to any other job, really. For many of us, regardless of what we initially seek to get out of porn, it's just something we love, a job where showing up for work is generally a lot less mundane than most other jobs we could be doing. And just like stereotypes about porn stars are off base, so are the unfounded beliefs that porn sets are somehow unprofessional, unsanitary, or oppressive work environments. By and large, porn sets have been pretty much the most equitable and safe work environments I've ever had the privilege to work in. Compensation for time rendered is reasonable, personal limits are articulated and respected, safety considerations are addressed (i.e., testing, barriers, safe words, and communication, for starters), and respect and professionalism rule the day. Safe spaces beget creative spaces. And yes, porn is a creative endeavor.

For me, making porn has been about social justice, of activism through the creation of imagery, the imagery being my body. In truth, and having done a lot in my thirty-five years, I can say beyond a shadow of a doubt that porn touches and changes more lives than any professional discipline or any form of activism or social change. And that's part of the reason why I started, and why I continue, to make porn. As I've written about more extensively elsewhere, I started making porn because I saw a dearth of realistic representations of trans women in porn. I wanted to see more trans women like me, as I think I wrote back in 2009 before shooting my first scene. So for me, making porn was a very conscious and intentional choice. I wasn't oblivious to the enduring stigma surrounding porn. But I also figured that the stigma around porn was probably no worse than the stigma attached to being a trans lesbian. And after having given hundreds of hours to lectures, workshops, and journal articles about trans inclusion, I felt that there was a "cotton ceiling" of sorts (a term I would go on to coin later) and that sexual inclusion—of trans women as well as fat women, women with disabilities, racialized women, you get the point—was the elephant in the room nobody wanted to really talk about. It seemed worth the risk. It seemed like the next best thing a good feminist should do!

It's worth pausing at this point to reflect on why I, or anyone making porn or doing sex work, should have to "come out." You ever wonder why we have to come out about certain things and other things are just, you know, assumed? The question reveals the answer. How we are understood by others has been an enduring legacy of the human condition. We are social creatures, and ideas and beliefs are written onto our bodies all the time; people make judgment calls about what and who they think we are. For better, and mostly for worse, when people look at us—our skin color, our body shape, the way we walk and if we use any assistive devices, our genital configuration, and the list goes on—assumptions are made and judgments are cast onto our bodies. These can be about our values, our behavior, and in particular for trans folks, our gender identity or the validity of our gender identity in the eyes of some cis people. As alluded to earlier, "coming out" is a term that exists for all aspects of our self, so we can come out as a porn star. There are always decisions to be made. The notion of "passing" has its origins in racialized communities, of being able to "pass" for white. It's a term that's often been used in trans communities. In some respects, "passing," while it can afford tenuous access to privilege of being part of a normative or dominant group, can also serve to recapitulate these imbalances in power. Coming out and being out can be a powerful act and can destabilize these power relations through allowing one's very identity to be an embodied critique of the myths and stereotypes about a particular group. As I'll talk about for me, this has been something that I've consciously tapped into by being out as a trans woman making porn. Being out as a porn star is something that is more of a work in progress. I recognized the power in being out as a porn star with a graduate degree and working as a health professional, but it's not without its significant risks.

Beyond these assumptions and meanings written onto our body, I would argue that the simple act of making one's body visible in its entirety is an often-stigmatized act unto itself. Of course, nonpornographic film has a great deal of nudity (and I've done this work as well), but in making porn, the risk for stigma associated with our naked bodies is far greater. I've often wondered why this is the case. Is it because we enjoy this? Is it about the sex? Is it about, God forbid, enjoying sex? Is it because porn represents another transaction of money for time that can include sex, among other things, that thus makes it a form of sex work? Are we really still living in a society that thinks doing sex for work is any less important or legitimate than other forms of work? Are we still that squeamish about sex? The fact that this book exists probably answers all these questions, I suppose. The reason why a book that compiles stories such as this is so compelling is because stories of coming out as a porn star (among other things) is a potentially dangerous act; telling the truth about who we are potentially can make us vulnerable.

What's also rather irksome is the way that coming-out stories focus on how others "handle" our "secrets," how they are able to manage the arduous burden of bearing the weight of all that we've told them. And this is sort of messed up. In telling coming-out stories, there is a nearly ubiquitous focus on the, let's just call them "comee" (the person to whom one is coming out), their reactions to coming-out stories and their ability to and deftness with which they "handle" the truths of the "comer" (the one who's actually coming out). I contend this focus comes from most of us identifying with the comee more than the comer. The comer, after all, must be part of some marginalized group: a sexual or gender minority (or, like me, both); or a person with a health condition or disability, whether it be addiction, being HIV-positive, or living with depression; or any number of things that the comee isn't (or shouldn't be) expecting.

In telling our coming-out stories, we're telling stories of difference, stories of those of us on the outside, and in these stories you can trace the boundaries between what is "normal" and "expected" and what is not. People rarely come out, after all, about being straight or about never having shot porn. In telling coming-out stories, I think it's more interesting to hear the stories of the comer, of what makes them come out, to whom, and when, of what makes them unique, and how they feel about that which makes them different but which also makes them special. I want to hear the stories of how they came out to themselves—how they made a decision to accept that they may be into other women, or other men, or getting tied up by their genderqueer escort lover, or when they decided that yes, shooting porn is something they really want to do, it's actually something they have to do, and why the hell did they wait so long to do this. It's these stories that I choose to tell because it's these stories that I want to hear.

We are implicitly and sometimes explicitly taught to think that porn, or sex work, represents a potential liability. When I started making porn, I had friends ask me what would happen if someone "found out" about this, what I would do if I wanted to run (again) for political office (I actually did run as a teenager in a federal election here in Canada). Let's look at this notion of "liability," if our confidentially and de facto anonymity is that, a little bit more closely. First, I can't underscore enough that there is a difference between feeling shame about our work and having this be a reason to not come out, and of not coming out because of the stigma and misconceptions laid upon us by others. I'm out to the extent that I can be, because I am really proud of my work as a porn star. I've worked hard. I've done some cutting-edge shit. I've shifted some seemingly intransigent attitudes about trans women's sexuality and broken down some pretty entrenched barriers experienced by trans women in the porn industry. I'm proud of this work. Anyone I date has to be not only okay with this, but join me in celebration of this. I refuse to cleave off this part of my identity simply because others are stuck in the last century.

For all intents and purposes, I'm out. Does this mean that I come out to every nursing job I apply for? No. It's simply not relevant, although I'd contend that my accomplishments in porn show my ability to adapt to new working situations and achieve to a high level in all that I do, but it just never seems to come up. Part of me does wish I could be out in all contexts, all the time, but it's simply not relevant 99 percent of the time and not worth confronting on a constant basis all the anachronistic beliefs others hold about what it somehow "means" to be a porn star. If you want proof that being a professional or aspiring professional and being a porn star is big news, just look at the case of eighteen-year-old Belle Knox. When that twit at Yale decided to out his fellow law student actress Belle Knox as a porn star, overnight Belle was outstripping Justin Bieber on Google searches. She eventually took the unwelcome coming-out party by the reins, and if I may say about her work, she's acquitted herself way better than I would have at age eighteen in dealing with the slut shaming and discrediting she was faced with. My porn work has fed into my nursing work. I find myself actively challenging other providers' views about sex work, and many providers with whom I work are familiar with my other work. But I'm lucky in that way and an exception to the rule.

What I see so often is that others use the shame they affix to our work as porn stars and then use outing or threats of doing so as a weapon against us. We've all seen this happen and it deserves no link or reference or fucking citation. One side benefit of being out, although not without its risk as well, is that we can defuse this potential bomb that others can use against us. If we are already out, then we can control the timing and manner in which this gets conveyed. If we're already out, then there's nothing to hide that hackers or haters can use against us.

To be sure, being a porn star requires accepting some degree of risk that our work can be used against us. Moreover, the extent to which one has success in their porn career introduces more potential vulnerability as our image and impact as porn stars has a greater reach and we are often outed by accident, if not on purpose. When I won the Feminist Porn award for Heartthrob of the Year in 2011 (basically the biggest individual award given out at these events every year), I was thrust into the spotlight, so to speak, and had to make decisions about accepting interviews for national magazines and weeklies read by everyone under forty in Toronto, where I live. I had to make a decision that risked my family finding out about my work. As it turns out, my brother saw some articles written about me, and although I don't think he will ever fully appreciate my reasons for doing porn or ever understand what it is to be a woman, or a trans woman, he accepts that it is important, trusts my judgment, and respects that I'm able to make informed decisions about my life and work.

Being a porn star (heck, even making a single porn video) requires thinking about how one is going to relate to this work and who they will tell about it. When I started making porn, I had to ask myself, "Who is Drew, and what is Rebecca's relationship to this person?"

Porn names and their ubiquity both signal a way that we can create separate performer identities and can help provide a buffer, allowing disclosure about our work to others outside of the industry to take place at a time and place of our choosing. I know, for myself, having a separate porn identity, as it were, has aided in helping me get into a heightened state of physical awareness that accompanies a performance. Drew has always been more outgoing, more vocal, and more confident both socially and sexually than Rebecca. And although Drew perhaps may be more performative, this isn't the same as saying that Drew is any less of an honest and authentic part of my total self than who and what Rebecca is. In some respects, I see my porn identity as an embodiment of myself freed totally from the weight of past trauma and of insecurities related to my body that Rebecca carries. By creating and getting to know Drew, I've been able to give myself the space (from myself) to heal and effect change in how I relate to my body. Making porn has been profoundly therapeutic and confidence-building. It's something that I found out, perhaps surprisingly to my former self, that I was actually damn good at.

Creating Drew was a way to provide a layer of distance, to protect the extent to which I disclose that I am a porn star. And creating Drew, as the name actually implies, has allowed me to discursively create a new part of myself to heal and to reach my full potential as a human being. I've only ever felt proud of the work I do, and by and large, I'm happy to scream to the heavens that I'm a porn star and I love it. But this attitude is tempered with recognition that not everyone feels this way about porn. There is still a great deal of stigma associated with it.

Yet I suggest that coming out is not just an act filled with risk but also an act laden with significant potential for positive change in our lives and the worlds in which we live. In a perfect world, I'd like to see everyone be out about everything, all the time. As a trans woman and porn star, I believe that coming out and continuing to live out goes a long way toward changing beliefs about sex work and porn, about who trans people are, what we do and look like. If everyone came out, it would likely mean we had a society in which stigma wasn't affixed to particular bodies or particular forms of work. It would also mean that we lived in a society where particular assumptions weren't placed on us. People have to come out as gay or queer because of heteronormative assumptions. These sorts of assumptions are placed on us, often from a young age. That we need to come out as a porn star, or as any form of sex worker, illuminates that there are assumptions placed on us that we wouldn't, and perhaps shouldn't, be doing this form of work.

Perhaps if everyone came out, there would be fewer stigmas. That's a part of it. We also need to strike down laws criminalizing sex work. And last, we need to hold the media as well as film and TV producers accountable, and get them to show women and men who are sex workers as the powerful and intelligent creatures we are, rather than as hapless victims. Only then can we rewrite the notion that doing porn or other forms of sex work constitutes bad choices or bad professions. Maybe one day, having your child say that they want to be a porn star when they grow up could be met with gentle support and encouragement. It seems almost absurd to suggest it, but if doing porn isn't by and large the bad, scary, oppressive work environment that some would argue it is, then why shouldn't families and friends be excited and supportive of their daughter/son/brother/sister being a porn star? I can envision a day when this is the case, but we're obviously not there yet.

It's perhaps ironic (but really not that surprising) that I've found it easier to be out as a trans woman in my porn work than in my work as a registered nurse. Perhaps this relates to normative assumptions placed on nurses as a result of them (us) occupying a space of power in our society. Generally, trans people (or porn stars, for that matter) are seen as people with whom we work, not people we work alongside; they are seen as recipients, rather than providers, of services.

When I started making porn, I had a rather unique decision to make: Should I be out as a (post-op) trans woman in my work, or should I simply not talk about it and ostensibly be assumed to be a cis woman? As a trans woman who passes for cis pretty much all the time, I am afforded a certain amount of conditional cis privilege (that privilege afforded to those who are cis, or at least perceived to be). Because one of my main motivations for doing porn was that I wanted to see more diverse and realistic representations of trans women, it only made sense to be out in this work. Despite making this decision, it hasn't stopped cis fans or directors from assuming

I am cis. Their reaction when they "find out" that I am, in fact, a trans woman, is often ugly. I've been trained to not read comments to articles that have been done on me or reviews of my work. With that said, my work and attitude has always been "take it or leave it," and for every person who feels that trans women feature I'm in should not be considered girl-girl or lesbian, that it represents some fetish (as if fetishes are bad, but I digress), I have another fan that loves the body of work that I've done. I'm especially elated to have so many other trans women as fans who've been inspired by my work and who can connect with me and how I live out and talk about my sexuality on camera.

I never set out to be a "porn star," but I wholeheartedly admit to being one now. With the help of allies in the director chair, I've broken down some significant barriers and helped redefine what "trans women porn," or more accurately, what "trans women *in* porn" means as we move forward. I'm so proud of my work and recognize it to be so important that I feel no shame or carry no fear about it ever coming back to haunt me, whatever well-intentioned friends or colleagues may say.

Porn is the medium through which sexual culture is both reflected and reshaped. It can be educative, transgressive, and just really fucking impressive. I've shot with cis men and women, genderqueer folks, trans men and women; with my porn work, I've helped to reshape the place of trans women in the broader queer community and helped to show that there is space for full inclusion of trans women—not just in porn, but in all aspects of queer and straight sexualities. I've done as much work, if not more, than Rebecca has accomplished giving talks, leading workshops, or writing journal articles.

In a lot of ways, my whole porn career has been about coming out—coming out and showing that post-op trans women exist; that queer trans women exist, that switchy genderfucking trans women exist; that trans women can cross over into queer porn and mainstream cis porn; that we're sexy and smart and pervy and vanilla. I'm excited to see other trans women come out and show us all who they are and how they love to fuck.

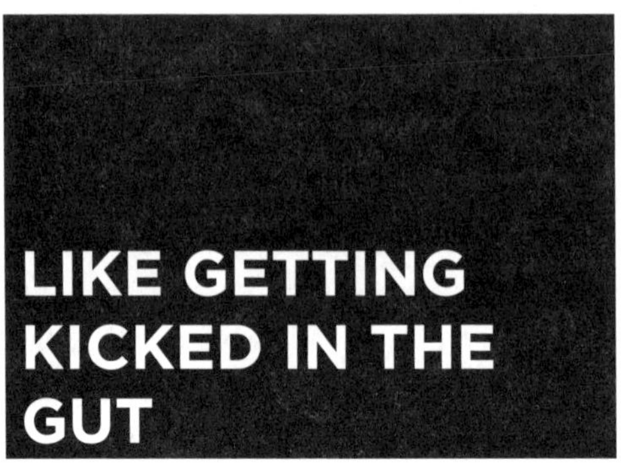

LIKE GETTING KICKED IN THE GUT

D. R.

D. R. has requested to submit this essay in anonymity.

It was like getting kicked in the gut and then being dipped in a cold bath of fear.

On the other end of the phone, a good friend and fellow performer was telling me in a frantic tone that there was a website that had just gone up that listed over 15,000 performer's real names, as well as their personal details: addresses, names of family members, children . . .

I was sitting on the couch as the sound of her voice went in and out in my hearing, terrified thoughts short-circuiting my brain: What? That can't possibly be real. Holy shit, I wonder if my name is on there too. She went on to say something about how the people that created the website got the information, shrieking something about "leak" and "medical records."

I was about a year into dating an amazing new person. He and I had been friends for years and had transitioned our relationship into something wonderful and nurturing. He darted out from the blur of my peripheral vision to half catch me as I tried to stand up and couldn't quite manage it before losing my legs at the weak knees. I managed to garble out, "Where is your computer?" and tell my friend thank you and that I would try and call her back and that I was sorry, but I couldn't get the words out of my scared mouth to tell my boyfriend why I was so suddenly messed up. I grabbed the computer, typed one key at a time, wishing with each tap: Not me, not me, not me, not me, please, not me, not me. A few moments later, there it was. My porn name and my given name. On a website that called me a whore and a hooker. A website that exposed over 15,000 men and women. A website that wanted to hurt. A website that wanted me to feel exactly what I was feeling in that moment.

Many people think that porn stars and adult performers pick names because it's a fun thing to do. They think that we pick names to reinvent ourselves. That we pick new names to hide and because we are ashamed. Are all those thoughts true? Sure. For every choice there are a thousand reasons, and stereotypes come from a first choice made by one person at some point. But while those reasons might be true, what is also true is that new names protect us. From stalkers, from people that think they get to find us and hurt us and ruin our lives because we choose to share our sexuality publicly and onscreen. New names protect those we care about from suffering the consequences inflicted on them by a world that thinks our friends, family, and children should be punished because we have sex on camera. New names allow us a tiny modicum of freedom from the oppression of judgment, shaming, hatred, and retribution brought on by a world that thinks that what we do is wrong and that we don't deserve the same kind of privacy and respect as everyone else. New names give us a way to feel okay for even just a few hours, to love what we do and not have to live in abject terror that that enjoyment, those choices, those scenes, these movies will get us killed, get our parents fired from their jobs and our children kicked out of school.

And for some people, new names give them a chance to try something new, try it only once, decide it's not for them, and move seamlessly on to other jobs. It was these people the website punished the most.

Still sitting on the couch, still completely chilled with a fear that was getting steadily worse as I read more and more pages of the website, I began to discover an even sadder truth to which my friend had referred on the phone: The content for the site, all the names and addresses and personal details had been leaked by someone at our very own performer-testing resource. At that time, testing was maintained by a single organization that standardized the process and worked to keep the industry well-informed and healthy. It had been someone from inside that had passed along all our information. This was how one-time performers were on the list. People whose scenes may have disappeared into the ether of obscurity were now part of something much bigger than their singular choice.

Now, at this point you either know the site of which I speak, or you really, really want to know. Either way, you won't catch me writing its name here. You won't catch me giving the wretched, homophobic, racist, abusive man who created it any more publicity than he has already, unfortunately, received. You won't catch me telling you what it's called so you can run to your laptop and Google it, moving it up the page stats and closer to something that people care about and want to feed again. And in your curiosity, you might be saying, "I still don't understand why it's so bad, isn't it better to be out and not ashamed?" It's a question many people have asked me. And to you and to them I say, imagine something you do that you know people wouldn't understand. Imagine having to tell them about it. Now imagine someone else telling *everyone* about it on the World Wide Web with a picture of you next to it. Imagine the feeling of coming out about it, in your own time, in your own ways, crafting a hopeful privacy for yourself that you can figure out when the time is right. Now imagine having none of that. What are we entitled to as far as privacy? Because we perform on camera, do we get none? Because we bare our bodies, are we owed nothing of respect and space and boundaries? Regardless of your politics, your religion, consider the shreds of control you hold onto when you make choices every day. With the tap of a computer key, that can all vanish. This is being outed in the modern world.

It's been years since that day on that long, green couch. I can write about this now with only the smallest pit of bile in my stomach. Many legal battles have been fought over the website and its resulting exposures. That healthcare foundation is gone and others, hopefully safer ones, have risen in its place. Jobs have been lost, families have been torn up and shifted around, and people have dealt with the fallout and found ways to move on. There is no happy ending here.

I eventually put down the computer, allowed the fear to turn into wracking sobs and then decided that I would give it no more of my energy. This is the first time I have written about it. You are the first people who have gotten to hear my story of that day, my thoughts about what was done to us. But even after all this time, healing and growing and getting over it, one thing has not changed.

You still do not get to know my real name.

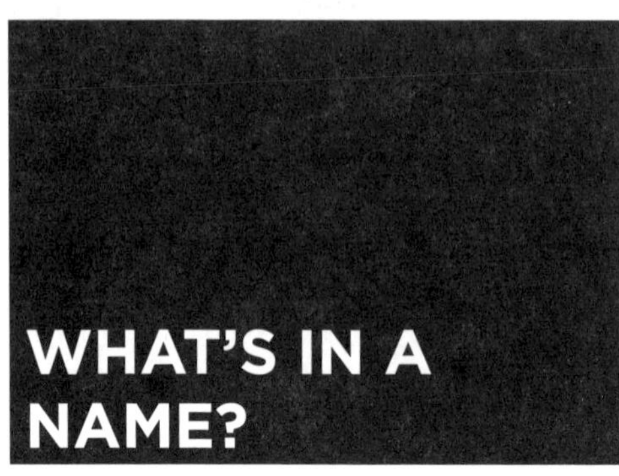

WHAT'S IN A NAME?

Edward Lapple

Edward Lapple has worked as a producer/director/editor and every other production job over a forty-five-year career. He worked on over 200 adult films for a host of companies. In the straight world, he won six Emmys and numerous other awards while working for ABC, NBC, KCAL, KCOP, ET, PBS, Prime Ticket, Disney, ESPN, and a slew of advertising agencies. Infomercials he has worked on have grossed over $50m and he conducted eBay's most viewed auction, selling the town of Bridgeville for $1.75m, with 1.3 million page hits. He is semiretired, living in Humboldt County, California, and writing for BareFootMusicNews.com.

I spent about seven years in the adult video business. I'm speaking about seven years as a professional, getting paid to do it. I have no tally of the time I spent during my high school years, sneaking into dark theaters on self-authorized field trips, attempting to gain an education into the taboo subject of sex. Sometimes you just have to take the initiative because you're growing up in the early '60s and your mommy won't tell, your daddy won't tell, your religious school sure as hell wouldn't tell, not to mention that MTV and the Internet were a quarter of a century away in some place called the future. I needed to get educated so I wouldn't look like an idiot the first time I tried to do it. I was able to check out my dad's *Playboys*, but they were just still pictures; there were no how-to sections. So I admit that I got my Sex Education 101 from underage visits to X-rated theaters. When I was up late at night, I'd watch all-night movies on television, and there was this one cowboy car dealer that ruled the all-night airwaves. Wait, what does he have to do with this? Well, fifteen years later, I found myself directing his commercials and directing those kinds of movies. Who knew?

I spent those seven years behind the camera rather than in front of it. Sure, I had the standard male fantasies that when the urgent cry of "Stunt cock!" came from the set, I could rip away my Clark Kent disguise and swagger out onto the set like Godzilla in a rapacious mood, dragging my schlong along; however, unfortunately, that particular mental fable just had to remain in Fantasyland, the reason being that while my folks did endow me with the funds to obtain a college degree, my physical endowment was more wanting than wanton. I am certain that even Howard Stern would not be in awe of this member. I understand that the male segment of the human race has succeeded in deluding the female portion that three inches is actually a foot, but cameras do not lie (although they may fib a bit). When the standard comparative size device of a United States quarter is placed in the shot and Washington's head exceeds the altitude of your own phallic monument, let's just say that you are not going to be chopping down many cherry trees.

So now you know why I remained with my trusty camera, but there was still the problem of my name. Each of these one-day wonders that we shot had credits on it when it was released to the public, and people who were associated with adult films could very well be shunned by the industry where I made the other half of my living. Not to mention by their unions, euphemistically called "craft guilds," those blood-sucking vampires would rain on you like a ton of bricks if they thought you were working a nonunion gig and I never worked an adult flick that was a union signatory. So crew names on credits were invariably pseudonyms. Heck, my weekdays had moved up from car commercials to where I was a director/editor for the Walt Disney company, and an association with productions bearing titles like *Days of Our Wives*, *Backside to the Future*, *Crocodile Blondie*, *Funky Brewster*, and *The Beverly Thrillbillies*, to name but a few, would have given that adorable rodent mascot of my overlords a coronary which could only achieve resuscitation by the termination of my employment. Oh, he may appear to be soliciting laughs in those lovable cartoons, but trust me, that little rat ain't got no sense of humor.

Early in my career, I had worked at a PBS station with a Mormon program director—half of the people in broadcasting are either Mormons or hippies—and he made the mistake of telling me that if he ever worked as a DJ, he would use the name Eddie Lawrence; since the initials were the same as my real name, when I had to come up with a nom de plume, in a hurry I quickly appropriated Larry's invention for his alter ego and embraced it as my own. He never worked as a DJ, so he never missed it. That's the story behind how the name "Eddie Lawrence" turned up on a couple hundred porns. As an aside, I must tell you that when you take a hot date to an adult motel, the kind that you rent by the hour, and you switch on the TV in the room, which normally has a couple of porn channels, and the show that comes on is one that you made, there is nothing erotic about it at all.

Many of the crew dogs on these shoots had straight gigs during the week, so their credited names were changed to protect the guilty. One of the great DPs of this business (get your mind out of the gutter, DP is director of photography, not double penetration) was named Dink R., but I always used the credit "Sucof Kind" for him, which spelled backwards is "Focus Dink [*sic*]." The man who lays claim to having directed the first triple-X-rated video and probably a thousand more, Roy K., used his real name about half of the time for his directing credit, but when he was also the writer, he was credited as "Hugh Guesedit." I had a young camera operator whose father was a billionaire, and this kid was already worth millions but he wanted to run a camera because he thought it would be "hot." Actually, shooting one of these shows is similar to covering wrestling matches for ESPN, except they are shot in living rooms and bedrooms and there is no stripe-shirted referee nor time limits or a bell. Also, you have to dodge two C-light operators, and the WWF has yet to add those to their crews. This fellow's camera credit was "I. Cansee." I had one pain-in-the-backend performer whose real name will not be mentioned. He gave me a really hard time on the set and took five hours to finish his scene. When the flick came out, his credit read "A. Hole-e." I know, sometimes I can be a bitch.

So many performers used different names, but that wasn't really to attempt to conceal their participation in the biz. I mean when your face, among other parts, is up on the screen, plausible deniability is difficult to maintain. In fact, porn stars probably changed their names in no greater percentages than actors in straight Hollywood films. Would John Wayne have been as popular under his real name, Marion Mitchell Morrison? Or Natalie Wood as Natalia Nikolaevna Zakharenko, or Woody Allen as Allen Konigsberg? How about Ben Kingsley as Krishna Pandit Bhanji? I think you get my point. If Olivia Wilde had done porn, she probably wouldn't have had to change her name from Olivia Jane Cockburn. They can have many weird reasons to make a change. I did an infomercial for a psychic hotline with Kreskin; he had his name legally changed to T. A. Kreskin, so now he's The Amazing Kreskin.

There is a delightful study of porn performers done by Jon Millward called *Deep Inside*. You can see it at http://jonmillward.com/blog/studies/deep-inside-a-study-of-10000-porn-stars/. He has created a database of 10,000 porn stars. When I was working, I thought that I knew half of everybody in the biz. Well, with that number I didn't know 2 percent of the people. Plus, it turns out that Mr. Millward only took a small sampling because the Internet Adult Film Database contains a list of 115,000 adult actors/stars. Mr. Millward's analysis of the averages among adult performers makes fascinating reading, but for the purposes of our discussion of adult pseudonyms, I'll skip right to the bottom line. The vast majority of adult performers employ false names; the most popular last name for female performers is "Lee," and the most popular for male performers is, perhaps you guessed it, also "Lee." I think that is pretty amazing, and I feel a kindred spirit because my great-great-great uncle was Robert E. Lee.

The most popular male first name is David, and the five most popular female names are, in order: Nikki, Jessica, Lisa, Kelly, and Angel. I'm not sure if a pseudonym is adequate protection from having your profession outed to your folks. I can imagine a scenario where Poppa sneaks off to the above-mentioned hot-sheet motel to enjoy a libidinous liaison with his mistress, only to observe his little darling performing some impossibly kinky act on the in-room TV. What's he really going to say that evening around the family dinner table? Just how is he going to explain his source for that information? I personally never had a problem over my involvement in the industry with my parents. My father died while I was still in high school studying to be a preacher, and my mother, always being the frugal entrepreneur and quick to embrace every source of dollars, appreciated the business as just another way for me to pay my video equipment lease payments, but she never did get the pronunciation correct. She always asked me, "Are you making another one of those promo films?"

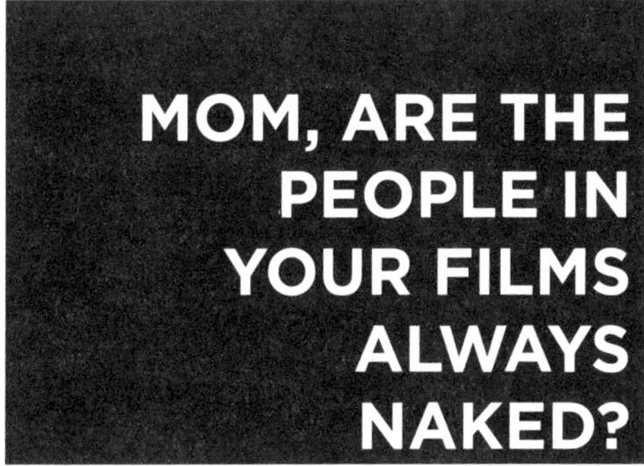

MOM, ARE THE PEOPLE IN YOUR FILMS ALWAYS NAKED?

Erika Lust

Erika Lust (b. Stockholm, 1977) is an independent erotic filmmaker and author based in Barcelona. She graduated from Lund University in 1999 with a degree in political sciences and founded Erika Lust Films in 2005. A staunch feminist dissatisfied with the portrayal of women in mainstream adult industry, Erika is committed to infusing intimacy, modernity, and beauty into her explicit films. Her latest multiplatform project, XConfessions, grabs inspiration from the audience's own sex stories, resulting in a totally new genre of adult film.

My name is Erika Lust and I am a film director. I make explicit films.

I was born in Sweden and before making the choice to specialize in erotica, I studied political science, feminism, and sexuality at the University of Lund. There, I came across the 1989 book *Hard Core: Power, Pleasure, and the Frenzy of the Visible* by Linda Williams. This book was hugely influential on the modern discourse of pornography, and on my personal impression of the genre as well. Sweden has a strong culture of sexual liberalism, and just like everywhere else, feminists were dividing themselves on the issue.

Me? I am a sex-positive feminist. I think women should enjoy sex as much as men. I've always considered myself free and open-minded toward pornography. Yet, during my first furtive experiences watching porn (either at a pajama party with my preadolescent friends or at college with my boyfriend), I couldn't help but feel disgust. It was tacky and ugly, the women did not look like they were enjoying themselves, and the sexual situations were totally ridiculous.

On the other hand, I was a cinephile. Whenever I watched a feature film with erotic content, I felt aroused and delighted. I especially recall watching Jean Jacques Annaud's *The Lover*. It was clever, it was artistic, it was *hot*! So I wondered: Isn't it possible to shoot real sex with such care for details, with more complex characters and situations we can actually relate to?

When I started my career a decade ago, female voices were practically nonexistent within the porn industry. To me this was outrageous, leaving the most important discourse on gender and sexuality in the hands of only men who weren't often the most talented people, and who were definitely total strangers to that exotic idea of women having the same rights as men.

This inequality was never far from my mind, and deep inside of me, I knew that if I didn't like porn as it was, I should stop complaining and start shooting the adult films I wanted. But I had studied political science, not filmmaking! So I moved to Barcelona in 2000 and began working in production houses. I served coffee, drove actors, bought batteries—whatever it took to be on a film set. I was also inspired to take filmmaking classes. In 2004 the opportunity arose to make a short film. "It's now or never!" I thought. So I shot *The Good Girl*.

My main character wanted to be pleased rather than please. She was a modern woman who fucked the pizza guy. It was adult entertainment but with a twist. The casting, the decoration, the clothes, the styling, the music, the script, the photography—all of these were key elements for me. "Why put so much effort into videos for jerking off?" many asked. "You are such a brilliant student, why are you wasting your life like this?" said others. Yes, I had doubts. But then I uploaded *The Good Girl* to the Internet, for free. As days went by, I saw the number of downloads grow faster and faster until it reached almost two million! OMG! I was on fire. So there were other people who felt the way I did, who wanted a different kind of adult cinema, and everything was still ahead of us!

I sent the short film to the International Erotic Film Festival Barcelona (FICEB) where it won first prize. I immediately felt the urge to go back to the set. So I founded Erika Lust Films in Barcelona in 2005 and shot *Five Hot Stories for Her.* The title says it all! And little by little, my work attracted media attention worldwide and I got in touch with other filmmakers who were on the same wavelength. I managed to shoot *Barcelona Sex Project* (2008); *Life, Love, Lust* (2010); *Cabaret Desire* (2011); and the short films *Handcuffs* (2009) and *Room 33* (2011). To sustain theoretically what I was doing and make it accessible to others, I also became a writer and published *Good Porn: A Woman's Guide* (2008) and *Let's Make a Porno: A Practical Guide to Filming Sex* (2013), among other titles.

But now it's time to "come out" to my daughters! I have two, Lara (seven) and Liv (four), who are very intuitive. Lara already asked me, "Mom, are the people in your films always naked?"

My partner, Pablo, and I have already started to teach them about sex. We bought a great classic book, *Where Did I Come From?*, and they are loving it. All new trends say that it's a lot better to start talking about sex and gender at their age than waiting until they are ten or eleven, when the shame starts shaping their preadolescence minds. It's been easy coming out to my children, who are open to whatever we decide to teach them. It's easier than talking with certain adults, who have very conditioned ideas and prejudices about sex and pornography. Because I not only have to teach my daughters about sex, but also teach them about porn. And this is a huge advantage they will have because many parents will have the sex talk but avoid the porn talk. And that's a mistake because porn does matter. Porn is becoming today's sex education, which is dramatically influencing today's gender education.

I talked about this and other relevant issues around the influence of pornography in our society in the TEDx Vienna Talk "It's Time for Porn to Change," and I am now involved in spreading this message: #ChangePorn #ChangeTheNarrative!

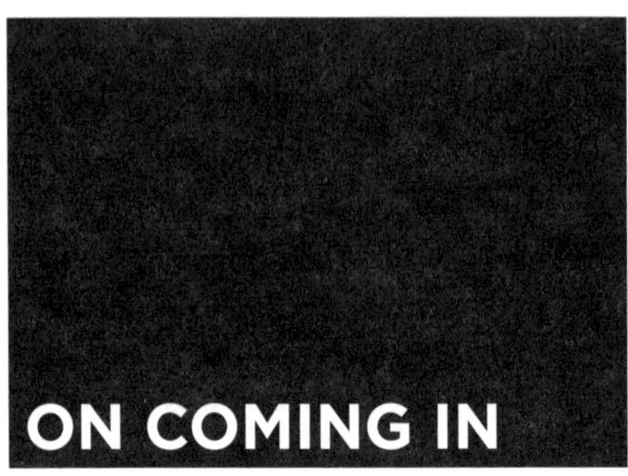

ON COMING IN

Gala Vanting

Gala Vanting is an Australian erotic film producer and performer, professional BDSM practitioner, educator, pleasure activist, relational anarchist, and erotic imaginist. She draws from a diverse background in the sexuality field and brings a queer, nonbinary, feminist approach to her work. Central to all of this is the core value of intimacy and the democratization of sexy. You can find her at MsGalavanting.com, SensateFilms.com, and MsGalavanting.net.

I have as many coming-out stories as I have relationships—romantic, bureaucratic, medical, familial, professional, sexual, commercial, and others. Long-term or fleeting, troubled or treasured. There are so many I'd like to document, and each of them speaks to the complexity with which our culture deals with the work I choose to do in the world.

I tell the hairdresser, and she spills out all of her baggage about her own barriers to pleasure and wants to be in one of my films. I tell my (former!) high-school math teacher, and he buys me a lot of beer in a short period of time and we make out in the car park of a dive bar patronized by half of the high school football team from my graduating class. I tell my partner, and he thinks it's pretty cool until three years later, when he insists that the end of our relationship rests on the fact that he just doesn't see the mother of his children being a sex worker.

But every time I think of a particularly memorable coming-out story, I second-guess my agency to tell it; when I come out with our story, I out others too. Changing names to protect doesn't mean all that much once you have a certain degree of public profile, whether or not it's attached to your legal name. If you know who I am, you know who you are in a story I've written for an anthology about the time I told you I was a porn performer and you proceeded to fuck me too hard because you figured that's what porn stars like. (Thanks again for that UTI.)

So who owns these coming-out stories? And who do I stand to hurt in the process of telling them? They're written by us both, in the moment, as I choose how to filter my reality for your consumption, ye baristas and immigration agents, ye artists and accountants. But they're also written by each of our individual and collective experiences, and how they have coalesced to shape that moment. And what's the truth about how it all went down, anyway? I have my experience, and you have yours. In many cases, I'd suggest they're at least somewhat disparate.

Is it my place to share our private interaction with everyone whose eyes pass over this page? What's at stake in me telling these stories? In what other ways do I come out when I write them as a whole bunch of things other than a porn professional? As a lover, a daughter, a whore, an owner of several fake teeth (it's relevant, but I can't put that one to print), the biological sister of a perpetrator of gendered violence, one of those girls who made 'special friendships' with male teachers and university professors, a would-be scholar, a welfare recipient, and so on. Telling these stories is revelatory in ways one wouldn't necessarily expect. And sometimes it outs a whole lot more about the person receiving the information than it does about me, the humble messenger.

As much as I'd like to live in a world where the virtues of what I do—as a porn performer and producer, a sex worker, an educator, an activist—are as obvious to others as they are to me, the degree to which I can be out in any given situation sits on a rather wide spectrum and is peppered with all kinds of privileges. In being willing and able to come out as often as feels safe and not too disadvantageous, I've done some work toward the creation of that world. I've challenged a few stereotypes and changed a few minds. Probably made some friends, or at least had some conversations that I wouldn't have had otherwise. The novelty of the porn-industry-identified goes a long way. Or a short one, depending on who you're talking to.

A few years ago, I listened to my dear friend Sam talk about coming out to a room full of people gathered for our local monthly sex-positive event. Sam is a fabulous queer flying high in corporate education administration, who manages to bring their ethics and politics with equal force to high-rises and marathon board meetings as to kinky, gritty, queer spaces. They described the various othernesses and outings they'd experienced in their years: lesbian, kinky, queer, diversely gendered. On it goes. Many of us share this sort of serial and intersectional coming-out experience.

What stood out for me about what they shared was their reframing of the whole matter of coming out in the first place. We, the Others, are quite occupied with the process of projecting ourselves out into the world, with the ways in which our various identities are either read or invisible to the outside. We're concerned about the ways in which representations of our communities are interpreted, and sometimes we even try to exercise some control over this. We're anxious about how those individuals we interact with will receive the news that we are what we are. We end up devoting a lot of time and energy to what's happening outside, perhaps to the detriment of what's happening inside; inside our lives, our relationships, our communities, our fucking, and our politics.

So Sam decided to talk instead about "coming in"—coming into their own delicious confluence of identities, spending more energy exploring and loving it, filling it up, poking at its peripheries and looking for the give. Accepting it as the already-perfect starting point it'll always be. Spending less energy iterating it to others or caring much about their response. Coming into a glorious shared space with others who share those intersections, and those who don't care what kind of thing you are as long as you're good people. Coming into an era of just being themselves.

Not a dry eye in the house after that one, as you can imagine. What a beautiful idea. How freeing. And deeply self-loving. And queer as fuck. Since then, I've thought about how this idea might function for me. What might it look like for me to come in?

Like many of my peers in the sex industry, I've cultivated quite the lovely bubble of sex-working, porn-performing, sex-positive, kinky folks who offer me something to come in to. Because I'm white, middle-class, first-world, choose a career in the adult industry, and so on, I am able to be out enough in the places I go to be able to identify others like myself, to form friendships and loverships and collaborations with them, and to be able to come in enough to feel (mostly) nurtured and supported in so doing.

There are plenty of people who don't have this option, and this is crucial to acknowledge. It's important for anyone who hasn't developed a nuanced understanding of the sex industry, some of whom may even be starting that process by reading this book, to know that some of us never even have the option to come out. That the act of doing so could have consequences that threaten physical and emotional safety, financial security, and one's familial, social, and religious networks. Just the act of talking about this at all is a privilege, one I want to see more and more porn performers and sex workers all over the world be safe to claim.

When I began my career in the adult industry as a porn performer, my mission was political. I wanted to diversify and destigmatize pornographic bodies, starting with my own. But, of course, I carried plenty of stigma in with me; no amount of unpacking I would have been able to do at that time would have prevented this. I performed for "alternative" sites, which I thought gave me virtue, a virtue framed by de-valuing those involved in the 'plastic' production of that wicked mainstream porn industry, as though they were somehow less human than I was. Then I realized that whores of all stripes were heroes—whether they made pictures or films or sexy dances or real-life encounters (thanks, Annie Sprinkle). I remembered that watching porn performances by Cytherea had sparked a small revolution in my own sexual expression. I began to acknowledge that mainstream porn had the capacity to offer just as much as alternative or niche imagery to our collective sexual consciousness. And this was part of the process, for me, of coming in: knowing and owning the history of my peers and my industry, learning to accept their diversity, and placing myself in a context of sex work that wasn't so wrapped up in stigma.

One of the sentiments most frequently expressed by those

who've come to be aware of my porn work is, "Wow, you just don't seem like a porn star." They reiterate that myth of the virtuously unmodified body, the "natural" girl next door. They marvel at my ability to articulate myself in discussions about the industry. They like it when I sound academic, until I tell them that I quit my BA to take a job in a porn company: I'm a drop-out for smut. They see my body hair and congratulate me for not conforming. I use the words "ethical" or "feminist" or "cross-genre" to describe my work, qualifiers that I do believe are applicable, and it becomes more acceptable to them. At the same time that I'm providing an accessible point of entry for them to humanize porn professionals, and potentially making my future interactions with them much less strained, in my mode of coming out, I'm also allowing some of their core stigmas to perpetuate.

I should probably mention here that it's not always like this; my mileage has varied on others' responses. But I interface with that much less often these days, because I've become more skilled at deciding when to offer some version of disclosure, and when to just say, "I'm a filmmaker."

Once I began to consider this process of coming in, I started to quietly shift my focus away from needing to be a palatable representation of a porn performer to those on the outside. I became less available for the labor of answering countless repetitive and stigmatic questions about my work. I began to devote energy to contributing to the community of my colleagues and allies to make coming in a more active and accessible process for all of us. I helped to cultivate peer support networks and worked to uplift the work of my colleagues. I started to care a lot less about how people responded to what I entered as my occupation on forms. Sometimes I'd even declare it in a completely matter-of-fact, almost deadpan way. I told my osteopath, "I'm a sex worker," and that's all I told him, and I chose not to own any of his discomfort.

More often, these days, I put the onus on them: your stigma, your labor. My work is to love and care for and celebrate and come into myself and my smutty community. This is not to say that I don't have those conversations anymore. I'm just more choosy about where and how I have them, and what basic conditions I require from others in order to engage in them. This is why there are still members of my very immediate family to whom I can't talk about work because I can't even remember what I told them I do. And why my partner's mom thinks I make music videos. Not everyone has what it takes.

The experiment of refusing to frame my multi-whore identity as peripheral—to insist on its centrality and normality—can be hard to wrap one's head around. The suggestion that I could spend my time digging into that identity, and all my others, with gusto and fascination and self-inquiry, and to make that process as loving as possible, is something you perhaps don't have to think about so much, ye baristas and immigration agents, ye artists and accountants. Have you ever reflected on how weird it is to, say, go to the same place at the same time every day, to have someone else regulate the amount of time it should take you to, say, eat a sandwich or complete a task? Have you ever been called to question whether or not your work was ethical or valuable, whether it could make or break your eligibility to love, procreate, choose where you live, feel self-worth? Why don't you ever skip a beat when you tell me, "I'm in finance"?

What if I concerned myself more with coming in to me than on how to best come out to you?

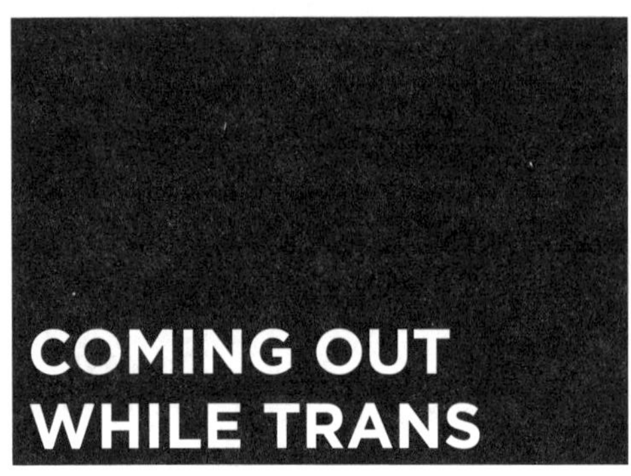

COMING OUT WHILE TRANS

Emma Claire

Emma Claire is a transsexual dyke, porn performer, dominatrix, sex worker, activist, and smut maker. She works at St. James Infirmary, the United States' only peer-based sex worker clinic, advocating with clients and on policy, such as fighting against the bill mandating condom use in porn before the California legislature in 2014. She is currently producing and directing TransLesbians.com, a site run by queer trans women portraying hardcore trans lesbian sex.

All coming-out experiences I have been a part of have been seriously loaded. My experience coming out has been no different. It's been layered. Layers made of years, experiences, trauma, and whatever force that binds me to my ancestry. It's also been informed by intersections of my roots in class privilege as a white person, and as a dyke-identified transsexual woman. For those of us who have come out many, many times in different ways, we cannot divorce these experiences from who we share our lives and our occupations with—whether that be sex work, porn, or something decidedly less stigmatizing.

When one asks about coming out in my life, I go back to when I was eighteen years old, freaking out because I had just hooked up with a boy for the first time in my life, and I thought I had gotten a sexually transmitted infection. I turned to my mom, and she was only somewhat helpful. She didn't validate my experience, she didn't ask me about my sexuality, but she also didn't tell me how messed up it was to get drunk the first month of college and hook up with your dorm-mate. She told me to wait and see what was going on and simply said, "Just please be careful," as if I knew what that meant besides wearing a condom. I ended up having an ingrown hair and an embarrassing nonrelationship with my dorm-mate. Since then, I came out in succession to my blood family as bisexual, then queer and nonmonogamous, then as a transgender girl, and most recently clarified my gender expression and sexuality as a trans dyke. Coming out has never been so much an end goal as much as a continuous process—a kind of evolution/devolution of my body and self.

Shortly after coming out as a trans girl, I worked to make my home with other queer women, in the kink community, and wanted to express myself through sex work that I loved to consume: queer porn. I took several trips to New York, San Francisco, and Oakland to do porn while I was living in the Midwest. I was working in a restaurant and would occasionally moonlight doing dominatrix work afterwards. I kept these things from everyone except for close friends and some of my partners. Even though I felt that I had just reasons for what I was doing, I was never out to the restaurant, and later, youth center workers, about my new path of work. In terms of what I really desired to be a part of, I needed to move, as I had several times before in my life, to open myself to more like-minded queers and trans people who were more enveloped in sex work.

Moving to Oakland, California, I came into a community of queer folks who were intensely comfortable about having done or being currently engaged in sex work. It seemed like every other dyke or fag or genderqueer homo I met had been in some kind of porn and was also willing to chat about it with me. My day job as a coordinator at the United States' only holistic clinic for sex workers, St. James Infirmary, has given me an intensely fulfilling and comfortable space to inhabit my multiple sides: sex worker, dominatrix, porn performer, harm reduction advocate, queer radical. Suffice it to say, I am completely out as a sex worker and porn performer to my community of friends, lovers, and even strangers who I share space with. These are some who I can identify as chosen family, and working and being identified with my magical sex worker clinic has also given me some of the foundation of how I move about in the world with my identities.

My job at St. James has tacitly outed me as a sex worker because of its peer-based model; however, it hasn't seemed to catch on with my blood family. While it's true that some workers at the clinic are not current or former sex workers, most of us are, and certainly one would hope the person training peer counselors, which is part of my job, would be a peer themselves. My conversations with family have been solidly around my work as an advocate, a kind of social worker that is firmly rooted in harm reduction, and someone who works with the dispossessed—those pushed to the margins of society. Because I haven't come out as a sex worker and can show my family members some source of sustainable income, I have operated under this unspoken assumption as a social-worker type, which can be unduly clinical in its approach and, at worst, a gatekeeper to resources for those who are marginalized.

My desire to come out as a sex worker to my family is superseded by celebrating me as a trans woman and as a dyke. Nearly four years after coming out as a woman, despite the occasional awkwardness of using the wrong pronouns, they have finally done the work of not just accepting, but starting to celebrate me. I would be lying to myself if I didn't fear that coming out as a porn performer and sex worker to my blood family would undo all of these years of relationship building. I heard, "We will love you no matter what" when I came out as a woman, which kind of sounded like I did something wrong rather than, "I have unconditional love for you and celebrate you." I've been lucky to start these conversations around sex work because of my job at the clinic and have carefully toed the line of "out" and "closeted." My criticisms to my blood family have waned and tolerance has increased over the past few years, and I think it has also for them toward me.

Sex work, and porn in particular, is continuously derided by many in our society as shallow and unfeminist, and it comes loaded with character judgments about those engaged in that work. My ideas around queer porn and transsexual porn have developed into something different. I integrate what works for me in my work and have developed my own website where all trans women work behind the scenes to create trans-women-on-women porn. The creation of TransLesbians.com is an extension of my sex work, where

I'm trying to create something financially sustainable and safe for trans women sex workers. I imagine that new work and the possibility of more recognition will put me more in danger, where blood family will find some hardcore sex scene and not understand me. Yet my coming-out process has been my own, straddling a fine line of pushing boundaries and also protecting myself.

COMING HOME

Harley Hex

Harley Hex is a witchy, queer, full-time webcam model and occasional porn performer. They have been working in the adult industry for two years, primarily in the hairy/unshaven niche. When they are not working, they enjoy hiking, consuming all the queer sci-fi they can get their hands on, and cuddling their two cats, Freya and Artemis.

"I think I'm going to quit my job." Matt pulled his girlfriend into his arms, the two of them leaning in close to the fire. Cracking a smile, he glanced over the fire pit at me. "Maybe I can get into what you've been doing. It seems to be working out well for you."

"Yeah, it's been great so far but it's still work, ya know." He playfully shrugged his shoulders and we both laughed. It was a lovely night. I was sitting in the backyard I more or less grew up in with my friend Jessa and her brother, Matt. The only unfamiliar face was Matt's new girlfriend, whom I was eager to get to know. This visit had been a long time coming and I was ecstatic to find that it still felt like home.

"So what do you do?" There it was. I was so comfortable that I forgot this stranger had no idea what my job was. Whenever I get asked the work question, I pause to assess the situation. A few checks I go through before making my decision to either answer, avoid the question, or stretch the truth are: (1) Does this person feel safe enough to disclose to without there being excessive discomfort or conflict? (2) Am I emotionally prepared to handle discomfort or conflict if they happen? And (3) Do I have an escape route if things end up not going well?

On this particular night, my anxiety about coming out was low. I was around friends who both knew what I do for work, and I had been getting along fairly well with the new girlfriend up to this point. Without much hesitation, I smiled and said, "I'm a full-time webcam model and I sometimes fly out to California to perform in porn. So basically, I'm a professional naked person." In the time it took me to close my mouth she had already slid out from under Matt's arm and pushed her chair about as far back as it could go. I sat there for a minute. Something I learned about coming out is that sometimes if you give people a minute, they realize they've completely overreacted, and if anything, social norms will keep them from turning an already awkward situation into an actively confrontational one.

Unfortunately, this was not the case. I sat for a few more minutes while she rattled off everything everyone had ever told her about how sex work is degrading, dangerous, and just plain not nice. Her reaction wasn't anything I hadn't heard before so I took a deep breath and said something to the effect of, "It's really more complicated than that. How I make my money is my business—and doesn't have much of an effect on you—so let's go back to not talking about this." I had decided early on in her rant that we were never going to be friends, but for the sake of enjoying the rest of the night I chose not to take it to heart. Simple: You don't like this, so let's change the subject. Except navigating negative reactions to personal disclosure isn't always simple. As I turned to my friend Jessa in hopes that we could change the subject, the barrage of questions began. I swear it's times like these that I wish I had a sex worker bingo card handy.

"You said you're a feminist. Aren't they supposed to hate porn?"

I rolled my eyes. "Like I said before, it's more complicated than that." I was determined to stay calm and not get into a heated argument about feminism and the adult entertainment industry.

"How can you allow yourself to be degraded like that? I'm just curious."

I felt my body language shift as I sifted through past experiences, searching for something to say to diffuse the situation. Past experience had told me that she wasn't looking to ease her curiosity; she was looking for a fight. The muscles in my shoulder tensed. I was sitting up straight in my chair. I guess my friends must have noticed. Matt inched back over to her, putting his hand on her shoulder. She pushed him away. "No. I really want to know." Against my better judgment, I decided to answer her question. "I don't feel degraded by what I do. I chose a job that meets my needs and I've had a lot of great experiences. Sure, there are shitty clients and photographers out there, but overall, I love my job." I have a hard time with conflict. For someone who takes their clothes off for a living, I'm honestly quite shy. I was hoping that giving her an answer would end this interaction so I could move on to ignoring her and chatting with the people I had actually come to hang out with.

"What does your family think about what you do? I mean, I was raised better than that so I know my family wouldn't be okay with me being a whore."

Before I knew what was happening I was on my feet. I have a hard time with angry feelings. Aggression scares me. As much as I hate being on the receiving end, feeling like I'm about to be aggressive toward another person scares me even more. I had no idea what I was going to say.

Luckily, my friend had my back. "How about you stop being an asshole? I think we were all raised better than judging someone for something that is none of your business anyway." I turned to look at her and mouthed a "thank you" before kicking the chair I had been sitting on out of my way and storming inside the house.

My friends' mom was sitting on the couch, watching TV. After coming out to my family about gender and sexuality stuff went badly when I was a teenager, she become like a second mom to me. I curled up next to her and told her what happened. She wrapped her arms around me and told me I didn't deserve to be treated badly in my own home. Jessa came inside and sat with us, leaving her brother and his girlfriend outside. She told me they were arguing about how she handled the situation and that everyone here had my back, that we're family and we take care of each other. I still felt the anger swirling around inside my chest, but I knew that I was surrounded by love. Something I've learned about coming out is that it isn't always easy—but if you are able to fill your life with people who love you, even the bad times somehow end up okay.

Later that night, the girlfriend approached me, attempting to apologize. "I'm sorry I offended you. I was mostly talking about those other girls who do what you do." I didn't say anything. Maybe I should have stepped up in defense of other sex workers instead of simply giving her the cold shoulder. Maybe I should have never engaged with her in the first place. Either way, I know she was wrong. My friends knew she was wrong. Her opinion didn't matter. I let her go. As she slipped out the door, I went back to the couch and enjoyed the rest of the night with my family. It was nice being home.

CONCEALMENT

Hayley Fingersmith

Hayley Fingersmith is a queer porn performer. She likes strawberries and elevated trains, and was irrationally excited to find her very first grey hair. She came out in San Francisco and recently gave up her hedonistic West Coast lifestyle to live amongst the grunge and unrelenting energy of New York.

I used to wear a mask every day. I wouldn't step out the front door without it. I wore it to get the mail. I wore it to do laundry. I wore it to go to the gym. It is difficult to sweat under a mask—the bands come loose and flop around—so I did not go to the gym very often. I never swam.

I wore the mask to work. I wore it to see my family. I put it on before dates, carefully gluing down the edges so they wouldn't show. I worried what would happen if I slept over and the mask fell off in my sleep.

I worried that people would notice the mask. Not that they would see it—they were supposed to see it, after all, that's what masks are for—but that they would see the fact of it, that it was a mask. I tried not to speak too much, fearing it would slip. I avoided eye contact on the street. People still looked sometimes. Sometimes I knew they could tell. Sometimes I thought they couldn't. Sometimes people smiled. Perhaps they thought the mask was beautiful.

I think now that I did not have to wear the mask as frequently as I did, or as fervently as I did. I wore it so protectively because I knew I would die without it, and knowledge is a powerful thing.

Under the mask, my face slowly changed. I do not want to understate the importance of this, for as my face changed, I found the mask less and less tolerable. But neither do I want to overstate its importance because the mask is about concealment as much as appearance, and I still felt I would die if anyone saw me.

They say that doing porn turns you into an object. In the lens, you are not a person with love and sadness and needs and mortality. Instead, you become a doll, something to be looked at and lusted over, masturbated to, and eventually forgotten. And I do think this is something cameras do. This, in fact, is what allowed me to perform in my first porn. I would not have to wear the mask. The lens would suffice.

By that time, I had begun to tire of the thing, the isolation, the ritual of putting it on, the time it burned every morning and night. I had just moved to a new city. I wanted to smile and talk and flirt with people I met. Occasionally, I had failed to wear it, and I had not died. I began to question my assumptions. I downgraded certainty to probability: I would *probably* die.

Still, once you've worn a mask for five years, it becomes as comforting as it is stifling. I wore it to my first shoot, and I wore it back. During the shoot, I wore only my makeup.

People have asked me why I decided to perform in porn. I've said it was for the money, and that's true. I've said it's because I like having sex with pretty people—also true. I've said it was a political statement, to be a visibly out trans woman, a model for other trans women who, like I once did, feel like they have to hide.

What I haven't said, and what I had not realized until I sat down to write this, was how queer porn gave me the space to come out. The hours I spent on set were some of the very first hours I spent in public, as my whole self, without fear. The sets of the queer porn producers I've worked with have been, without fail, safe and affirming spaces, and it was on those sets and in seeing myself through their lenses that I began to discover that I could be seen and safe. It was there that I experienced the profound healing of being invited to exist.

I am in another new city these days. I still have the mask, but these days, it mostly collects dust.

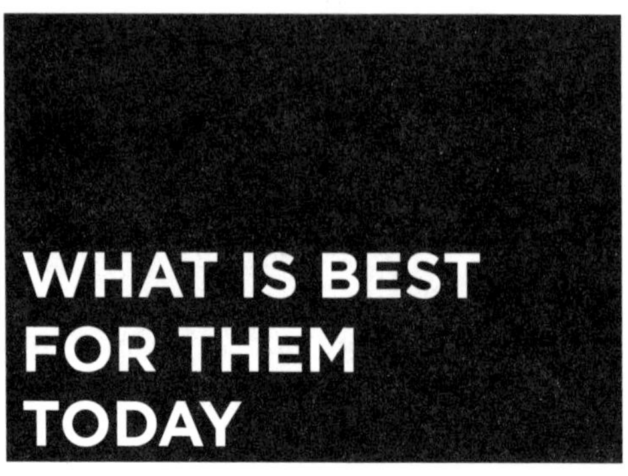

WHAT IS BEST FOR THEM TODAY

Jaffe Ryder

Jaffe Ryder is a pen name.

Anyone who knows me personally knows what business I'm in. It's just a normal fact of my life. For acquaintances, I go with my instincts and the instinct is usually just to say I do corporate video, and that sounds dry enough to people that they usually don't follow up with any more questions. And I never bring up what I do at my kid's school.

That is, with one exception.

I had recently gotten some press in a mainstream paper, and the next day a parent came over to me as I was picking up my kid and said something like, she saw me in the paper, wink-wink. I think all the blood drained from my face at that moment, but she went on joking that she was going to tell everyone what I did. I burst out an oddly sharp-toned, "No," then quickly back-pedaled and said it was really nothing, something a long time ago. It was all very awkward. I'd been outed in an unexpected way. If we had this same situation in my neighborhood, I would have had more composure, but being at my kid's school within earshot of other parents, I freaked. Not because I'm ashamed of what I do, but because I don't trust outsider opinions of the industry and what actions they might take based on that opinion. I also want to give my kids the opportunity to choose whether or not they want to take on this challenge for themselves.

So far, my kids know I make movies, and as they get older I'll give them what information is appropriate for their age. It's my hope that one of them will carry on the family business. I want to leave it up to them whether or not they want to come out about having a parent in the industry. Being a part of the adult industry was a big decision for me and I went into it with my eyes open. My kids should get the same opportunity. Some might say that having more visibility as a parent in the industry would normalize things and make it less of a stigma. I get that, and the way I see it for my family is that my kids already have other challenges, and I don't need to add one more right now. My life is all about their lives, so I do what I think is best for them today.

I negotiate whether or not to come out on a pretty regular basis. It's not a one-time thing where I say, "I'm in the adult industry," and there, it's done. It's an almost daily negotiation based on how I'm doing that day, where I'm at, and if my kids are involved.

COMING OUT ABOUT PORN FROM INSIDE OPPRESSION

Ignacio G. Rivera, a.k.a. Papí Coxxx

Ignacio Rivera, a.k.a. Papí Coxxx, who prefers the gender-neutral pronoun "they," is a trans, genderqueer, two-spirit, Black-Boricua-Taíno. Ignacio is an activist, filmmaker, kinky-sex-positive sex educator, sex worker, mother, and performance artist. They blog about, among other things, sex and gender on WhatTheySaidBlog.com and is the founder of Poly Patao Productions (P3).

There are similarities that continue to occur for me when I think of the multiple identities I carry and how I balance them. Specifically, how sex work shifts the positioning of what is being juggled. What does it mean to be queer and a person of color (POC) in porn? What are the implications of being a parent who works in the porn industry? What does it look like to be a trans-identified person in porn? All of these questions help inform who I come out to, how, and why.

Coming out is a lifelong process, and so is dealing with the overall oppression and opponents of porn. Porn has been viewed as offensive, degrading, and as an oppressive tool against women. I don't disagree with this, and yet there are other sides to porn. This outdated, one-sided view continues to construct the porn performer as victim and desire-less. Whether we come out or are outed, whether the experience is negative or positive, those who work against porn help shape the indignity that many must navigate through.

"Coming out" indicates a process tainted by discrimination and societal disapproval. Those who do come out, come out of necessity, to crush stereotypes, refocus the dialogue, create change, and combat systematic forms of oppression. Coming out can be empowering and it can be exhausting. Even when someone has been out, sex work, porn, and/or public discourse on sexuality and desire can be used against you. Employment and institutions may accept porn thrice removed, but not when it's standing at the helm of their work. Anti-porn proponents, fueled by religion, conservatism, and "in the name of feminism" beliefs have maintained an ongoing battle against pornography. Exposing ourselves for the greater good shines a light on a controversial subject that some of us will withstand. The greater good in this context is the act of exposure for the purposes of de-stigmatizing, education, debunking shame, and reconstructing desire, or reframing the concept of legitimate work. Porn has come a long way, but it's still one of those touchy subjects that will always fuel debate.

I came to porn from a privileged vantage point. I had an out. Even if the out was undesirable, it was there nonetheless. I came at it from a position of empowerment, not desperation, although desperation introduced me to other forms of sex work long ago. Before porn, sex work as an undesirable but necessary option came to me off and on for years. I grappled with the idea of sex work but only chose to do so when I had "security." Others haven't had that luxury. I had always seen sex work as a legitimate and quick way to make money, but fear of losing my child held me back: "Sex worker" equals "unfit parent." I was a young, queer parent on welfare, and living in and out of shelters. Sex work provided an option to navigate within these rigid systems, have time with my daughter, and supplement my income. However, if I were ever caught engaging in sex work, I'd lose my daughter, partial income, housing, and insurance. I decided that I had the "security" of welfare for the time being, so I maintained the scrutiny of that system and put sex work on the back burner for several years.

When the question of sex work came up yet again for me, I opted in. I went in drag, put on wigs and heels and went by names like Nena (Spanish for "girl"), and Mistress Isis. Although this portion of my sex work history was anonymous, my friends knew and so did my daughter. I've always been open with my daughter. My daughter was aware of my anonymous sex-work encounters. I kind of just told her, this was where the extra money came in. She understood, asked some questions, and helped me put my make-up on. My daughter was practically raised at rallies, pickets, and community organizing circles. She is well-versed in oppression, its manifestations, and how some have grappled with surviving in them. Sex work was not a hands-off topic, and she had informed knowledge about almost everything in my life. My chosen family and friendship circles consisted of poor queers, poor trans people, people of color, poor people of color, activists, artists, and writers. The ideas and reality of sex work were not foreign. It was a sad reality, a wonderful option, a quick fix, fast money, emotional work, dehumanizing, liberating, and legitimate.

While engaging in sex work, I picked up a few things. I talked with other sex workers; we shared stories and skills. All of my hard studying worked and I was really good at it. I wanted to learn more and, within my work, I found sex education. I became more knowledgeable on safer sex and how to negotiate. These skills not only helped me in my sex work but in my personal life. As a survivor, this transformed me. I was negotiating the sex I wanted and exploring new relationship structures.

While working at a New York sex shop, one of my coworkers, Morty Diamond, asked if he could film my partner and I. This was where my private sex work transitioned to public. Morty had already released *Tranny Fags* and was looking to film his next. We agreed, and what ensued was an upstream of positive reactions. The docuporn, *Trans Entities: The Nasty Love of Papí and Wil* exploded. I was wonderfully overwhelmed by the want and need for desire-positive, sex-positive, POC, trans/genderqueer, negotiated kinky porn. Just like that, I was Papí Coxxx. Not soon after, because of the sexuality education and sex liberation work I was doing, my name quickly became Ignacio Rivera, a.k.a. Papí Coxxx. The two were very publicly one and the same. It was terrifying and necessary. I came out like a porn star as a form of empowerment, education, and visibility.

It was time to break those rigid frameworks and ideas about how queers, POC, and parents fit into this industry. For-us-by-us, indie, and feminist porn provided the vehicle to do the kind of porn I wanted to be in. It was the porn I wanted to see. This porn is art. It is political. In many ways, I had a level of protection with indie/feminist/queer porn. Engaging in public sex work has its own challenges, but none like private sex work. The worker risks are higher and so are the state and societal ramifications. Porn is legal. Stigmatized, but legal. Indie/feminist/queer porn took it many steps further than the legal privilege and dove deeper. It challenges how we use our bodies, how our bodies look, and who we are. It has allowed for the porn performer to be multidimensional. We are performance artists and social justice agents. It helped change the landscape of queer eroticism and made it easier for me to be open and out about it.

Even within that "protection," the outness of porn is naked. It is vulnerability. You display your imperfect body, your impure thoughts, and your unnatural actions on screen.

It is there for all to see, to enjoy, to feel empowered by, and for all to judge. This is not a secret. Private sex work was easy to tell my daughter about, but the public sex work was not. There was no more secret. Only after we received a Feminist Porn award for *Trans Entities* did I approach the subject. I took the passive way out and put the glass butt-plug Feminist Porn award on my dresser and waited to see what would happen. When I finally did begin to talk about it, she laughed, cut me off and said, "I already know, Papí." I was taken aback and relieved. She'd noticed the butt-plug and waited for me to tell her. We talked about what me being in porn meant and what she needed. This was a hard coming out, but the reception was good. Our previous discussions had paved the way to this understanding.

The coming-out process is a never-ending story, like that of queerness. Sometimes we choose whom we tell. Some porn stars choose anonymity; others, like me, go all out.

I didn't choose my queerness or transness. One could say that I didn't "choose" sex work. According to the Oxford Dictionary, to choose indicates that you "pick out or select (someone or something) as being the best or most appropriate of two or more alternatives." I "chose" within systematic forms of oppression. Whether we view it as empowering or legitimate rests within the confines of a sexist patriarchal system that, at times, applauds our sexual entertainment value and, at others, demonizes the very acts that get them off. If we are privileged enough, coming out like a porn star challenges those discrepancies, creates dialogue, makes visible and offers new opinions on sexuality.

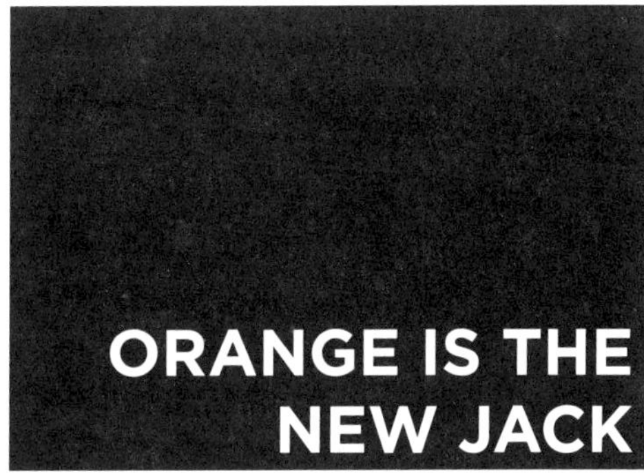

ORANGE IS THE NEW JACK

Jack HammerXL

Jack HammerXL directs HardTied.com for the company once known as Insex.com (Intersec.com). He served in the Marines for eight years and is also an avid practitioner of Brazilian jiu-jitsu and was at one time a cage fighter. After finding out about BDSM in the late 1990s, he played in private for some time before starting to work in BDSM porn for Kink.com in early 2008. During that time, he acted in many shoots as a submissive and later as a dominant male figure. You can see all of his work at JackHammer.xxx or on Kink.com.

When I applied to work in porn, I didn't think I'd even get cast. I was just chilling at home, drinking a bottle of wine, owing the IRS, and someone was like, "You should apply." I sent my application to Kink.com and chose the name Jack Hammer. I didn't realize there was another guy, a white guy, by the same name who had just been released from prison for armed robbery. Even though he's back in prison, Los Angeles porn agents still wouldn't want girls to shoot with me because of this confusion. But I never really considered it a setback because mainstream porn wasn't what I was into. This let me focus on BDSM, which I actually prefer. I've been in porn for eight years now, but BDSM is basically all the porn I've ever done. It's how I got my start.

For eighteen years and six months, I also worked as a sheriff's correctional officer. Just eighteen months away from retirement, I was terminated for being a porn star.

And then I was diagnosed with stage 4 urothelial carcinoma (bladder cancer). They told me I'd be dead in two years, but here I am, five years later, in remission. After I made it through the hardest part of my cancer battle, I had just gone back to work. I'd only been back to my job for a few months when, through an anonymous tip, my job was informed of my connection to pornography. They put me on paid suspension. It took a year and a half for them to figure out what they were going to do. While combatting this personal attack on my professional life, I was also fighting a battle against my very own body in the form of cancer.

What happened next, I imagine, was the difficult process of them tracking down my porn work. Of course, they didn't take the time to look back at all the lives I saved and all the good I had done. They just dug into random sites on Google and Kink.com to find my performances and warped it to fit their agenda. They accused me of engaging in workers' compensation fraud because they didn't understand that when you film a shoot, it comes out at a later date. I tried to explain that to them and they wouldn't listen. I repeatedly said, "When you work, it doesn't come out the next day!" And even though the shoots are in the daytime, and my shift was 5:45 p.m. to 6:00 a.m., they'd try to say that I called out sick so that I could shoot porn. They ignored the production dates and times on all the scenes they collected. I was being stonewalled.

The worst is that they tried to say that I was abusive because I performed in BDSM scenes. The picture they painted made me out to be some type of liar or woman beater because of performing in BDSM scenes. They're idiots because they didn't try to educate themselves, occasionally pulling out their Christian cards. As they brought up each new scene, I would counter with things like, "That was my partner at the time," and, "That's my girlfriend." They just assumed BDSM is the same as abuse. But despite the scenes with my partners, the main thing they seemed to take issue against was the gay and transsexual porn. I never even saw the complete list of scenes they had collected against me.

I wasn't aware of the policy at my job that stated I couldn't do porn. It's one of the last things on a very long list of stuff you're not supposed to do. You can't be a bouncer, things like that. A couple of times they sent out a paper that you're supposed to fill out, asking if you have secondary employment. The one time I signed one was back in 1999, long before I was working in porn. I don't even remember signing that. My lawyer was like, "Look at the date!" She made them look so stupid. She used to be a prosecutor for sex crimes. She called them out for how they lied, and called them out for all kinds of shit they were trying to pull on me. They went to Kink.com and told the site owners that they were doing a criminal investigation against me, and they were given all the information they needed—without a search warrant. They said I lied, that I got money—when what happened was Kink.com's owner, Peter Acworth, held a fundraiser for me because I was homeless with stage 4 cancer. My lawyer told the prosecution someone did the fundraiser for me and gave me the money. But they tried to say I did tax evasion. They violated my rights by having my supervisor call me directly for my tax records, rather than going through my lawyer. I could easily just walk away from all of this, but where's the justice in that? What they did was wrong and they need to know that. Fighting for my life is something I've gotten very good at.

They eventually decided to terminate me. I never lied once. I still remember one of the guys who interviewed me, because I trained him. He ended up having a desk job, while I was deep in the trenches. I worked in the worst places there are to work in prison. If you watch *Orange Is the New Black*, it is spot-on. Especially in the federal system, there's a lot of horrible shit going on. If you look at Baltimore, a bunch of officers got fired because inmates were getting pregnant. Fraternization will get you fired. I knew some people who had done that too. Yet here I was, being dragged through the mud because of porn scenes.

I had to tell the mother of my fifteen-year-old. She couldn't believe that I was let go. She knows what it's like there. You can *kill* someone and not get fired. I've seen it happen.

Being fired meant I had to come out to her about the nature of my termination. Since then, I've wanted to attend my daughter's cheerleading events, but she told me she didn't want anyone to know that I was my daughter's father, out of fear that someone there might recognize me from the porn that I do. I've only been to four of her birthdays because I was working. I was always working, and not by choice. Christmas, Thanksgiving, school plays, all of it, 5:45 p.m. to 6:00 a.m., working mandatory overtime. They make you work. I still have some of my pensions, but I have lost most of it. If you get fired, they can take their portion of it back. I've lost my health benefits; I would have had Kaiser for the rest of my life. My daughter was also on my plan. Now I have to pay for that. I'm a stage 4 cancer survivor of urothelial carcinoma. I need that level of health care. Now, I am without the safety net of my job's insurance. I'm lucky enough to be in remission, but I've already seen how fast things can go bad in your life.

I have suspicions about who outed me. If it's who I think it is, it was a friend of mine who wanted to direct scenes for Kink.com and was never offered a position. He tried to use me to get the job but it didn't work. He was one of the few people who knew me working at the prison and he had the most motivation to use it against me. He wanted to get back at me. Jealousy. Nothing but jealousy and hating on someone's good fortune and notoriety. Green-eyed monster, as Othello would say.

Now I'm a director at Insex (the company that put porn on the Internet) with its creator, PD. If you've ever seen the documentary *Graphic Sexual Horror*, you know of them. This is a company that existed long before Kink.com. Live shows and everything. So I work there now. I still do scenes for Kink.com if they call me, but at Insex, I'm a director. I make less money now without the pension, health insurance, and I can't get my pension until I'm fifty. (We'll see about that.)

Before I got fired, I was making $150,000. I'm still paying child support for three more years. I'm not a materialistic person, like the people I suspect outed me. I lost seven figures worth of money. And that doesn't include my benefits, which I'll now have to pay for, right before my retirement.

For the first few days, I was upset because I had just been through a lot and I did my job really well, and the people I worked with, folks who knew my reputation, knew that if they called me, things would get handled, the job would get done. I used to tell people all the time, I have more respect for murderers than I do rapists and child molesters. Creepy pieces of shit that are the biggest, whiniest people in the world. I had to deal with Cary Steiner,

Curtis Dean Anderson, Scott Peterson; I've dealt with all those fucking guys. Couldn't stand them. But if you had a problem at work, I was there to help you. You can't fill these shoes. Compared to the average guy, I guess you could say, I'm a man's man in the vanilla homophobic sense of what that's supposed to mean. I served in the Marines, fought as a cage fighter, and was in law enforcement; I was a total ass-kicker at work. I was *that* guy. You had a problem, you called me and that problem was taken care of. I grew up in West Baltimore in the worst neighborhood. I was in combat in Kuwait. I survived stage 4 cancer. I sat across the table from people attempting to tear my life apart, and I couldn't help but think: "What have you done with *your* life?" I risked my life for what I believed in, and I was being punished because of outdated stereotypes.

There are some people at work who are like, "You're okay with me."The ones who are still cool with me don't care. The ones that are still cool sent me messages while I was on administrative leave. They called and said, "Dude, I don't care what you do." But a lot of people, guys who I knew for eighteen-and-a-half years, stopped being friends with me. Law enforcement is like this *box*. It was like lighting a match to gasoline.

Not too long after I got fired, I was watching *Orange Is the New Black* with my girlfriend and I started crying. She asked, "What's wrong?" I was like, "That's how it is." She said, "What do you mean?" I told her that's what I dealt with for the past eighteen-and-a-half years, I've met all those types of people. I'm glad I don't have to deal with that shit anymore. I get up, go to work, have sex, and get my paycheck.

You can't ask for a better job than that.

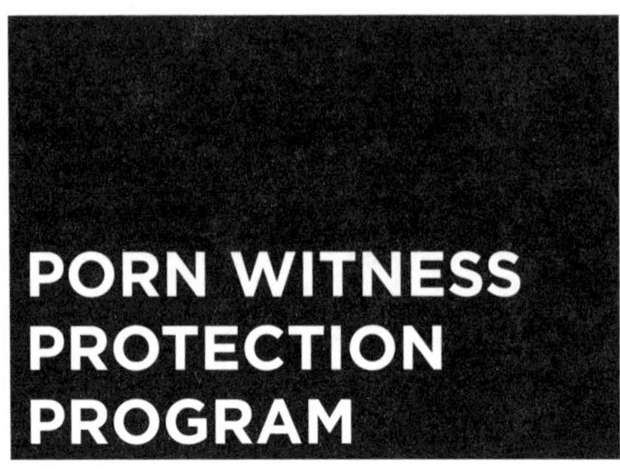

PORN WITNESS PROTECTION PROGRAM

Jackie Strano

Jackie Strano is the executive vice president of Good Vibrations, the legendary sex-positive retailer (GoodVibes.com) and executive producer of the video-on-demand site (GoodVibrationsVOD.com). Strano is a trans butch singer-songwriter and feminist pornographer. She cocreated with her wife, Shar Rednour, the cult phenom Bend Over Boyfriend *and queer butch/femme favorite* Hard Love & How to Fuck in High Heels *(AVN Best All-Girl Feature 2001)—the first time an all-queer, all-woman indie production company had won the industry lesbian feature title, paving the way for queer porn to become a viable genre. She loves her kids more than anything. Follow her on Twitter @JackieStrano.*

"Listen to me carefully: If they come for our kids, I will disappear with them quickly. I will head north with them, and I will contact you safely to tell you where we are and how you can find us. Do not let them follow you or get information from you."

I said these words in a serious, low tone, looking intensely into my wife's eyes. She knew I was serious and that I was capable and that she could trust me, and I knew I could trust her. We were outlaws, and we were afraid of our children being taken from us, so we were planning for the worst while hoping for the best.

As a matter of fact, we were not outlaws. We weren't breaking any laws. We had made explicit movies, mostly educational in tone but explicitly sexual nonetheless, and had put ourselves on screen. To some, we were porn stars; we called ourselves revolutionaries and feminist pornographers.

We wanted to be parents but because we were queer, poor, and porno people, we didn't dare dream that the state would allow us to have a child. We were foster parents and got certified at exactly the same time we decided to stop doing current production and work from home. We had taken down our website and left San Francisco for the redwoods of Boulder Creek to lead a quiet life by the river. I found us a rental with a hot tub and sweet neighbors. We were the lesbians next door; the spirits of the two gay men who had built the cabin we lived in kept us company as we prepared our little Shangri-La for a baby.

I had been performing, touring, and recording for a decade with my rock band. My wife is a performer and writer who'd gone on spoken-word tours and published books. Together we'd produced events, parties, and productions, and raised money for the community with benefits and galas, while running our digital video production and distribution business. We had received awards and critical acclaim, but we wanted to be parents most of all.

We'd always known we wanted to adopt, and were excited when we signed up at the local fost-adopt agency. Wanting to give and share love was stronger than our fears. We were at a street fair/gay pride event when we visited a booth run by friendly feminist social workers, and we mentioned that we were interested but thought that being in the sex industry precluded our eligibility with the county or an agency. We knew of people who had lost their kids to the court system; we were fearful, yet knew we were going to be great parents.

Several months later, after getting fingerprinted, taking classes, getting a home inspection and CPR certified, and prepping the house, we waited. We were only "pregnant" a few months and had an empty crib waiting in our room when we got that phone call saying we were certified. We weren't supposed to get a phone call so soon; other people had been waiting longer—but we didn't care about gender, race, or circumstance, we just wanted a baby. We were blessed with a beautiful two-week-old baby straight from the hospital. Our social worker loved us, knew we wanted more children, and was supportive. We felt like we were in the witness protection program with our new life and new address and new routines, yet we were so blissed out being in the woods with our baby, listening to the sound of the river flowing outside.

We were featured in an HBO documentary, and the phone rang. Our social worker wanted to know how to best defend us in case a nosy social worker or judge or lawyer came around. We never broke any laws. Nothing we did was illegal. We paid taxes like any other citizen, but because we were involved in the sex industry, we knew that the social welfare system could turn against us and make an example of us. Even though we hadn't been involved in any production since we'd become parents, and we were nothing but kind and loving and completely devoted to our child, they had to remind us that because we were currently just foster parents, we had no protection, that the baby was legally a ward of the state, and we were basically just glorified babysitters. I was ready to fight, to lawyer up and take on the system, but in my heart I knew the first step would be to not let anyone enter my home and forcibly take my child from me. We were all he'd ever known and he was my entire reason for being, and he was helpless against all of this. I would protect him and never let him get lost.

Until the day that the judge stamped our adoption decree and legally declared us a family, I held my breath. I finally fully exhaled on that day and was grateful I'd never had to put my plan into place. Now I work in executive management on the retail side of the business, but it's still a bit of a dance when I tell someone what I do for a living. I feel relieved when they tell me they have heard of Good Vibrations or that they are a customer and they love the business. I mostly keep it under wraps until I think I can trust someone because, now that our kids are older, I don't want other parents to judge or think twice about having our kids over to play, especially if their child has become fond of our children and vice versa. My wife and I have always been out and proud about what we do, but we don't expect our children to come out and to have to explain every time they make a new friend or someone inquires, "What do your parents do?"

So I just say I'm in management and e-commerce until I get a sense that the person won't start asking goofy questions when it's not appropriate. Most often, I find myself giving parents advice on products and personal topics like intimacy, and am more than happy to keep it simple for my kids' sake. My wife is usually more forthcoming and at ease about giving information, as she is a writer and works at home.

I am proud of the work I do. I know that I have personally helped people have healthier lives and helped them accept their authentic sexual selves. I know this because people have told me this. I have reached people through the movies we have made and with the retail business I have helped run. I am proud of standing for safe, nonjudgmental access to sex information and quality products, and I am not in the closet about my sexuality or gender identity. I work hard and I have made my own way in life with no trust fund to help me along. I am fiercely protective of our children and would do anything for them. I do not suffer fools gladly and do not care about the opinions of hypocrites and fear mongers. Our children are a true blessing and a gift from the Greater Spirit, and although I have been called a lot of names in this life, I love being called Mama most of all.

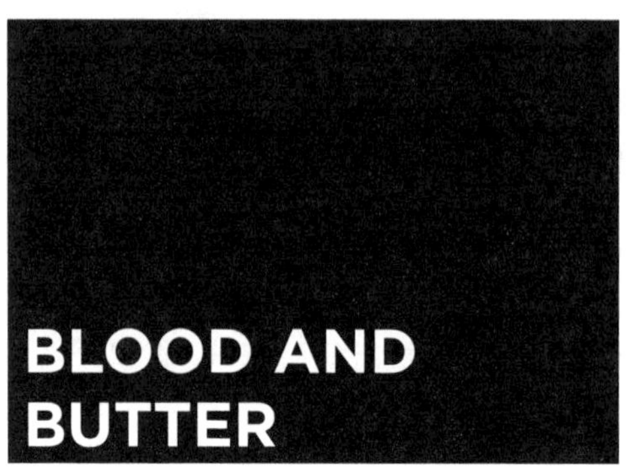

BLOOD AND BUTTER

James Darling

James Darling is a Bay Area–based, multiple award-winning adult performer, educator, and director from the Dirty South. He won the Feminist Porn Awards Heartthrob of the Year 2012 and most recently was nominated for 2015 AVN Awards Transsexual Performer of the Year and Cybersocket's Best Sex Scene. Darling's rise in porn began with his performance debut on CrashPadSeries.com, and continued with queer and trans porn studios including T-Wood Pictures, TROUBLEfilms, Alternadudes, and Buck Angel Entertainment. In 2012, he launched FTMFucker.com, one of the first all-FTM porn membership sites. His work has been featured internationally at film festivals, universities, and conferences on topics related to trans issues, sex worker rights, and privacy. You can find more of James Darling's adventures on Twitter @JamesDarlingxxx and Tumblr at JamesDarlingxxx.

"Have you ever had a butter burger?" My dad and I are driving from the Indianapolis airport through the endless miles of Midwestern farmland to where my grandmother is in an assisted living facility. We pull into a Culver's; he is so relieved that I'm no longer a vegetarian. Honestly, being a vegetarian was so much worse than me being gay, and almost as bad as not being a Christian in my conservative Midwestern family.

My dad was the black sheep of his generation. Growing up in the clean-cut suburbs of Indiana, he and his father didn't speak for many years when he decided to drop out of the Air Force and move out to California to ride motorcycles and be free. I'm a queer transsexual man, and my father and I rarely spoke for years when

I moved out of the house, transitioned, and took a Greyhound bus across the country to make my own life in California. I see so much of him reflected in myself the older I get, it kind of scares me. Despite our same grey-blue eyes, jawlines, and sordid histories, I sincerely doubt that my father ever did porn.

For the past half decade, I've been carving out a spot, piece by piece, scene by scene, for myself and other transsexual men in the adult industry. I launched the first all-FTM hardcore porn site, have directed several feature-length films, performed in countless porn scenes, and have been nominated at most major adult industry award shows. I love porn, and I always have. I used to sneak into my friend's parents' closet and read their books about sex and took every chance I got to see scrambled porn on the Spice channel or on Internet forums. As I came into performing, I found that I had a captive audience who appreciated my boyish brand of nontraditional masculinity and commitment to ethically produced porn. Each scene challenged me to push myself further, and what started as the occasional indie queer porn gig grew into a career. I love that I get to meet all kinds of people, and that I have complete creative control and can breathe life into fantasies in a physical and visual medium most people only dream about. I imagine that I will be making porn and performing in it for quite some time, and it is work I'm very proud to do. However, my family has no idea what I actually do for a living. The more time goes by, the more I know that I need to say something. I keep imagining one day dying and my family finding out about my double life after I'm gone, a parade of sex workers showing up to the funeral with nothing but gang bangs and filthy transsexual porn to fill them in.

At this point in my life, I've come out as different identities countless times—as a lesbian, as a trans man, as someone with multiple partners of multiple genders. My family no longer asks me any questions about my personal or romantic life when we talk on the phone with a safe several thousand miles between us. My life is too much and too confusing for them to understand, but at least we are able to be a part of each other's lives again. I love my family, and I want so badly to be able to be honest with them about my life and to openly share the joys and struggles of this path I've found myself on. If I had been in any other field, I imagine my parents would be very proud of me for forging my own path against the odds, running my own business, winning awards, and being interviewed in magazines and podcasts and academic papers. Unfortunately, I don't feel safe telling my family about this because working in porn has a huge stigma for most people, and I know that my family would not understand why it is a good or important thing for me.

I entertain the thought of practicing my story to come out as a porn star with my grandma with advanced Alzheimer's. She is one of my last surviving extended relatives. She is a fierce eighty-year-old lady who raised three sons and was married to the same man for over fifty years. I can't imagine what it must be like to see all of the things she has experienced during her lifetime and to be so strong. Even though my grandfather stopped speaking to me when I transitioned, my grandmother was the first extended family member to use my chosen name. Her memory is gone and she can't remember how old her grandchildren are anymore, or even whom she saw a week ago, but she still remembers who I am, even though I am a man now. We watch TV, and she asks me if I'm happy. I tell her yes, but decide to keep the porn to myself.

My dad and I were at the airport bar, awaiting our departing flights. He was harassing me for the millionth time about how I need to go to college so I don't end up self-employed and always looking for the next gig like him. How if I got a degree, he might be able to help me find a better job. I tuned him out, and as my mind glazed over I thought about my business, my struggles as a transsexual man trying to make it in the adult industry, and the awards—and snapped out of it. I started to talk without really knowing what I was saying and just emotionally vomited all over my father: "Dad, I can't go to school. I don't have time. I already have a career and have for some time. I didn't know how else to tell you this, but I make porn."

I expected my dad to freak out, or walk away, or do . . . something. Instead, he just got really quiet, and after a pause he said, "Thank you for telling me. I love you."

Our flights were leaving, so we headed to our respective gates and parted ways with a hug. I tried to stop shaking on the plane, relieved and secure in the knowledge that my father still loves me, his complicated transsexual pornographer son.

JOB SECURITY

Jesse Jackman

Jesse Jackman is a writer, senior software engineer, and logorrheic dork savant who moonlights as a porn star—although he prefers the term "erotic illusionist." He blogs about his experiences as a forty-something gay pornographic actor at JesseJackman.xxx, and is also a regular Huffington Post contributor (huffingtonpost.com/jesse-jackman). Jesse lives with his fiancé Dirk Caber, a classical musician (and fellow industry performer), in Boston, Massachusetts.

It's Monday as I write this, and as most of us—myself included—head back to work, I thought it would be fitting to write about some adversity I once faced on the job. No, not at the studio, at my day job. Yes, I have one, and yes, they know about my other career as a porn actor. Well, they do now.

Porn is not my full-time job. I hold a bachelor's degree in computer science and have worked as a software engineer at the same large Boston-based company for the last twenty-two years. Porn is more like a hobby for me; it's an opportunity to do something new and exciting and fun, to give me a little extra spending money, and to have sex with some of the hottest guys on the planet.

I filmed my first scene with TitanMen in August of 2011. The scene—with Hunter Marx in *Surveillance*—wasn't released until January of the following year, so for a few months I was able to keep my newfound sideline a secret. Finally, on a chilly Saturday night in December, I made my first official hometown appearance at one of Boston's largest gay clubs to promote my upcoming debut. It was an amazing experience. Friends and strangers alike were really supportive, and I had a fantastic time.

On Monday morning I arrived at work to find the following email in my inbox (I've changed the names and removed any specific references to my employer):

> Hi Jesse,
> My name is Steve Richardson and I work in the customer service department. My office received a message that I wanted to share with you. Would it be possible to stop by my office so we can talk briefly? Let me know what a good time might be for you.
>
> Steve

Oh shit, I thought nervously. I work in internal support and don't have any direct contact with customers. Why would someone from customer service want to see me?

I met with Mr. Richardson that afternoon. "Call me Steve," he said amicably. Steve was an upbeat gentleman with a brightly-colored shirt and a firm, friendly handshake. I had a seat in his office, swallowed hard, and asked him what was going on. "I think the easiest thing to do is just show you," he said. Then he handed me a printout of an email. It read:

> To: Stephen Richardson, Customer Service Department
> From: Concerned Customer
> Sent: Sunday, December 18, 2011 3:01 PM
> Subject: Unacceptable Staff Behaviour
> To Whom It May Concern:
> It is absolutely appalling that your organisation would hire and employee [*sic*] an individual who openly participates and promotes such a despicable act as adult pornography. Tolerance of diversity and non-discrimination of an individual's race, sex, religion, political affiliations, and sexual orientations [*sic*] are to be expected but to knowingly employee [*sic*] such a perverse individual [*sic*] that engages in obscene and lewd behavior is reprehensible.
> In recent times, individuals have been castigated for sexual misconduct and or behaviour that is not to be

> associated with an organisation's philosophy. You should be more diligent in knowing what behaviours could be potentially damaging to its credibility and overall image. Patrons would be hesitant, philanthropists would be reluctant, media would be unforgiving, and staff would be stigmatized through association.
>
> Jesse Jackman (performing with TitanMen) may have his own reasons for participating in such salacious activities, but we hold you to a much higher standard and hope that a resolution can be achieved that does not adversely affect the organisation. Although Mr. Jackman does not have direct customer contact, the morals and ethics should be held consistent for all of your employees.
>
> —Concerned Customer

As I read the email, I got that terrible sinking feeling that comes with the anticipation of really, really bad news. What would my company's response be? I'd read the code of employee conduct thoroughly, and I was almost certain that I was well within my rights as long as working in porn didn't interfere with my day-to-day responsibilities. But I was not absolutely certain. Had I overlooked something? Was I about to be fired?

Steve had been direct with me about the email, so I figured it was best to be direct in return. After I'd finished reading the letter but before he got a chance to say anything, I told him that the message's statements about working with TitanMen were true. However, I explained, I'd researched my decision to work with TitanMen very carefully and believed that I wasn't in violation of any corporate policies. I also commented that whoever wrote the complaint certainly seemed to have very strong opinions, then reiterated my belief that I hadn't done anything wrong.

Steve listened attentively. I finished making my case, then gripped the arms of the chair with dread. It was the moment of truth . . . and Steve's words took me completely by surprise.

"I just want you to know that this email is absolute bullshit."

I love my company, but at that moment, I'd never been more proud to work there.

Steve reassured me that I'd done nothing wrong and that the organization was behind me 100 percent. Anticipating that I might want to keep my side job and day job separate, he explained that he hadn't followed the standard practice of notifying my supervisor. He'd already discussed the email with legal counsel, but other than that, the matter would be kept sealed. He was more concerned for my safety than anything else. He wondered if the complainant might hold some grudge against me (I told him that I don't know anyone who would) or attempt to slander me in other ways. He even offered my company's support should this type of harassment recur. Clearly, they were on my side.

Even though I've never received another complaint and haven't heard from customer service in over three years, I've always been curious: Who is "Concerned Customer" and what does he or she have against me, or against porn? I also occasionally wonder if something like this will happen again. But if it does, now I know that it'll lack teeth. My employer has my back, and there's no reason to be nervous anymore.

A few weeks later, I wrote about my visit to customer service on my blog. Within hours, someone posted the following comment from a fake email address:

> Author: queefs are more entertaining than this blog
> E-mail: lolz@yahoo.com
> Comment: bitch, bitch, bitch . . . just shut up and eat a dick you stupid whore.
> If you were a shitty employee, they'd fire your ass. But since you must be doing something right, they will tolerate stupid shit like this. Which is very unusual for most places.
>
> Now aside from your gripes about your CHOICE of side job and its cons, are you going to prattle on about some stupid shit related to your boyfriend? I can't wait for your ass to get dumped, then your blogs will haunt you.

Whoever "lolz" might be, he or she has my pity. My ass hasn't been dumped; in fact, Dirk and I are well into our fourth year together and are now engaged to be married. I still love both of my jobs, my family, my friends, and my life, and anyone who knows me knows that I'm happier than I've ever been. What I've come to understand is that anger such as lolz's often hides a much deeper layer of self-hatred, isolation, and shame. I truly feel sorry for him or her, and I hope that someday he or she is able to find inside his or herself the same kind of joy that I've finally found after all these years. Everyone deserves that, even him or her.

Also, I guess lolz forgot that he or she was writing to a software engineer. The next time he or she posts a vitriolic, anonymous message to my blog, he or she might want to consider masking his or her IP address. How's the weather in Pittsburgh, lolz?

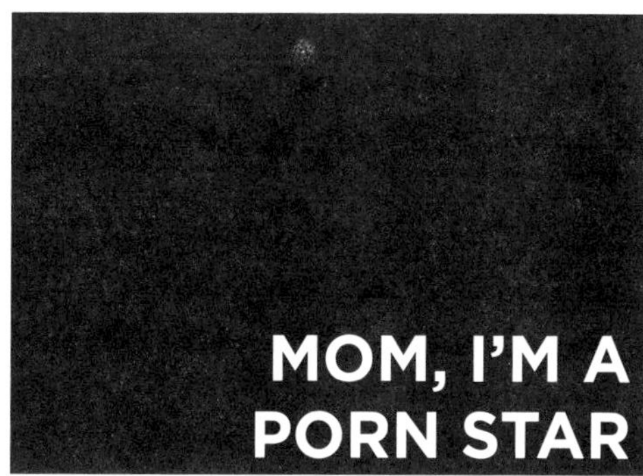

MOM, I'M A PORN STAR

Jesse Jackman

Jesse Jackman is a writer, senior software engineer, and logorrheic dork savant who moonlights as a porn star—although he prefers the term "erotic illusionist." He blogs about his experiences as a fortysomething gay pornographic actor at JesseJackman.xxx, and is also a regular Huffington Post contributor (huffingtonpost.com/jesse-jackman). Jesse lives with his fiancé Dirk Caber, a classical musician (and fellow industry performer), in Boston, Massachusetts.

When I plunged into porn at age thirty-eight, a lot of questions weighed heavily on my mind. Now that I was an adult film actor, would I be able to find love? How would this affect my day job? What would my friends think? And what would my mother think?

I'm the only child of a single parent. Mom calls me her "angel lamb," and I think she still sees me as the innocent boy I once was. As a gay man growing up in '80s suburban America, though, I've experienced plenty of guilt, self-loathing, and shame. Not wanting my mom to see me as anything less than perfect, I've always hidden those feelings from her, hoping to stay impossibly angelic in her eyes.

My employer and friends were all accepting, even enthusiastic, when I came out to them about my new side job. I decided, though, that I would wait until I retired from the industry to tell my mom that I'd been making adult films, if I ever told her at all. My rationale at the time was that I didn't want her to worry about my health (despite my studio's strict adherence to safer sex practices), but in retrospect I realize that was just an excuse. My real fear was how she'd react if she found out that her angel lamb is actually a gay porn star. Would she be disappointed in me? Would she be ashamed?

Well, she did find out. And her response was amazing.

It was a grey and rainy October afternoon. I was driving through my mom's neighborhood and stopped by her house to take a nap. She wasn't home. After a short snooze, I realized I needed to check something online. I went into her study, turned on her computer, and to my utter horror was greeted by a browser window that was open to a very familiar website: my blog. My *very* X-rated blog.

It's difficult to describe the sensations I experienced in that moment. My heart sputtered. I was instantly nauseous and felt like I was in free fall. The ramifications hit me at once: If she'd seen the blog, she knew everything. She knew that I was a porn star, that my husband Dirk (whom I'd met through my studio) was a porn star, and that my frequent trips to California were not just to visit friends. I felt completely exposed, as if the walls of the house had crumbled around me and I was left standing there alone and (figuratively) naked in the oak-floored study of my childhood home.

But then I got to thinking: My blog talks extensively about how porn has changed my life for the better. I'm happier now than I've ever been. I'm excited, empowered, and confident. And if I'd never worked in porn, I never would have met my amazing husband. If she had indeed read all this, she'd be sure to realize that my foray into porn has been a remarkable, life-changing adventure.

Wouldn't she?

I knew I had to talk to her. Dirk arranged to fly home early from his trip to Los Angeles, and we had dinner with my mom the next day. Pork loin, edamame, sweet potato soup. Delicious, in a way that only a mother's cooking can be. When we finished, I glanced at Dirk. He nodded encouragingly. I felt like the walls were about to start crumbling again, but I started in.

"Mom, there's something I want to talk to you about. I stopped by the house a few days ago and used your computer, and it was open to—"

"Your blog."

Gulp.

Her next words flooded me with relief.

"I'm so happy we're talking about this."

It turns out she'd known the whole time. Our bank accounts are linked because we co-own some property; several months earlier, she'd noticed a deposit from a source she didn't recognize—my studio—and traced it back to their website. At the time, Dirk and I had just released a BDSM film called *Loud and Nasty*, and our images were plastered all over the studio's homepage. With video! And in this particular video, Dirk shocks me with a violet wand, a device that's used to deliver high-voltage electric charges to its intended "victim." Mom said that it looked like I was being tortured, and she felt like a part of her had died.

Dirk and I couldn't help but laugh, though. Granted, it does look like I'm being tortured: I'm restrained, struggling, and doing a lot of screaming. But we explained to her that everything we did was consensual, exciting, and a tremendous amount of fun. Boundaries were respected and nobody got hurt. She still seemed skeptical, so we showed her a behind-the-scenes photo from the set of our "torture" scene:

When she saw the image, she understood. Dirk and I were in love. Nothing else mattered.

In essence, I'd come out to her a second time. It felt like a giant boulder had been lifted from me—just like when I told her I was gay some fifteen years earlier—and once again she was entirely caring and supportive. I don't think she fully understands my decision to make porn; she has difficulty grasping how I can be so open about something as private and intimate to her as sex. But that's not really the point. The important thing is that we actually talk about stuff now. If I can tell her I'm a friggin' porn star and she still loves me, then I can tell her anything. And I do. I tell her about my fears and pain and shame, and also my joy and love and passion, in ways I never would have dared before. She has shown me nothing but love in return. And I realize now that the walls of her study weren't the only walls that crumbled on that grey, rainy October afternoon.

PORN MADE ME LIKE MY PARENTS

Joanna Angel

*Joanna Angel is an adult film star, director, producer, and owner of the world's largest alternative pornographic empire, BurningAngel Entertainment, that pioneered "alt-porn," with a network of websites and hundreds of DVDs to its credit. Angel has appeared in every major adult magazine (*Adult Video News, Club, Hustler, Picture Magazine, Adam Film World, *and* Xtreme, *to name a few) and has graced the pages of several tattoo magazines. She has stormed mainstream TV and radio outlets, featured on Fox News, Playboy TV, Fuse TV, G4 TV, KROQ Radio, SIRIUS Radio, TLC's* LA Ink, *had a speaking role on Adult Swim's* Children's Hospital, *and starred in the drama* Scrapper. *Angel has appeared in the* New York Times, Newsweek, *the* Village Voice, *the* New York Press, Esquire UK, Details, *and* Penthouse, *among others.* Heeb Magazine *featured Joanna as their cover girl, naming her one of the "Top 100 Up-and-Coming Jews." The* New York Post *featured her as one of the "Top 25 Sexiest New Yorkers," and she has made CNBC's yearly "dirty dozen" (a list of the twelve biggest adult film stars) several times. Angel is a self-made star who has made her mark on the industry, and this is only the beginning!*

I am quite sure that the relationship I had with my parents growing up was far from normal. But it was also far from dysfunctional. People often assume that porn stars come from extreme family circumstances—trailer-trash homes, meth addiction, physical and sexual abuse. The story might be that a woman's porn career is the happy ending, her escape from a fraught home life. On the flip side, people could also think of a porn star's career as the tragic end for a normal girl with lots of "potential" who threw her life away. Neither of those stories describes me. My upbringing wasn't tragic or scarring, and it also wasn't picturesque or affluent. But I think I can safely say it was unique.

I'm a first-generation American on one side and third generation on the other. My mother is Israeli, and she moved to America just shortly after marrying my father, a Jewish American man from Ohio. My mother is a Sephardic Jew with Iraqi roots. Her parents fled Iraq with their six children and initially settled in a refugee camp in Israel, where they gave birth to two more children, one of them my mother. My mother's childhood involved sharing a tent with a family of ten. My father, on the other hand, had a fairly typical, fairly happy childhood in Midwestern America in the '50s. When two people from such different corners of the earth reproduce, the result is sure to be some shade of weirdo.

Growing up, I lacked whatever fear other kids had of their parents. If I did the right thing, it was because I felt like it, not because I was trying to please my parents. My English surpassed my mother's at an early age, which I guess gave me the sense that I was in charge. I helped my mother study to get her driving license. I translated signs at the supermarket for her. I taught her some basic American etiquette—for instance, shaving the mass of hair growing from her armpits before accompanying me to the local swim club (shaving razors were completely evil in her book, but she agree to get rid of the hair with homemade wax she made out of sugar and lemon).

What my parents really had to offer me was unconditional love, which wasn't exactly what I was interested in as a preteen. I was much more interested in getting a boyfriend, beating Super Mario Bros. 3, and obtaining a T-shirt that changed colors when you put your hand on it. I didn't hate my parents, but I didn't admire them, either. I didn't particularly respect them, and I certainly didn't fear them.

One day when I was fourteen, I carelessly lifted my arms and revealed to my parents the belly ring I'd recently gotten. My mother cried. As usual, I was mostly unfazed by my parents' anger and disappointment. The same was true when I started to come home reeking of cigarettes and when I was caught shoplifting at the mall. They didn't approve, but I wasn't seeking their approval, and life went on.

It was around that time that I met the people whom I would come to truly respect, the way kids are supposed to respect their parents. It was the world of punk. These were people whose approval was incredibly important to me, whose morals and values and traditions I followed dutifully, even religiously. This world dictated how I dressed, what I ate, what I studied in school, where I hung out, who my friends were, and what movies I watched. It was about so much more than just music. Punk gave me an identity and a purpose throughout high school, and then a real community in college. I didn't go to football games or frat parties; I went to punk shows. Punk became my family, and the family I'd been born to became more and more distant. My parents didn't understand me! They didn't know me. As far as I was concerned, they weren't my real family.

With the growth of the Internet, this punk family grew larger and larger. And like any large family, people fought, people disagreed, random people were married in who probably didn't belong there, and some people were disowned or ostracized.

Message board threads argued on and on over what was punk and what wasn't. Some punks prided themselves on doing drugs, while others went straight edge. Some punks were atheists, and some were hardcore Christians. Some were vegan, and some considered cows just a means to an end—the end being a spiky leather jacket. I stayed out of most of the punk drama. I read the message boards to find out about new music, where shows were, and on occasion to stalk a cute guy in a band. I was vegan but not straight edge. I was active in both animal rights and human rights groups, went to protests, and my record collection contained all the essentials. I was never the target of any message board that questioned how punk I was. That is, not until I started a porn site.

BurningAngel.com launched on April 20, 2002. My roommate Mitch and I started it ourselves. We had no funding, no investors—just us. I thought it was a pretty anticonformist move to start a porn site and work for myself instead of getting a "real job." No animals were harmed in the process of making our website, and no sweatshop labor was used. The launch of the website contained five different photosets of girls I knew from my own little punk community, and the photos were taken in my bedroom and basement by a guy who'd borrowed a digital camera from someone. In addition to the photos, I also included an interview with a local hardcore band. I truly didn't think I was violating any punk laws. I was proud of what I'd created and I assumed my entire world would be proud too. I had always supported my friends when their bands went on tour or when they put out their own records. Even if I didn't love the way a band sounded, I supported them if they were part of the punk scene.

The day of the launch also happened to be 4/20, and there was a party at my house with bands playing in the basement. The party had already been planned by one of my roommates before we ever knew it would coincide with the launch of BurningAngel. So what started as a celebration of pot accidentally morphed into a celebration of porn.

There was a lot going on that day, and at that time in my life I didn't even have my own computer. I used to use my roommate's or I would go to the computer lab on campus. Before I got dressed for the party, I went downstairs to my roommate's computer and checked two websites. First, I checked my own. My programmer friend had been telling me for weeks, "I think it will be up tomorrow," so I wanted to see if it was actually live or not. The good news: It was. Just like that, with a refresh of the page, I was naked on the Internet. The next site I checked was my favorite punk message board. I summoned my e-stalking powers to see if a guy I had a crush on might be coming to the party, which might determine how much effort I would put into my outfit. The bad news: The boy was not coming to the party. He couldn't afford the gas or something. And then the even worse news revealed itself: a nasty thread titled "Porn's not punk" with over 400 responses.

Photos had been taken directly from my website and pasted into the message board. This was technology that I didn't even know about at the time. How the hell did they do that? Then I started reading through the comments. Some were long-winded philosophical rants about domestic abuse and feminism. Some declared that it's not punk to make a profit off of punk (mind you, at that time our net worth was about $20). Some comments were much more straightforward: "She's fucking ugly." Mitch found me there, crying, with my eyes glued to the screen. I wanted to respond to the commenters. "No," he told me. "Just stop looking at it. People will be over it by tomorrow." I walked away from the computer and drowned my sorrows in a vegan pot brownie.

The evening proceeded to get more and more uncomfortable. Suddenly, all these people I thought I knew felt like strangers. Everyone was talking about me—well, maybe the pot brownie had a little to do with my thinking that. Everyone who approached me had something to say to me about porn. They loved porn. They thought porn was horrible. They respected me, they were disgusted by me, and they wanted to know how to get into the industry. When asked by someone if porn empowered me, I responded: "I really don't know! My website has been up for six hours!"

I went downstairs to the basement to watch some music. It was a local band I'd always liked. The lead singer was a girl who was in the Women's Studies Department at Rutgers. Before her set, she gave a long speech about sexual abuse and how it was tied to porn, and then in a nutshell she said that porn had no place in the music scene. My heart stopped. Was she directing this at me? Or did she just happen to choose today to air her grievances about pornography? Did she know that this was my basement she was singing in? Did she know how many shifts at Applebee's I had to work to afford my $220 portion of the rent, which included basement access? The next band played, and before their set, they dedicated a song to "a certain girl who stands up for what she believes in." Was that who I was now? A girl who believed in being naked on the Internet? What the hell had I gotten myself into?

I ran up the three flights of stairs to my bedroom and shut the door. I panicked on my Ikea twin bed, and the walls seemed like they were closing in on me. (Okay, so maybe the pot brownie had a little to do with that too.) I wasn't ready for this. I wasn't expecting any of this. A part of me wanted to take down BurningAngel, move far, far away and never speak of this again. And another part of me felt that this strange thing I'd started had the potential to become something really amazing. It had to be one or the other. I had to make a choice. And then I thought to myself, for the very first time in my life: I need my mother.

I drove to my mother's home the next morning. I didn't tell her I was coming, and she was thrilled that I'd come. When I walked through the door, she gave me a big hug and immediately cooked me a meal. She lectured me about my veganism and told me I should really consider trying to just eat fish or eggs because my diet didn't have enough protein. Then she asked me to help her write a letter to the police department because earlier that day she'd gotten a ticket she didn't think was justified. She said, "My English is not very good, and if you can write them, I am sure they will understand." Then she told me about how a recent storm ruined parts of her basement and she was hoping to get money from the insurance. It was a regular day at home, and it was comforting. I had already told my mother several weeks beforehand that I planned on starting a porn site, and she certainly wasn't thrilled about it. But she was able to put that aside and just be my mom; she wouldn't even know how to not be my mom, even if she wanted to. My mother definitely hated porn and me doing porn. She still does. My decision to do porn probably hurt her more than anyone else in my life—certainly more than the punk kids at Rutgers. But having a daughter was more important to her than fighting. That was the moment I realized how important and rare unconditional love really is. I spent the next few days being fed and tucked into bed. I felt more like a child than I ever had in my childhood. When I left, I hugged her and said, "I love you," which was something I'd never actually said to her before.

It's been about thirteen years since the launch, and this college experiment has since grown into a real alternative community that has changed the face of porn. And by the way, the punk world and I are on perfectly good terms. Even most of the message board trolls would agree with that nowadays.

Not too long ago, my mom came to visit me in Los Angeles, and she stumbled on my Fleshlight. She obviously didn't know what it was—she was fussing with it, trying to get the "flashlight" to turn on. "Joanna, how do you work this?" she asked. Then we exchanged a look, and I could see that she realized she didn't want to know anything more about it. She set it back down and we went about our day.

This is my life. It hasn't always been easy, but it's mostly been a blast.

Thanks, Mom.

BRANDED: THE PRECARIOUS DANCE BETWEEN PORN AND PRIVACY

Kitty Stryker

Kitty Stryker is the production assistant at TROUBLEfilms, Courtney Trouble's queer porn femmepire. Particularly interested in the intersections between explicit materials, politics, and ethics, Stryker has written for the Guardian, *the* Daily Dot, *the* Frisky, *Fleshbot.com, and more. She blogs at KittyStryker.com.*

I decided to become Kitty Stryker when I was about 30,000 feet above Ohio, or maybe Minnesota. I wrote up a list of what Kitty Stryker was like—who her friends were, what she did for fun, her life goals, what sort of people she dated. I was leaving behind Katy, an insecure goth who spent most of her time behind a computer screen and masturbating to a long-distance relationship because Katy, I reasoned, was Unknown, and therefore Boring. Instead, I was going to be the far more glamorous Kitty, who was extroverted, who was invited to all the parties and went on all the dates, who was in the spotlight. Kitty Stryker, I decided, would be Known. I was determined, on that plane ride as I moved my life from the East Coast to the West Coast, to step out of the shadows.

Little did I know the path that would take.

Google my name and it's all me. I've been living my life under my porn name since before I did porn, and it seemed like diluting my brand to pick another when I was already writing about sexuality and speaking on sex work. The photos you uncover will, for the most part, not be pornographic, although I've been in the industry for several years. You'll find photos of me riveting a forty-foot-tall rocket ship, or cosplaying as Tank Girl, or experimenting with shades of lipstick that make me look dead. Kitty Stryker, as a persona, has been pretty multifaceted from the start, as I consciously wove together my sex work and everyday selves into one being.

It seemed like a good idea at the time.

I knew that being outed as a sex worker could be problematic when it came to family, lovers, other jobs. I figured that in order to blackmail someone, they had to feel ashamed, so I made it my quest to be as open about my work in the adult industry as I could possibly be. I was privileged in that my family knew and accepted my career path, and I only dated people who knew what I did for work. I didn't feel I had anything to be embarrassed about, and so I refused to be embarrassed.

But interestingly, it was in the financial arena that I had to be the most secretive and careful.

My legal name is a blank slate, and I keep it that way for multiple reasons. As a woman on the Internet, having my legal name out there can lead to me being harassed near my home, stalked, and threatened with various types of harm for writing about my experiences. As a sex worker, the threats become a lot more serious, with a lot less sympathy or room to pursue legal assistance. I've had text messages asking me if I found it strange how many women end up in dumpsters every year, followed up by, "I know where you live." Yet Facebook insists users give out their "real name" (by which they mean the name on a legal ID). PayPal will give those who donate to you the name you use on your account, and will delete you if they don't think the name you're using is a legal one. Many crowdsourcing sites will similarly demand that you use the name that checks can be written out to when using their services.

Despite my work in porn being completely legal, my openness about it puts me at risk for having my bank account shut down, as Chase threatened last year. PayPal has long had a history of freezing funds to any account they suspect as being adjacent to the adult industry, and other payment processors—Google Wallet, Amazon Payments, WePay—have followed suit, erring on the side of shutting out sex workers rather than risking the rage of Visa's extensive and punishing fees. My legal name being linked to my work name could shut down multiple methods through which I pay and am paid for everyday things, like the therapeutic massages I get for my injured back, or being able to raise money through a fundraiser for my Consent Culture project.

This creates quite a bit of tension. In order for me to advertise my brand (which is myself, as a porn performer and now director), I need to utilize social media. For that to be effective, I can't really afford to hide my face alongside my porn name. Realistically, anyone with some time on their hands and a bone to pick can report me for being a sex worker to these payment processors and shut down necessary streams of income—even though the income going through those venues is not for explicit materials, but for eBay items. By branding myself the way many entrepreneurs do, I am branded as "the wrong sort of worker"—yet I cannot avoid it and survive in a competitive market. And so I take the risk and pay the price.

Our economy is pretty terrible right now. Everyone I know has multiple hustles going on, often instead of a traditional nine-to-five job. Some are starting small businesses out of their homes, selling stuff on eBay, making mobile apps, crafting things to sell on Etsy. And of course, more and more people are trying their hand at something in the adult entertainment arena to help them get by—perhaps camming here, maybe filming a porn there, possibly stripping or selling their dirty socks. Yet we live in a culture that stigmatizes us permanently for dipping a toe into sex work while simultaneously insisting sex workers should leave the industry and do other work.

With PayPal and WePay controlling most of the online payment market and Facebook harassing people for not using "real names," having a scarlet letter banning sex workers past or present from using these resources can mean that any other sort of small business idea is made impossible for us. I may want to stop doing sex work and write instead, but if I can't process online payments because of my porn work, I can't utilize Facebook or other social media outlets because my brand name isn't legit enough, and companies won't hire me because they can Google my sex work history, then I'm stuck in the business whether I like it or not.

It's strange, being so comfortable with being out as Kitty

Stryker but so paranoid about being outed by my legal name. I don't believe that showing your privates in public should mean you sign away your right to privacy, though. We all deserve time off, and a secret identity that's just for us.

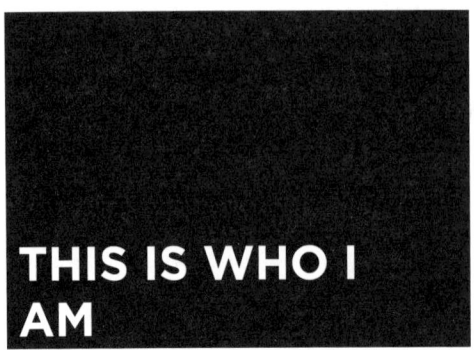

THIS IS WHO I AM

Lily Cade

Lily Cade is an adult film actress, an award-winning porn director, and "Porn Valley's gold star lesbian." She's been shooting smut since 2008 and specializes in intensity, hardcore strap-on scenes, and adult movies with real stories. She also runs her own website at LilyCade.com.

I'm Lily Cade, and I'm a lesbian and a porn star. Back in the day, when I'd meet other gay people, one of the things we'd ask each other was, "What's your coming-out story?" I encounter this less now, or less quickly, in a friendship. Maybe it's easier to come out now, or I'm just older and coming out is less proximate to myself or the people I hang out with. Still, it's one of those things. It's part of the gay experience. It's been part of my experience as both a lesbian and a pornographer.

The first time I came out to anyone I was in eighth grade, at a sleepover with friends from my small, Catholic middle school. We were playing Truth or Dare, which I both loved and hated. I loved dares and other people's secrets but I hated being asked incessantly about which boy I liked when the answer was none of them and would always be none of them. I was dared to run naked down the street yelling, "The British are coming!" and as I stripped to complete the task the other girls stopped me and gave me a truth instead. "What's your deepest, darkest secret?" My chest felt tight and hot and over the pounding of my heart I said, "I'm gay." Everyone was silent for a moment. They didn't ask too many questions—I think it made the others feel weird, but it also made sense—and we really didn't talk about it again.

After that, I just was gay. I usually didn't go around telling people, but if you asked me I'd be honest about it. I'd often answer questions in a way that made it obvious, without exactly saying the words. Someone would start to ask me, "When you get married—" and I'd stop her and say, "Well, that's not legal for me." I cut most of my hair off around the same time I confessed my homosexuality; I didn't shave my legs until I got into porn; and when I wasn't wearing school uniforms I mostly wore clothes that hid the female body I wasn't entirely comfortable with. I think it was pretty obvious to everyone, except my mother, who was the one person I ever worried about coming out to in the first place. I knew she wasn't going to kick me out or stop loving me, but I also knew my mother wasn't going to like it.

Mom was entirely oblivious to the lesbian subtext of my life, even though it was really on the nose. For some reason, I decided it was very important that she be the one to prompt the coming-out conversation. As high school wore on, I started to become frustrated that it had never come up, and I began to push her as hard as I could without directly admitting my lesbianism. I would stare pointedly at waitresses' asses. I would bring up gay rights issues in the news. I would talk about how much I liked the liturgical dancers at our church because you could see through their dresses. None of it worked, and finally on my last day of high school a friend of mine saw me off with, "See you later, dyke." My mother overhead this and asked me why someone would say that to me. I told her, "Because it's true!" My mother pulled the car over and in a panic, bellowed, "Is that what you think?" I said, with all the drama befitting a seventeen-year-old lesbian, "No Mom, it's not what I think. It's what I am!"

She didn't really accept that I was gay until I got married. She used to introduce Sten—then my girlfriend, later my wife—and me as "her," which would prompt us to make out so she'd have to admit it, because the only thing worse than one gay daughter is two gay daughters who are fucking each other. She wouldn't let me come out to my grandparents, even though having to lie about so much of what I was doing—"No, I don't have a boyfriend; I'm just focusing on my studies right now"—made me less close to them, until I graduated from college and the presence of Sten had to be explained. She claimed they would be devastated, but in fact, they didn't care and told my mother they'd known for years. I think, in the back of my mother's mind, that she thought the whole gay thing really just might be a phase. The wedding changed things. She threw my reception. She was great. She likes my wife. She's entirely over it, but it took her years to stop feeling uncomfortable about it.

I got into porn in 2008, at first on a whim, and then semiprofessionally until making it my full-time career in 2010. This is what I do. I'm a performer and director and the owner of LilyCade.com. For the most part, I'm out to everyone. I don't always tell the cashier or the taxi driver who makes small talk with me, but the only name I go by is the one I use in porn. I don't have any interest in developing relationships with people who can't handle my career, or my sexuality for that matter, so I'm upfront about it. The only person who doesn't know what I do is my mother.

I had a few coming-out moments with regards to porn. I hid my involvement in it from my roommates at first because I wasn't sure how they'd take it. I didn't tell my sister until I was sure this job was important to me, not something I was doing for extra cash and sexual thrill, but something to which I was going to devote the major part of my energy. Just like with being gay, it eventually became necessary to continue the relationship that I not attempt to hide a big piece of my life. Lying all the time is exhausting, and it makes it hard to connect with people and difficult to be around them.

Coming out is about telling people (or maybe also yourself) something about yourself that you're worried will upset them. It's an admission of a part of oneself that not everybody understands. I know that my mother wouldn't understand. Like when I worried about telling her I was gay, I used to have a significant amount of anxiety about her discovering my job. I thought it might make her hate me. I'm pretty sure she is going to yell at me if or when she finds out about it. Even talking about sex bothers her. She gives me shit about wearing "low-cut" tops, meaning anything that shows any cleavage. The one time I told her that I was nude modeling for a life drawing class, she freaked out at me on the phone and then brought it up all the time. She stills asks me sometimes, when I tell her some tame version of what I'm shooting, "Will you be naked?" I know that telling my mother I do porn would upset her and make her uncomfortable, and I feel less invested in making her get over that discomfort than I did with being gay. My job isn't about her, and it's totally about my sex life. I get naked and fuck chicks. I certainly don't tell her about doing this sort of stuff off camera. At times, it can be frustrating when she asks me what I'm up to and I have to fudge the details, but it's not nearly so hurtful as hiding a lover. Porn is what I do. It's not who I am.

Our relationship is changing, though. We're both getting older and I'm much more able to simply tell her that her opinion of what I do is not my problem. At the same time, I have more compassion for her than I did when I was a rebellious teenager. At times she drives me completely insane, but I can see that she means well. She loves me, and she always will no matter what. I've been doing this so long now that I'm no longer scared about her finding out about it, although I'm not yet at the part of the story where I actually want her to know. I'll cross that bridge when I come to it. There's enough other stuff that I do—and enough details we can soften—to just not talk about it. In my ideal world, I'll let her know someday that I used to be a porn star and hope she'll find it amusing and not just uncomfortable.

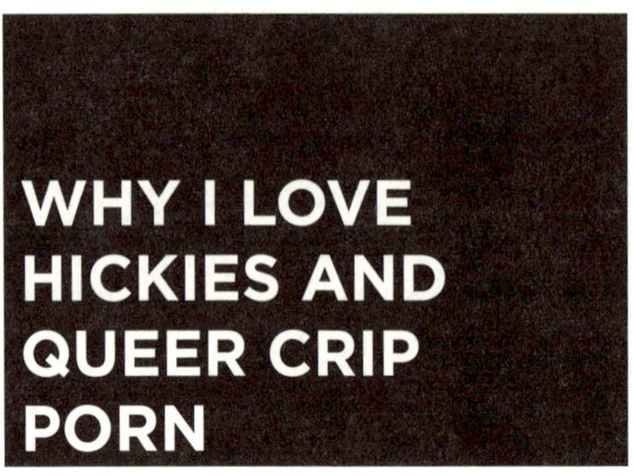

WHY I LOVE HICKIES AND QUEER CRIP PORN

Loree Erickson

Loree Erickson is a queer, femmegimp porn star academic in a doctoral program at York University in Toronto. She is the creator of want, *an internationally award-winning porn film, and a community organizer. She loves travelling to lecture, making queer crip porn, and facilitating workshops on a variety of topics including collective care, disability justice/radical disability politics, and all things related to sex and disability. She is also a fan of sun, sparkly things, and social justice. You can find her at FemmeGimp.com.*

I've never been good at being in the closet—any closet. When I first went to college in Richmond, Virginia, I immediately started volunteering with the Queer Student Alliance. I was tasked with calling people to remind them of the upcoming meeting. It wasn't until I was halfway through the list that I realized I maybe shouldn't be leaving messages. Then there was the time I left a message on my friend's parents' answering machine telling her, "The Lesbian Avenger meeting starts at seven—(awkward pause)—so you probably wanna come over afterwards since you are not coming to that meeting because you are definitely not a lesbian." Certainly not my smoothest or proudest moments. I have reimagined my ideas of normal so completely that I forget what is not considered commonplace in the mainstream world, that is, until I'm faced with the overt homophobia, femmephobia, and whorephobia I often experience as a white, academic, queer, femme porn star who is visibly disabled and an exhibitionist.

My body has taught me so many lessons. A great deal of these lessons have come through having a body that connects with and relies upon other bodies in order to perform daily tasks: go to the bathroom, get out of bed, take a shower, and so on. I can't even begin to name all of the ways these embodied experiences have enriched my understanding of bodies and how bodies relate to each other, ways they've helped me refigure ideas regarding care and independence, as well as providing opportunities to confront body shame. From an early age, I was used to being naked in front of and with other people. I often joke (with a modicum of seriousness) that being an "out body" combined with my exhibitionist leanings served well as a foundation for becoming a porn star. That I don't have a choice but to be out about certain needs of mine definitely feels like it has created a comfort with outness that I bring into making porn.

Picture, if you will, a sassy blonde with tits spilling out of her leopard-print tank top and fishnet-clad legs held tight by a red and gold miniskirt. She's cruising down the sidewalk in her power wheelchair with a smile on her face until a voice calls out. It's some variation on the same refrain: "Slow down there, speedy" or, "You're going to get a speeding ticket, if you're not careful!" I don't endorse the nonconsensual shouting of sexualizing salutations, but I equally tire of desexualizing patronization. This is as much about the privilege of my white skin as it is about sexism and disableism. And then there is also the infamously insulting, "You look too good to be disabled" sentiment. My crip of color friends who are also visibly disabled often describe the ways that they are routinely hypersexualized. After all, as Jin Haritaworn pointed out to me, hypersexualization and desexualization are just opposite sides of the same coin.

Because of homophobia, transphobia, and ableism, people often don't see my queer sexual and romantic relationships, repainting them as family or care relationships. Certainly, the expectation is that we aren't banging. I am, after all, the asexual poster child, white, innocent, and wholesome, and therefore deserving of being saved. For many people, the only understanding of disability they have regular contact with is the sad, unlovable person in MDA ads or cystic fibrosis poster campaigns. Poster children never grow up and they certainly don't grow up to be porn stars—but of course, this one did. This constant desexualization is why I love hickies and why I started making porn. I first started taking dirty pictures of myself as a way to finally see my body, my self, as hot and sexy. I started making porn to expose people to bodies that flaunt asymmetrical curves, bodies that move differently than the nondisabled desirable norm. I started making porn to give other queer crips a chance to see something a little closer to their lives depicted on screen.

I call what I do "porn" because I love how it causes a rupture. Ideally, people can no longer pity or patronize me after they know I make porn. Take the following (sadly typical) exchange with a stranger: "So what do you do?" (Pity and lowered expectations dripping from her voice.)

"I'm doing a PhD."

"Oh! That's so nice!" (Like the university was just letting me do a PhD to be nice.)

"Yeah, I make porn and then write critical cultural analysis of the ways porn made by and for queer disabled people transforms and interrupts systems of oppression."

(Stunned silence.)

In workshops and in classrooms, I use the porn I make to teach the necessary and important skills of reimagining disability, desirability, bodies, and what we think of as sex or sexiness. The students I present to consistently challenge whether the videos I am sharing with them are indeed porn. I think this is due in part to the context of an academic environment, but certainly another aspect of their resistance to my work is that they're unaccustomed to seeing hot, antioppressive porn that features nonnormative bodies and sexualities. The two main reasons students give me for why the videos I make are "not porn" are (1) they're "not offensive," and (2) there is no "explicit fucking." I find both of these responses incredibly significant and telling. I firmly believe that the ways (primarily mainstream) porn has become culturally linked with oppression and dehumanization in the popular imagination serve to undermine the historically rooted potential for porn as a vessel for transformation and resistance. Also, for most people, porn is seen as being fairly self-evident, the old "I know it when I see it" approach. This approach, which is also how many people understand disability, serves to render both as fact, not cultural constructs. This thinking serves to undermine the fluidity and complexity of both porn and disability. Furthermore, when students only understand sex as penis-in-vagina intercourse, they are not only missing out on some really fun and sexy activities, they are reinforcing larger structures of cissexism, heteropatriarchy, and disableism. At times, I strategically use disableism and the ways that my work is not considered porn to mitigate whorephobia. Whereas sex work and porn are criminalized, pathologized, pitied, and seen as illegitimate, my porn video has been purchased by many university libraries, taught in several courses, and screens in numerous spaces that typically avoid association with porn. It is still a work in progress, and probably always should be, to navigate this particular intersection of marginalization and privilege. I remain committed to organizing and talking publicly about the ways we need to fight back against the marginalization of all sex workers. I am incredibly indebted to sex workers in my communities who have shared with me their knowledge and expertise in resisting whorephobia.

I use my given name rather than a porn name partly because my first porn, *want*, was made as part of an activist video production class. I certainly did not expect the work to become as widely known and awarded as it now is. My academic work has always taken knowledge, wisdom, and inspiration from my life and community, meaning that even if I used a porn name, I would still be talking about and analyzing the porn that I make (and support others to make) in my academic work under my given name. Furthermore, due mostly to the hypervisibility that comes with being visibly disabled, I've never really found anonymity or confidentiality to work in my favor.

At times, I really wish I could choose to use a porn name, if only because there are just so many creative possibilities. There are also times my life would be easier if I could separate my porn life from my other life. I am currently attempting to get permanent residency in Canada and doing so as a queer, disabled, poor person is already a giant challenge, as I will inevitably be considered a drain on social resources. I'm sure being a porn star won't boost my attractiveness in the eyes of Canadian immigration. An additional struggle is that my family knows I make porn. Mostly it works out fine, in the sense that my WASPy family, for the most part, has a "don't ask, don't tell" policy in effect. My dad will ask how my school work is going, but he never asks what I'm actually studying or writing about. My mom for years referred to *want* as my "racy video." Then, one day, I caught her in a good mood and we started talking about my work and what it can accomplish in transforming cultures of undesirability. At the end of the conversation she said, "So you're a porn star. Well, I'm very proud of you."

Echoing Nic Bravo's critique of National Coming Out Day in her blog, *Stick Up for Yourself, Son*, "Coming Out is based on a presumption of being able to pass as normal, as cis/straight/binary/whatever. The focus on Coming Out narratives belies the existence of queers who ⋆really⋆ exist on the margins, who don't get to come out because they read as abnormal all the time" (http://stickupforyourself.nicbravo.com/). Like I said, I have never been very good at being in the closet, in part because I have never been able to pass as normal. Fortunately, I've never wanted to be normal. I'd much rather flaunt all of those messy, beautiful, complex, tough, and tender things about me and the people I love that transform and disrupt!

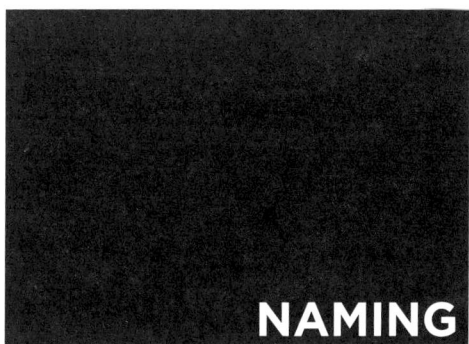

NAMING

Lorelei Lee

Lorelei Lee has been an adult film performer since 2000 and a director since 2009. Her writing has appeared in Salon, The Rumpus, Wired, Denver Quarterly, The Los Angeles Review of Books, *and elsewhere. She is a contributor to* The Feminist Porn Book *and the cowriter of* About Cherry, *distributed by IFC Films. You can find her tweeting about politics and books @MissLoreleiLee, and about naked people @XOXOLoreleiLee.*

In Las Vegas, I was twenty-one. We'd been there three days, and I was learning my new name. A stranger was teaching it to me in the ballroom. The women changed their clothes again and again; they passed in parades of Technicolor latex, in white dresses and nurse hats, in fishnet and lace. On a table nearby, a woman climaxed. I was at the booth with Seven. We posed beside a table of free sample DVDs and a television that played ten-minute loops of us being tied and untied. She wore a black silk overbust corset and sucked on a cherry Blow Pop. Pink rope impressions were pressed into her wrists and shoulders. I thought she was the most beautiful woman I'd seen. I was wearing her boots. They were a size too small, knee-high, stiletto, black patent. My toes had been numb for hours. You couldn't have paid me to take them off.

A man said, "You're Lorelei."

I paused a moment before saying, "Yes."

He said, "I've seen you."

That was the first time.

If you talk to a performer—say her name is Lily Black (remember, I am making this up)—at some point, Lily might say,

"Sometimes I have to take Maria out for a night. Sometimes Maria needs a night out." When she says that, she'll be talking about herself. She isn't crazy or confused. She knows exactly who she is.

I know exactly who I am.

We calculate and divide to keep ourselves safe—in the tangible ways, sure, but also safe from unguarded inquiry.

Every time I meet a stranger, I do this math: How much do you know about me already? What, if anything, do you deserve to know? At a holiday party surrounded by women my age, by mothers in Saturday lipstick, I won't lie exactly, but I will evade. If you tell me a dirty joke, I'll pretend I haven't heard it before. I never cash my checks with the teller anymore. My name is the last thing I will tell you.

It isn't that I don't trust you—but I don't. It isn't that my birth name doesn't fit me anymore—but it doesn't. Everything I'll tell you is both true and not true. There are a few things I was born with, but most of what I own, I made up. Most of what I own, I earned. Day by day and scene by scene. This isn't about confusion, it's about context.

I'm thirty-three, and for fourteen years, I have sold my naked image. I have made my body public. At this point, I have been a whore for nearly as long as I wasn't one. I've spent my entire adult life hustling. Pornography has made me who I am. I am Lorelei Lee—and also, I am not. I'm big sister to four siblings, thirty-three-year-old child of a single welfare mother. I'm a queer woman, a porn star, a dominatrix, a stripper. I'm a wife in Saturday lipstick. I've done nearly everything a person can do without clothes on. I am paid to lie to you, but I often tell the truth.

For a while, there were places where I would use my birth name, and there were places where I would be Lorelei. I divided it up—public and private—until the division became more rigid, the private more precious. There was a day when I decided not to be promiscuous with my origin. There was a day when I decided that I had earned my new name. It belongs to me now.

Here's what I've learned: Our names are constructs, just as our bodies are. It was by stealing a name, by hiring out my body in performance, that I truly began to own both.

I took on the name Lorelei at twenty-one. It was three years after my first naked performance, when I'd used a name the producer had given me. When I was nineteen and naked in a stranger's house in Chula Vista, spreading my legs on a washer-dryer, they called me Carolyn, but that name was never mine.

I sold cigarettes in bars as Lulu. I'd grin out from my pink dress, click my high-heeled shoes and proffer my heavy box of chewing gum and tobacco, king-sized candy bars and light-up silk flowers, pressing my breasts into the goods to make them cost more. I'd say "I'm Lulu," and the tourists and the boys stumbling into bachelor parties at the North Beach strip clubs would say, "Did your mother give you that name?" And I would lie and lie. The dancers on break, smoking in the doorways, bought packs of Parliaments with ten-dollar bills they peeled off hairband-secured rolls of cash.

"I'm Lulu," I'd say.

"Me too," they'd reply.

I became Lorelei tied up in someone's living room in Sacramento, wearing three-dollar thongs from the sidewalk bins on Mission Street. I became Lorelei in a red leather jacket and nothing else, squatting on a staircase of perforated metal in the dark, holding for the flash. I became Lorelei in Chinatown, high on Vicodin just to alleviate the boredom of posing. I became Lorelei in a basement in Livermore, faking orgasms badly in knee socks, fucking myself in an old elementary-school desk chair with a cheap plastic vibrating dildo. I became Lorelei on my knees in front of four naked men in a shoot house kitchen, clinging to pink satin beside a swimming pool at a Los Angeles mansion, tied in rope and hung upside down from a tree in upstate New York, on a green felt pool table with spit sprayed across my face and loving the strangeness of strangers' bodies in close-up, loving the seamed scars and discoloration and dimples and forgotten hairs, scent of salt and flowers and smoke, infinite variation. I became Lorelei in cars, in trains, and taxis and buses, hungry and tired at 2:00 a.m., at 6:00 a.m., at 3:00 in the afternoon, fingering a new white envelope of hundreds, pulling a twenty for cab fare from a just-counted stack, pressing my forehead to the cool windshield in slow traffic on the 405 with five days' worth of thousand dollar checks in my shoot bag. I became Lorelei in the restaurant at the top of the Hard Rock Hotel in January, fist-sized goblets, plate-glass wall glossing the neon, white linen in my lap, when I leaned over to Seven and whispered, "I will never wait tables again."

Naming a thing makes it real.

In Las Vegas, I was twenty-five, in a rhinestone dress on the red carpet, holding Annette's hand. The line of photographers held out their microphones and flashed their camera lights.

The reporter from *CBS This Morning* said, "Are you a porn actor?"

I said, "Sometimes I act, and sometimes I don't."

We were scared and young. We wore cheap silk and paste jewels. I thought Annette was the most beautiful woman I'd seen. I was still so easily shamed. If you called me a whore then, I'd flinch.

My entire family saw that red carpet footage. They called my mother and asked her, "Does she hate herself?"

I resent even having to tell you that the answer is no.

Here's the thing about coming out: It doesn't happen just once. It isn't a thing you do and get done. It happens again and again. It happens over and over and over, and it is never over.

I earned my name in Washington, DC, where the summer steamed the bushes and sent waves of green heat into my face, evoking my childhood. I had traveled there to be a witness in John Stagliano's obscenity trial, and my attorney argued that I should be allowed to use my name in court, that my safety relied on it. The prosecutor objected, said that to use my name would "legitimize" me. As though illegitimate were my appropriate status. I'm still angry. Every day, around the world, the legitimate humanity of sex workers is dismissed. We are told we should be punished and then policies are enacted to punish us. Or we're punished by those who know that committing violence against a whore is too frequently state sanctioned. I know, she was just doing her job. The judge never ruled on my name. The case was dismissed before I could be called to testify.

I earned my name in 2008, traveling ill-dressed through six weeks of winter with the Sex Workers' Art Show, ice under my flats in Ann Arbor, in Williamsburg, in Asbury Park. Twelve of us traveled in two vans. All of us artists, all of us sex workers. All across the country we danced and sang and took our clothes off, we covered ourselves in glitter and lit ourselves on fire and read our stories out loud. ABC News called us a "traveling sex show." Protestors sang hymns in a circle outside one auditorium. At the College of William and Mary, police officers positioned themselves in the front rows of the audience, in case we might need arresting. All of it—every snow-calmed college campus, every Holiday Inn with its basket of apples, every epithet and dirty joke reversed, every roadside toilet, dusk rush of dark trees past the passenger window, Midwestern strip club cup of ginger ale, backstage sequin and chalk dust and sweat, and the terror and thrill of standing up on that stage night after night to tell one true story to hundreds of hushed faces—all of it was hard and beautiful. At Harvard, the walls were old brick and polished wood, a gleaming gold-pale I will forever associate with academic wonder. If you licked those beams, they'd taste like money. A flavor recognizable only after you've starved for it.

Before we left, I had considered using another name, a third name, a writers' name. But Annie Oakley, the visionary woman who ran the show, told me she had already sent out materials that said "Lorelei." That I ended up using the name I'd already made, the name I'd been earning for years—the name under which I'd done a thousand things the world still wants to shame me for—this experience changed my life. This six weeks of coming to know myself as an artist, of learning my name one more time, this time as an artist's name, this, finally, is what allowed me to understand that I was never splintered, that whatever I am—slut, whore, sister, freak, artist, wife—all of it is truly, wholly me.

If you call me whore now, I'll tell you: You have no idea.

And still, I may be making a mistake, telling you anything.

At a bachelor party in 2010, I'm giving a lap dance. I kneel between a man's denim legs, look up at him. He says quietly, searching my face, "Do you really like this?" He says, "What's your real name?" I smile, bat my false eyelashes and cover his face with my breasts.

Whatever name I choose, that is my real name.

HOT PINK HANDBAG AND OTHER GARISH THINGS THAT CRY OUT, "TAKE ME!"

Lyric Seal

Lyric Seal is the porn alias of Neve Be, a punk performance artist and writer, choreographer, filmmaker, educator, advocate, and spacemaker creating [queer] family and home between the Bay Area and Seattle. The great, great, grandchild of the author of The Velveteen Rabbit, and the child of an art teacher and mystic scholar, they grew up on fairy stories, are a bit of a character, and are, with love, becoming real. Raised on a river in New Jersey dairy country, they honed their powers and gathered their heat. They would go on to attend New Jersey Governor's School for Creative Writing and later Hampshire College for literature, disability and performance Studies. Their favorite pro-body groups to work for are Pink and White Productions and Sins Invalid. You can find their writing in Maximum Rocknroll, Plenitude Magazine, *ModelViewCulture.com, and on CrashPadSeries.com's blog in the advice column Slumber Party! Their first book,* Taking it Lying Down/Crawling Like an Animal *is coming out through ThreeL Media in Summer 2016. You can find them on Facebook and on Twitter @FancyLyric.*

If you want to slip in and out, real quiet, calm, unnoticed, don't come with me. My body has never been the camouflaging type, so I chose to roll with it.

I grew up rotated and brown and with a taste for glitz and roses. Looking at a photo of me from when I was seventeen, plunging neckline Jessica Simpson hot chartreuse dress, purple circles painted on my cheeks, behind the ears wet with some Night Queen oil, my mom tries to find humor in her own anxiety at my outlandishness: "They're going to remember you for fifty years in this town!" It's a small postcard town in New Jersey, a mill town, but also not really surviving off the mill anymore, other than its red face in paintings sold in novelty shops. A bit Gilmore Girlsy, and though my mom hates the fast, quippy way the Loreleis speak, we are a single mother and an only daughter. We do drink a lot of coffee, and crawl headfirst into the nest or cavern or corn maze of one another. We were always teetering on this sweet hysterical edge of laughing and crying, heads thrown back or held tight on our necks, trying to decide how we really felt about something before it was too late.

The purse is hot pink and it makes her nervous or agitated or afraid. Maybe we are a family of animals, that we could both be so sensitive. She makes a joke about my fur cape, to show we still share a mythology, saying I look like a beaver from Narnia. This is in front of my partner whom she is meeting for the first time, at the airport, who is also queer, who knows me too, and I say, "That's not all that beaver means."

There is a tale of a woman who could take off her head and make soup from one grain of rice. Sometimes she is an old woman in rags and sometimes she is a haughty princess. You must serve her aims no matter what.

She tested girls' generosity, humility, modesty, obedience, and faith.

How the good girl chose the plain eggs and not the ones covered in jewels. Or she brought the pitcher of water to the woman's lips. Or she did not laugh or make a sound at all. Good girls are tactful, subtle, obedient, quiet, agreeable, and pretty.

Girls who advocate for themselves, say no, shine it on, make noise, or react are bad. The bad girls get frogs falling from their mouths.

I guess I wonder if it is possible to do what you want—disobeying orders respectfully, lovingly even. Breaking rules is always seen as a sort of violence, but never their existence in the first place. Circumstance doesn't matter. If you break code, slippery amphibians follow you all your life like a cursed reminder of your boundary-crossing ways.

If I do something you believe to be offensive, inappropriate, self-obscuring, or self-destructive such as get tattooed, identify as an anarchist, identify as queer as in fuck you, not gay as in happy—although queerness in its possibilities that I've already seen have made me happiest of all—genderfluid/multigender/genderqueer/genderfuck and not woman, at times even act as a separatist of something I need to protect from something I need to protect it from—and worst of all, perform in porn made for the Internet, that sieve: If I do these things that you don't respect, does it mean I don't respect you? If you don't love it, can't I still love you? Even if you can't believe these actions are the stuff of love, can't you still believe me?

As Maureen so beautifully put it in her plea-bargain love duet with Joanne, "Everybody stares at me." Who knows if this was always a favorable experience. People have paid attention to me since I was a child. Sometimes doting and sweet attention, sometimes pity, sometimes resentment that somehow the nature of my existence and the entire shape and function of my body required their attention, positive or negative. The combination of my will, charisma, disability, race, gender, and pervasive and confusing visibility commanded the attention of others, even when my and their needs were left uncommunicated or ignored. I learned I was a princess early on. Race and class aside, I was a princess because I was a little girl; I liked pretty, bright, floral things and fairies (and bugs, really), and often my style of playing was to sit in one place while I made up stories and people brought me things and I added to the story. I was a princess because people did things for me, whether I wanted them to or not. People adore princesses; they loathe them; they tolerate them; they mutiny.

No, that's on ships, but I was always also at sea.

For my whole life, my mother has held in her freckled, golden head the most important mind of this or any age. She fed me the mythologies that run through my veins: She built for me ethics, how to care for cats and birds and fish, boil rice, stew meat, wash the dirt patterns (she called them kitten markings) from my neck and chest, and stretch my curved joints. She supported all of my academic, artistic, and even some less-informed social endeavors. I have never known how to convey to her, as I exploded outward and upward in growth, that my attractions, desires, expressions, and aesthetic were not inspired by my anger or pain but by just that, my desire, my inner fire, my joy, which sometimes, as Clarice Lispector says, is a difficult joy, but is still called joy.

There is an anger in there too. But it's not an evil, it doesn't poison me, and it's not the point.

One day, I decided I wanted control of what people saw. Maybe that's how I justify it now, like the eating disorder it was about control over my out-of-control body and visage. Not just out of control, but if people were going to interact with my body anyway, try to control what they believed I was, then I would be something else. Maybe there are ways that is true; and can it also be true that I am a creatureling with weird taste, and I can't help it any more than you can help craving a normal human life? But I dyed my hair blue like beaches on the East Coast in winter and I tried piercing everything at least once, even though each time I remembered hating try to stick my face in saltwater. I tattooed down every creative and less than creative thought in my head and I tattooed my face, I did, I'm sorry but I'm not sorry that I like them. They are like antenna, horns, fern fronds, new legs, river bends. I follow them and reach with them. They are a sensitivity.

I have come out to my mother many times, as many sorts of creatures with different powers and disempowers. Coming out is much more like a partner dance than a PowerPoint presentation. I am frequently testing waters, even though I am always already swimming. I don't think I ever really came out as a porn performer. I knew just the word, "porn," would pierce her eardrums and sit heavy in her mouth. She noticed that it was something I was close to. The way she notices a new tattoo, a fur cape, a Facebook status where I say the word "fuck" or talk shit about something, when my hair is dirty, when my lips are red, when my gender or sexuality are morphing yet again, unfurling, settling, unsettling.

The Internet is a new tentacle to contend with, I know. A new extension of my different body and different life. While I try to shut out some people, I don't shut out my mom from my Internet life. She doesn't comment online, but on the phone, she wonders if I limit my opportunities with the advertisements for events that show a costar's naked thigh, my hand, my smiling face.

I tell her my possibilities are more expansive than she knows. I tell her I hope she'll move to me. I tell her, but also, I don't know who writes me off. Do I need them? Might they need me?

My mother is a private person, and shy, self-protective, protective of me, subtle, modest. But whimsical! Imaginative. She is also proud; she is also a genius. And she is not a prude. As an artist I always hoped to appeal to her finer sensibilities. But even artists have art they think isn't worth it. Art that just makes them say, "Why?" Why is the word for my decorated body, for my public sexual performance, for my volume, for my visibility.

The answer is, why not? The answer is yes. The answer is, I have always been a container and a vessel. I am bubbling with fire water and I am carrying it out into the world. To you. Take it. Take it from me. I have more.

Things that are antisocial or societally interruptive are considered either violent or self-destructive, and eventually, tragic. I can sense the furrowed eyebrows like they have their own pulse, their own smell. Potent. The your-shame-should-be-so-deep-it-makes-me-feel-sad eyebrows. We must already hate ourselves if we could do such things to our bodies. We must already know what punishment is coming. We must actually crave the stones thrown, the hot shoes, the toads and snakes, ostracism, imprisonment, exile, scrutiny, disgust. To be born with a queer (also meaning "odd, strange," and in my case, "disabled"), weird body is one offense. To perform queer, weird desires is to add insult to public injury.

When I move and the shock of my form hurts you, I can't kiss it better. Consider the erotics an attack and a gift.

All I can tell my mom is that there is joy and love in what I do, in how I perform and live who I am, in how I fuck on camera, even though she can't hear that word, and how I dance onstage. How I settle and unsettle. I tell her about the love because there is anger too; there is a rage so wild it might have colored, stained, tattooed me on its own. There is anger there, and she knows about it. She has always known. I think the anger is what I have the most pride and defense around because she could always see it, all aflame. Sometimes, more so lately, she tells me how she sees the light and sweetness too.

Maybe I can't relate to the story of the good girl and the bad girl and the plain eggs filled with virtue and the bejeweled eggs filled with filth because I am closer to the dangerous egg, to the unlikely and ugly magic itself, than a human girl, good or bad.

I can come out, I can show you, show you, but I can't make my body subtler. I can't deescalate my me-ness. I can't make it less.

Mama, I love you. I know you love me too. We don't have to share everything, but know that the sweet things you teach me are in everything I do. The tattoos, the choreography, the writings, the relating, how I put my body where I do. You have taught me that it is possible to make my own life, to save myself with magic and resilience, to love through it all. And I have, and I do.

I am the sorceress, and I am not in disguise. I am a mainshow freak. I am the gingerbread house, the Venus flytrap with nothing but love and teachings and madness inside. I am the head that keeps talking after it is removed. I am the grain of rice in the pot. I am the toads that spill from somewhere wet. I am the sun after it has been raining for too long. I am the muck and the sugar too. I am the egg that cries out, "Take me!" and if you do, I'll take you too.

Take me.

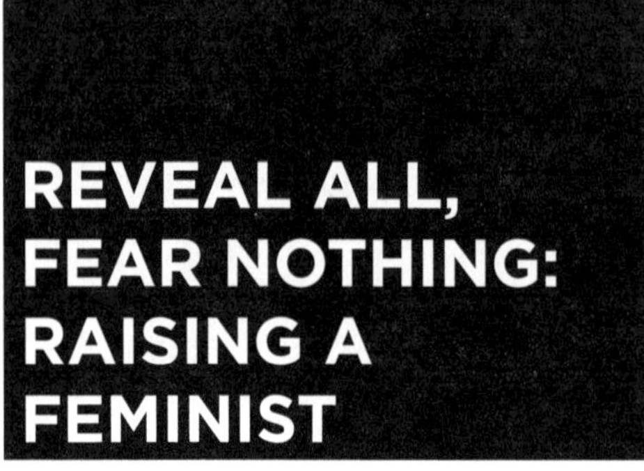

Madison Young

Madison Young is an author, artist, feminist pornographer, certified sex educator, and mother. Young has presented on the topics of pornography, feminism, and sexuality internationally, including at Yale University, Northwestern University, and the University of Toronto. Young's writings have been published in books such as Best Sex Writing of 2013, Subversive Motherhood, Daddy: A Memoir, *and her forthcoming* DIY Porn Handbook: Documenting Our Own Sexual Revolution. *Young has been featured for her expertise in sex-positive culture on such media outlets as Bravo TV, the* New York Times, *and HBO. Young is currently working on her third book,* The Ultimate Guide to Sex During Pregnancy and Motherhood. *Madison Young lives and works in Berkeley, California.*

Growing up in the conservative Midwestern landscape of Southern Ohio, I was born deep inside my own personal closet. In those closets we kept our fears, our differences, our desires, and bodies hidden from the public.

Closets are dark and scary places. Growing up a young girl who found herself experiencing queer and kinky sexual desires when I had yet to ever hear an open conversation about sex—I found myself amongst tremendous feelings of isolation, anxiety, and depression. I thought there must be something terribly wrong with me to have these thoughts, yet my thoughts and fantasies of an alternative life in which my body was paired next to that of another woman was one of the only slivers of light in the darkness of my pubescence.

I daydreamed frequently and found escape in worlds that I had built in my head that were different from the one that surrounded me. I knew that I had to leave Ohio in order to find any kind of connection and freedom from my closet. I dedicated myself to my schoolwork and had a talent for memorizing and regurgitating the lessons that my teachers outlined in school. By doing so, I graduated at the top of my class and made my way to college in Chicago, where I followed my love of theater and began to step out from the shadows of a closeted life.

In Chicago, during my freshman year of college, I phoned my mom and told her that I had started dating women. I listened to her cry over the phone, " Why would you make your life more difficult? Why would you choose this life? What did I do wrong?"

I listened to my mother's pain that my freedom had cost me, but felt the heavy veil of shame that I had been carrying around for so many years start to lift as I slowly uncovered my own identity and room to explore who I was and who I was meant to be.

In 2000, at the age of twenty, I decided wholeheartedly to dedicate my life to creating space for individuals to express and explore their authentic selves. I decided to open my own queer feminist art gallery and performance space, Femina Potens Art Gallery, in San Francisco, California.

While serving as the artistic director of Femina Potens, I simultaneously launched a career as a porn performer and feminist porn director with an emphasis on BDSM performance. I quickly found that this powerful pornographic medium was a way to empower others to explore and embrace their own sexual desires while dismantling shame around sex. I discovered that in committing to loving myself, and openly and publicly exploring my own sexual desire, I would be empowering others to do the same. Within my career, in the realms of art and sex, I developed a primary mantra—a code of ethos—that I refer back to in all that I do: Reveal all, fear nothing.

To reveal all and fear nothing is not to say that fear wouldn't exist or I wouldn't encounter it, but that we persevere through the fear, that we live through the fear and find our way to the other side of it. I've now been performing and directing in erotic film for well over a decade as well as presenting and leading sexuality workshops at conferences and universities since 2005. My parents have come to accept who I am as both a queer woman and feminist pornographer in my very out and public life.

In 2011, my life changed in a way that was both terrifying and beautiful: I became a mother. I was raw, exposed, and more vulnerable in my essence than I had ever experienced, and I felt fear.

The moment I went public about my pregnancy, interview questions poured in asking, "What will you tell your child? What will you tell the mothers at the PTA meetings?"

Considering both my child's father and I had appeared on national television multiple times talking about pornography and sexuality, and their grandmothers were the iconic Annie Sprinkle and Beth Stephens, we weren't going to stay discreetly unnoticed in a quiet corner somewhere as we pretend to be someone we are not.

I didn't have all the answers four years ago, and I don't have all the answers now. But I always knew that no matter what, we would not live in a closet. My entire adult life, I had worked to dismantle my closet as well as hold peoples' hands as they bravely stepped out of their own closets. I wasn't going back in because I was becoming a mother.

I was more motivated than ever to raise this brilliant little person and give them the space to express their authentic self and their authentic gender—to express and explore who they are in their own time, at their own pace.

My child, Em, is well practiced in coming out daily as their gender fluctuates through different spans of the spectrum, sometimes in a single day. Em has also honed in on the skill of facilitating gentle practice for others to come out, asking warmly to me, their father, babysitters, and friends: "What is your preferred gender today?"

So how does someone who works in the realm of sexuality and creates art and film on the topic of sexuality come out to their children? How do I reveal all and fear nothing in the face of parenthood around such loaded topics as sex and pornography?

Sex and pornography are two highly emotionally-loaded topics. We pack them full of more shame and power than any other topic. So first, let's unpack these two terms. "Sex" is a natural human expression of affection and gifting of pleasure either to oneself or to others. "Pornography" is the creation of film or photography that captures the natural human expression of affection and gifting of pleasure either to oneself or to others.

Coming out to Em has been easier than coming out to any other person that I have ever met. Em was born into an experience of living outside of a closet. When our bodies and sex are not shamed or stigmatized, it becomes so much easier to have an honest conversation about the context of documenting pleasure and sex.

For me, I realized that as a feminist and a mother, it was key to advocate for my child to develop a healthy relationship with their body. I also realized that for my child to develop a healthy relationship with their body, I would need to first develop my own healthy relationship with my postpartum body, which was challenging. I looked in the mirror at a body that looked foreign to me. Through meditation and affirmations, I grew to love the body that was proof of where I had been, that told the story of the journey to birth my child. I looked in the mirror, I looked down at my belly, at my stretch marks in wonder, tracing them with my fingers and thanking them for reminding me of where I had been, physical memories clawed into my postpartum belly.

As I came to terms with my relationship with my own body, I knew I was advocating for my child's healthy relationship with their own body. Em is growing up knowing the anatomical names of their body parts, snuggling up with their plush vulva toy, Val, which is adorned with silk, velvet, and sequins, and not fearing their body but embracing their body with love and curiosity.

It's very natural for kids to want to run around naked, yet in our body-negative and sex-negative society, we consistently get the message to cover ourselves up. We give Em the knowledge that we wear clothes when we are cold or to protect against dirt or unwanted germs entering our body. If Em is warm and wants to run around the house naked, that is okay. If we see a naked child running around, we don't make a big deal about it, and if Em shouts out that they see a naked child, we might also point out a child that has clothes on and make note that the child without clothes must not be cold, or bring the experience back to how Em thinks it might feel for the child that we see without clothing on.

Potty learning also proved to be an excellent opportunity in cultivating a healthy relationship for our child around their anatomy. Potty learning begins with role modeling. When Em watched where I eliminated my urine and feces, it informed them about the process of bodies and elimination. This also gave Em an opportunity to see different genitals, where pee and poo go and where they come from. I've had exciting conversations with my three-year-old about our urine exiting our urethra, poop or feces exiting the anus, and where in the vagina the urethra is located.

When I'm menstruating, I use a menstrual cup that holds my menstrual blood. So when my child accompanies me to the bathroom when I'm emptying my menstrual cup, we have the opportunity to discuss what menstruation is, when it happens, why it happens, and in what bodies it happens.

As Em grows, they will have new questions. Life is a constant learning ground and every day I'm faced with new questions like, "Is this a microphone?"

"No, my love, that is Mommy's nonsharing vulva toy. It is only for me to use."

Or, "When I grow up like Daddy, will I have a penis too?"

To which I'm able to answer, "When you grow up, if you choose, you can buy something like a penis at Good Vibrations, or if you decide having a penis would better fit the way you feel about your gender you can take hormonal treatments in which your clitoris would develop into a penis."

All of these moments advocate Em in developing a healthy relationship with their body, intimacy, consent, body agency, gender, boundaries, and the natural humanness of pleasure.

My child can identify the anatomy of the vulva more succinctly than many of the students at my workshops and can ask for consent before giving you a hug. They know where their uterus and clitoris are located and know how to ask for privacy, please, in their bedroom if they want to explore their own body. They know that no one has the right to touch them without consent and that they need to ask others and gain consent before gifting affection.

Em knows that Mommy and Daddy are artists and filmmakers that make films for grown-ups, about grown-ups who are sharing consenting pleasure and affection for one another.

I remember when my child was two years old, they asked me, "What are you doing at work tonight?"

I was teaching a cunnilingus class. I was able to tell my child, "I'm teaching people about how to share pleasure, use their words to ask for what they want, and helping them to learn more about vulvas."

And my very wise two-year-old looked at me and smiled and said, "That is a great idea, Mom!"

I'm challenged and inspired on a daily basis as I engage in the practice of life and motherhood. But throughout those daily challenges, I strive to stay authentic and true to myself and my child as we forge forward in beautiful and fearful moments that make up who we are and what we believe in.

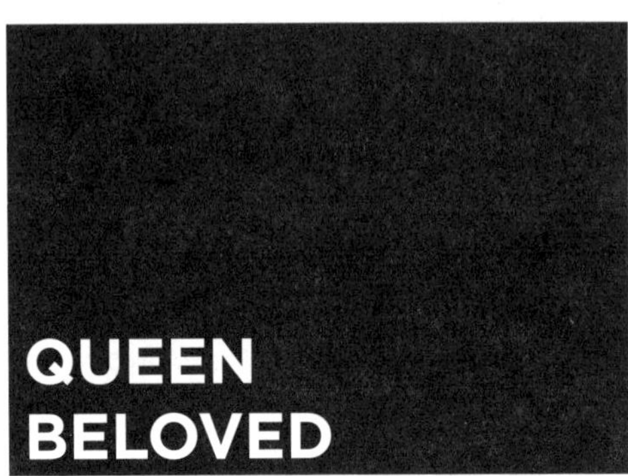

QUEEN BELOVED

Milcah Halili Orbacedo

Milcah Halili Orbacedo is a writer, publisher, performer, and entrepreneur living on the West Coast. She divides her time between Portland, Oregon, and the Bay Area, California. You can find more of her work at MilcahOrbacedo.com and follow her on Twitter @milcahorbacedo. Milcah's first book is Sisterhood: Ate *(ah-TEH).*

My legal first and middle name means "queen beloved." As a self-identified Oakland suburb hoodrat from the Bay Area, I so wanted this to be true. I wanted to be a beloved queen, and I believed, as a young woman of color from a lower-middle-class background, that to achieve this in a capitalist society I needed money to self-care like a beloved queen would. I needed money to house, feed, and decorate myself in radiant beauty.

I turned to sex work because Antonia Crane wrote a column for *The Rumpus* called "Recession Sex Workers." I've always wanted to be like the writings I read. Antonia was a self-identified stripper turned writer. I was obsessed and read anything I could read of Antonia's on the Internet. By my mantra, what you read is what you become, it was all in due time that this writer become a stripper. When I auditioned at a strip club for the first time, the house mom of the club asked me, "What's your stage name?"

"My stage name?"

I did not want to give her one. I didn't want to feel like my legal name was a secret or something to be uttered in shame. I wanted to give her my given name because I'd already built a following in the pornography industry with that name. When I fill out model release forms before porn shoots, on the line that reads "Stage Name" I write my legal first and middle name: Milcah Halili.

"My name is Maya," I said, as I acquainted myself in my titty bar with strange men from the neighborhood looking for naked bodies dancing under black lights, whiskey shots and beer, and, if they were lucky and polite, undivided attention from their favorite dancer. I had a hard time believing my stage name, often grateful I had picked a name that started with an "M" on the off chance I'd forget. I had a window of time after I sounded out the "M" to switch the incoming "i" with an "a," squeeze the "aya" out before the "ilcah" made its way.

During the beginning of my foray into web-camming (which warmed me up to the idea of pornography and, eventually, stripping), Antonia found my blog of writings and candid nude photos and wanted to interview me for her "Recession Sex Workers" column. I gave her my consent and we emailed each other questions and answers.

"Sex workers never use their real names," Antonia wrote. She asked, "Why have you decided to use yours? What if your family, grandparents or brothers find out? What will you tell them? What do you think their response will be?"

"I'm assuming my whole family will eventually find out," I wrote, "and if they should come at me with any judgment, I hope I have enough love in myself to say to them, 'Thank you for everything you've done for me. I am grateful. But I'm okay and you don't need to protect me. Only God can judge me. Please let me have my peace.'"

This is what I tried to tell my father. It was a few years after my father and mother left me with my then-fourteen- and thirteen-year-old brothers to run wild for a while to squat, steal, and sneer at the world. I was still angry. Despite my anger, I agreed to video call on Skype with him. I told him I was doing better, that I: had found community with open, sex-positive, and polyamorous people, and that I was taking care of myself. He nodded his head, said, "Hm."

"I read your interview," he said. Then he laughed. "You said I molested your mother?"

"That's what you did."

"Okay," he said. "And now you do this . . . web-camming?"

"Yes, it's just by myself. It's super safe and my community knows I'm doing it."

"Okay, Milcah. Just don't take it too far," he said.

"You have no right to say that to me," I said and broke into sobs. I pounded the keyboard of my laptop and my web-cam feed ricocheted with the force of my anger, causing the image of my tear-streamed face to blur.

"I finally feel like I've found family. You never gave me a sense of that. You abandoned your own family. And now that I've found mine, you have the nerve to tell me not to take it too far?"

My father's forehead creased at his third eye. His pale complexion blushed. His mouth frowned and his hazel eyes saddened.

"My family loves me. And I love them. Tell me that's unholy," I said. I punched the keys with each utterance. "Tell me that's unholy." Again. "Tell me that's unholy."

He stayed silent. I wailed more into my laptop and balled my hands once more into fists. The image of my pained face pixelated with each punch to the keys. He let me cry. Eventually he said, "You are right."

He said sorry and asked me for forgiveness.

There was another part of my answer to Antonia. I wrote, "As much as my parents have hurt me, I love them with all of my heart, and I want to rebuild a new name for them, honor them. I want my mother to be strong and my father to be understood, and the way that I feel I can do that is through taking their name, my name, and changing what it means with dignity."

What hurt me most, more than the memory of my father and mother leaving me with my younger brothers, was the image of my father pinning my mother by the wrists, his mouth nonconsensually on her neck as she cried in silence. Her hands were tight fists. That image of her clenched hands still haunts me to this day.

Seeing my name in porn gave me a sickening sense of faith. I was nauseous with the belief that now my name wasn't a symbol of some sad past, but of a woman strong enough to be submissive and vulnerable in the space of professional BDSM.

Once on the set of *Electrosluts*, Mz Berlin punched her fist into my cunt over and over again, the image that would become the cover photo of the scene. The bold red and green headline text in the cover photo read, "An Electrosluts Christmas." When I saw the cover photo on Christmas day, I felt proud.

"I'm literally punching your pussy," Mz said.

"Huh?" That day, the clenched hand was a thing of beauty, something that gave me joy. Mz's fist in me made me feel like a beloved queen. I left my drunken and dazed state to cast my eyes down on my pussy. I remember most the shock I felt when I witnessed Mz's black-gloved hand gliding effortlessly in and out of my own body. I felt like I was inside of a lucid dream.

Never had I ever been pussy punched before. The production crew lubed me up well, but it wasn't just that. I was extremely wet. No matter what Mz did, even if she humiliated me and cattle prodded me, it aroused me because she stayed within my limits, and I felt heard and held. The element of consent made me open with such a force, I could take anything in and alchemize it into a positive and pleasurable experience.

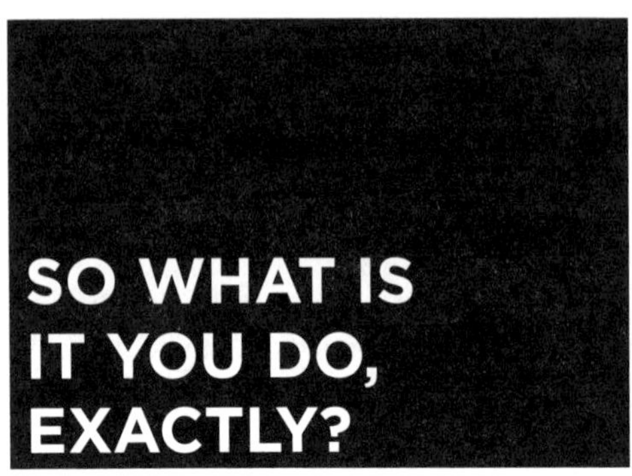

SO WHAT IS IT YOU DO, EXACTLY?

Ms. Naughty

Ms. Naughty is a writer, editor, blogger, entrepreneur, and filmmaker with a passion for making better porn. She's been curating and creating adult content online since 2000. Her site BrightDesire.com features her filmed and written work, and she also co-owns ForTheGirls.com, one of the first adult sites for women. Her short film Dear Jiz *won Best Experimental Short at Cinekink in 2014, and her films have screened at numerous international festivals. She lives with her husband in a small Australian town, surrounded by fundamentalist Christians.*

"So what is it you do, exactly?"

The conversation had moved on from "polite" and we'd had a couple of glasses of wine. I was feeling fairly comfortable and figured that these two friends of my cousin were open-minded. They were lesbians, after all, so I assumed they were fairly liberal in their views. I dropped the bomb.

"I make pornography."

There was a shocked moment of silence.

Trying not to panic, I went on to explain that I make erotic films and run an adult site for straight women. I gave a brief rundown of my efforts to make positive, feminist porn with a real effort to respect my performers. I did my very best to point out that no, I'm not like those other pornographers and that, really, I'm an artist.

One of my listeners went very quiet indeed. The other unexpectedly revealed how she'd been a stripper in her youth and then expressed her view that sex work always causes problems with one's relationships.

I nodded and then decided to change the subject.

After they'd gone, I felt the usual mix of bravado and regret. I wouldn't ever see these people again, so it didn't really matter what they thought of me. And yet I wondered if it might have just been easier if I hadn't mentioned my real job at all.

This is one of the dilemmas of working in the adult industry. In the course of everyday life, people ask your occupation. On top of that, it's a required item on customs forms, on tax bills, on government documents. Do you embellish the truth, lie, or just come out with it? Worse still, what do you tell your family?

I've been writing erotica since the '90s, and in early 2000 took up advertising porn on the Internet. This snowballed into a full-on career making porn, although I am not a performer. I have been very successful in my chosen vocation, with published stories, award-winning films, and two websites that are profitable enough to ensure I don't need to have a "real" job.

My parents know what I do, but they don't ever want to talk about it. It's interesting because we are not a religious family, but I think my Dad has a conservative streak. I originally didn't hesitate to tell them about what I was doing because I didn't see any need to hide it. I think they were impressed with the money I was making (back when the exchange rate was astronomical) but really didn't want to know the details. It's sex, after all. My mom once said she has no problem with the idea of people using a bit of porn in their marriage but that's the most we've ever talked about it. I occasionally tell them that I've got a film screening in Berlin or New York, and they'll just nod and quickly change the subject. I suspect they wish I had stayed a librarian or become a teacher like a "normal" person. When other people ask them what I do, they say I make websites, which is the official explanation given to all those who don't need to know the details.

My dear departed nana was proud of me, though. When I told her that I'd had my first-ever story published in 1997, she was thrilled. When I added with a tinge of embarrassment that it was a piece of erotic fiction in *Australian Women's Forum*, she boldly went out and bought a copy. She always told me she wanted me to write a Mills and Boon romance and become rich like Barbara Cartland but said erotic fiction was a step in the right direction.

I miss her.

I don't have kids, but I have twin nieces who turned eighteen recently. It's always been difficult trying to think of things to talk about with them because I can't discuss what I do. Given that we've done a lot of travelling to shoot things or go to film festivals, I've often fudged various explanations for it. Now they're adults, and I'm hesitating, wondering if I should spill the beans next time I see them or if it's best not to mention it. I'll admit that I'm curious about their thoughts on porn and sexuality, but I don't know if I should be talking about it with them. Am I a cool aunt because I make porn or a creepy one?

The occupation question is always a minefield when it comes to social situations. I find myself sizing up strangers, trying to work out if they're the type of person who is okay with porn and liberal sexuality or if they're the churchy, judgmental type. If they ask what I do, there can be an awkward moment when I hesitate and have to make a snap decision to lie or tell the truth. If I'm at a charity fundraiser, say, I might take the easy option and say I work in PR. But if I've had a couple glasses of wine and I'm feeling mischievous, the truth may well out.

This happened at a local film festival a couple of years ago. My husband came back from the bar to find me surrounded by ten women, holding court. "Uh oh," he thought, "she told them."

Telling the truth does two things: It sorts the wheat from the chaff and it acts as the perfect icebreaker. You can easily spot the people who aren't impressed; they go quiet, back away, or excuse themselves. I know then that they aren't the kind of person I'd want to talk to anyway. Unfortunately, I then have to worry about what they'll do with that information, but thankfully I've encountered very few of these people. Perhaps I'm just good at choosing my company.

More often than not, I'll spill the beans and find myself surrounded by new best friends. Once I tell them what I do, they raise their eyebrows and express the view that I don't look at all like a pornographer. I guess I should be bedecked in feathers and fishnets rather than the very boring cotton-and-comfortable-shoe type of clothes I usually wear. Indeed, I suspect I present as a homely, pearl-clutching bore at first glance rather than an evil purveyor of dirty, dirty smut. It's part of my successful camouflage.

In any case, after this first shock they smile, lean in conspiratorially, and want to know all about it. So I tell them, talking about the ins and outs of filming sex, of writing sex, and of selling it. A lot of people are genuinely fascinated about porn and they want to know the details of what goes on behind the scenes. It's such an out-of-the-ordinary thing that the conversation is instantly engaging and lively. We invariably end up in a philosophical discussion about porn itself and what's wrong with it. I've met real fans but also plenty of people expressing a frustration with mainstream porn and how it presents sex.

Perhaps most interesting is that revealing my secret seems to give people permission to reveal theirs. I've heard all sorts of private stories of porn use, masturbation, and sexual exploration from near strangers, despite not really wanting or needing to know about such things. I'll nod and let them talk but I'm not inclined to offer my own sexual history. Despite what I do, I like to keep that part to myself. It's a dividing line that I try to maintain, although it can be difficult, especially when it comes to drawing on your own sexual fantasies to write fiction or scripts.

I've been doing this for a long time now and there's not a lot that surprises me. I usually tell people that porn is a bit like working in a chocolate factory; what seems exciting to the outsider can become very humdrum after a while.

I tread a fine line, legally. Australian laws regarding adult content are complicated and often contradictory. My business is actually based in the United States so I have to comply with two sets of laws. Telling people what I do can be risky; there is a certain amount of trust involved in revealing my occupation. I live on a street surrounded by fundamentalist Christians and there's always the fear that if they found out, they could well decide I'm a criminal and call the police.

Despite this, I'm very happy with what I do. I like not having a "real" job. I'm my own boss, I work my own hours, and I don't have to commute or deal with office politics. I feel that I am doing good in the world, creating a vision of positive sexuality, going beyond the old ideas of what "porn" should be. Perhaps that's why I always feel a little bit proud and rebellious when I come out about my work because I'm doing something different and challenging and—hopefully—something that might help change the world.

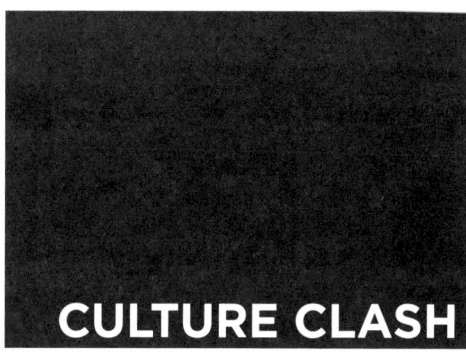

Nina Hartley

Nina Hartley is a pioneering feminist sex worker using her body in the service of promoting a sexually sane and literate society. Active as a performer since 1982, her rock-solid commitment to the importance of sexual autonomy has fueled Ms. Hartley's career in adult entertainment. As a performer, director, writer, educator, public speaker, and feminist thinker for all, no matter their orientation, she's traveled the world to deliver her message. She believes that sexual freedom is a fundamental human right and welcomes the new social media opportunities for spreading her message of knowledge and empowerment to the widest number of people. She's the author of Nina Hartley's Guide to Total Sex *(Avery Press). Putting to use her BS degree in nursing, she and her husband, Ernest Greene, have produced the million-selling sex-ed video series collectively known as The Nina Hartley Guides (Adam & Eve), currently in its thirty-eighth episode. Still active in front of the camera, she and her husband live in Los Angeles. She serves on the board of the Woodhull Sexual Freedom Alliance.*

I've made a practice of being out about my job as a porn performer for my entire career, now entering its thirty-first year. Sexual liberation being my core mission, it would have done little good to beat about the bushes when asked what I did for a living. I was one of the first modern video-era porn performers who was eager to talk to the public about my experiences, thoughts, and philosophy about sex, sexuality, and sexual expression. My openness has served me well even as the Feminist Sex Wars raged on throughout the '80s, only to fight to the standstill in which we find ourselves today.

Most of the attention I get in public is positive as fans recognize me even when I'm dressed in civilian clothes and without makeup. I enjoy bringing some cheer to their day by sharing the good news about sex, about which I'm a passionate ambassador. In short, being out about my job is second nature, and I've never had a bad experience because of it so far.

Over the course of my career, I've had the lucky opportunity several times to work in Europe. One time I was in Saint-Tropez and Nice, another in Munich. This time it was in Paris in the early '90s. I was at the height of my Big Porn look: tanned, toned, blonde hair teased to there, sparkling blue eyes, tiny waist, and a big ass. I was big-assed before big-assed was popular and my costume was custom-made to my specifications: denim bolero and a short skirt that was an odd marriage of tutu and ice-skating dress. Underneath I wore a front-closure bra top in white and red gingham and matching breakaway thong with the clips at the hips. If I bent from the waist, my ass was clearly visible. Smooth, bare legs with a fresh pedicure were strapped into high-heeled sandals the color of my skin. In short, I was a vision of *un grande-femme Americaine.*

French porn sets break for lunch to have a proper meal, complete with wine. We drove to a restaurant, me with the aforementioned costume on, and I found myself on the sidewalk as an old woman walked toward me.

She was the quintessential grandma: nondescript dress, white hair, glasses, and sensible shoes. She used a cane. Her companion looked to be middle-aged. When she saw me, she became very animated and made a beeline to stand in front of me. I shook in my heels, expecting a Puritanical tongue-lashing. After all, I did look a proper slut and stood out in the otherwise quiet neighborhood.

Imagine my delight and surprise when, instead of berating me, she patted my cheek and murmured, "*Trés jolie, trés jolie!*" I knew enough French to recognize a compliment: "Very pretty, very pretty!" I waited for her companion to speak to my guy, who in turn translated for me. It turned out that she had been a madam in Paris during World War II who had run a successful brothel.

She didn't know I made porn but she knew a good sex worker when she saw one. It made me proud, and the memory still sparks a smile to this day.

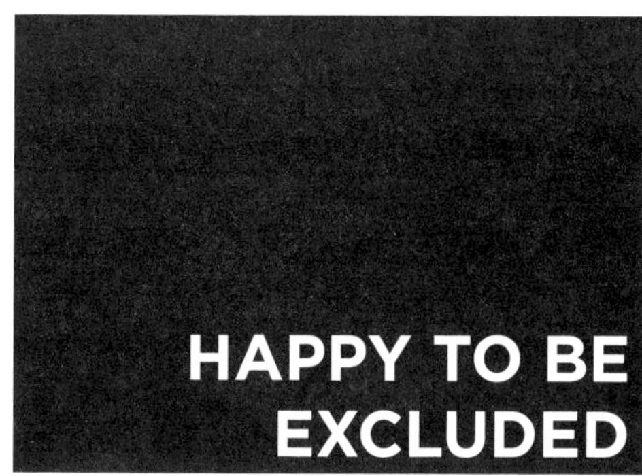

HAPPY TO BE EXCLUDED

Nikki Silver

Nikki Silver is a self-made hairy porn star and has been running her site, NaughtyNatural.com, for the past three years. She is at once a free-spirited wild woman and business-savvy entrepreneur. She enjoys pushing the boundaries of hair fetishism and creating erotic art.

"Coming out" has been a concept and action that's been part of my entire adult life and adolescence. Although I've come out over and over again, I've very rarely felt shame or personal discomfort with my various identities and choices. Coming out was and is part of figuring out how my relationships are to unfold: How much do I care about you knowing who I really am? How much patience do I have for possibly annoying or offensive questions? And how will revealing this information serve me?

At this point in my life, I have created a sex-worker-centric community and ethos around myself, in which I even include my parents and brother, where not being quite knowledgeable about the sex industry either by experience or proxy is quite rare. I'm completely uninterested in educating people around me about my lifestyle or job; that is what clients and fans pay me to do. It's true, I do live in an alternate universe where things that are problems outside it are not problems within it. In my work, I allow my clients and porn subscribers momentary access to my world, a privilege that they pay to access.

So I'll share two stories of travelling in other countries and coming out to strangers.

A good friend of mine and I went to Australia to shoot porn

for a few companies based there. After we were done shooting, we went to a small island off the coast of Melbourne to visit her friend. We had debated amongst ourselves about whether we would tell his dad and anyone else we met, aside from her friend, why we were in Australia. It was very important for us to not be seen as a rich Americans who were just vacationing, when in fact we had been flown to Melbourne by the porn company and were working while we were there.

So we ended up telling his dad and lady friend who were rather nonplussed (it is Australia, after all) and then an American man who was working on building a commune/hotel on the island. He actually employed us to do some manual labor for him—my first job outside the sex industry in seven years at the time—and we told him we were in Australia shooting porn. He expressed concern for us, as many patronizing men do when they aren't trying to sleep with you, but also went off on a ridiculous rant about how he was an expert in the sacred feminine. Once he had talked to us enough and came to his own conclusion that, indeed, we were not being forced to do porn and felt good about it, he said we were carriers of the "sacred feminine." This white man from Boulder, Colorado, even gave us a book he had written on the subject and told us we should go listen to his river on our break because that's where the Goddess lived.

More recently, I went on a vacation to Belize with my partner. We had tried to avoid interacting much with other tourists, but we inevitably ended up in a small island bar talking to a group of Lebanese Montrealers, and I decided to try telling the truth about my job to a group of young, drunk men. My partner looked over at me like I was a little crazy but stuck by my side for support. As usual, the one person that I actually liked and wanted to talk to was overpowered by his obnoxious cousin who asked things like if he could touch different body parts of mine and what my specialty was, what sex act I was really good at. I deflected and countered most of the things he said and had some fun sassing it up, but by the end I was exhausted by policing my boundaries and putting this boy in his place and felt much too vulnerable, so we left. Reifying that honest connection with the majority of the people in the world, especially straight cis men (the ones most likely to engage with me), is not something that's really possible for me.

There have even been a handful of times when I was traveling the country by hitchhiking and sleeping in the woods that I was propositioned in gas stations or by rides, and I told them I was a pro from New York City and would cost a lot more than they were offering me. My self-protective instincts haven't always been the best, but it has always been of utmost important not to hide who I am, perhaps more important than my self-preservation. Or maybe I've just never seen myself as vulnerable and never believed anyone could actually hurt me.

I tell these stories because coming out to friends or family isn't something I've done for a long time or was ever a big deal for me. I've always seen and created myself in opposition to the status quo and been quite comfortable with that. I would never wish to be "normal" or "acceptable" to the people who support the violence and repression we call "civilization."

Friends around me express shock and dismay at various governmental statutes discriminating against porn or sex workers (amongst other groups and issues), but I am never surprised. I think these things are very much worth fighting, but I've always expected the government and society at large to try to hurt me. By definition and action they stand against everything I believe in: joy, freedom, self-expression, nurturance, and care for each other and the earth.

I'm very happy to be socially excluded from a society that breaks individuals down so thoroughly they have to come seek out "criminals" to help them heal their emotional wounds. I will keep doing this work to create beautiful, expressive pornography, to let others live through me vicariously in words, photos, and videos. And perhaps the most intimate and intense work of all, connecting one-on-one, in person, with clients who have lived decades of repression. I am a respite, and I am so glad to be.

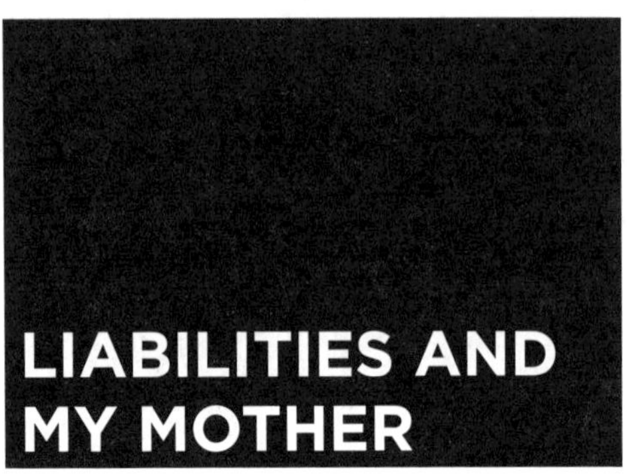

LIABILITIES AND MY MOTHER

Oriana Small, a.k.a. Ashley Blue

Oriana Small is a writer and visual artist from Southern California. As Ashley Blue, she appeared in over 300 adult films—including the infamous Girlvert series (JM Productions)—directed seventeen adult film features, cohosted Playboy TV's Night Calls Hotline, *and has won numerous adult film industry awards, including AVN's Female Performer of the Year in 2004 and Best Supporting Actress in 2005. She lives and works with her husband, photographer Dave Naz, and her cat and dog in the Hollywood Hills.*

The night before our trip, I was thinking of ways to get back at my mother—whom I prefer to call Cheryl—for being vile. She'd called me a few days before we were to leave, while Desiree was still in town. Cheryl knew about our planned Euro trip, but she probably didn't remember. Her brain is seriously deteriorated from doing drugs her entire life. She phoned while I was in line at In-N-Out Burger. Desiree had started her period in my car. She had bled right through her sweatpants, so she waited in the car with Tyler. I was trying to order all of our cheeseburgers correctly. Tyler wanted "no tomato, yes grilled onions, no special sauce, just ketchup only." He would throw a fit if it wasn't just so. Desiree's was simple: no onions.

I answered my cell phone and held it with my shoulder as I fished around in my purse for cash.

"So, do you have anything to tell me?" Cheryl's voice was angry. I could tell by her rhetorical tone that she knew the answer to her own question.

"What? What are you talking about?" I was handing the money over to the cashier and felt rude. I was rolling my eyes. I was annoyed at the bitchiness in my mother's voice.

"Well, do you have anything to say for yourself, young lady?" The voice got angrier. My mother hadn't been mad at me since I was in high school. There wasn't any reason for her to be; I'd been on my own since I turned eighteen. Nothing I did was any of her business. How dare she utter a demeaning phrase like "young lady"?

"Excuse me? What are you getting at? What's your problem?" I had no respect for her. I responded with the same volume of nastiness. Cheryl had put me through misery all of my life. It angered and saddened me when she tried to play "mother" with me now. She hadn't earned it.

"Well, I just saw my daughter on the Internet—with a mouth full of cock!" She said it with such mean, matter-of-fact evenness.

I was disgusted and embarrassed. I could tell that her sole intention was to hurt, humiliate, and expose me. I was ashamed of her. Somehow, to hear her speak "a mouth full of cock" was cruder than me even having one. A mother isn't supposed to say things like that. I wanted to vomit into the phone. Instead of "fuck you," I venomously said, "So?"

"I think you better start explaining!" She was feeling powerful, and that wounded me deeply. She was trying to corner me.

"So what, do you hate me now?" I asked her. I knew she didn't, but I had to ask.

"No," she responded flatly.

"Okay," I said back, in the same voice as hers. We sounded very much alike.

"No. Not okay. I'm so mad at you! You're all over the Internet. You fucking little whore. Your mouth's full of cock. I'm ashamed of you, to be your mother! You fucking little bitch!" Then she hung up on me. I didn't get a chance to rightfully respond.

When someone finally handed me the bag of fast food, I was weak in my legs, in shock. I shoved the phone back into my purse and walked out of In-N-Out. My hands were shaking. We'd only done one line apiece that morning, just to wake up. The tears came a few minutes later. I always knew that at some point I would have to talk about it with my family. Cheryl just had no right to be so vicious about it—she was probably with her grotesque boyfriend, looking at porn when she'd found out.

I've never been scared of letting my mom down. Whether or not she's proud of me makes no difference. Cheryl is a drug addict and a manipulator. It's impossible for me to trust her. Just when it seems as though she cares, she's got some ulterior motive to benefit herself. I've often promised myself that I would not talk to her anymore. Cheryl would have to wait.

Cheryl and I made up on the phone. She left messages on Tyler's voicemail, crying and begging him to have me call her. I was fully prepared to never speak with her again. I can be cold in that way; if I feel like somebody is doing more damage to me than good, I cut them out of my life. You have to remove cancerous tumors.

Tyler had a plus-sized heart when it came to family sympathies. He listened to Cheryl's pleas on the messages and argued with me about the situation: "She's your mother. You only get one in life. Call her. You can't go on like this."

I pointed out to Tyler than no matter how much he loved his mother, his own Cheryl, he still lied to her about his occupation. His mother was flawed, but Tyler was forgiving. She'd lied to Tyler about who his real father was and chose her lovers over her children—just like my mother. It's eerie how similar they are, in name and manner. Tyler forgave his mother for all of it. They even did coke together.

I had called my mother from Paris. It was an expensive call. It was our last night before we left for home. In such a romantic, inspiring place, where it feels like anything is possible, I thought maybe I could change and somehow grow to be a more compassionate woman by reaching out to Cheryl. I needed her at the time. Just the thought of my family's reaction to my porn career made me cringe, and I hoped Cheryl would be a gateway to get through to them. No one would be happy for me. My family always praised me for having a sharp mind. Now, to them, I would be wasting my gifts and exploiting my body. Everyone in my family is extremely modest about sex, except for Cheryl. She taught me everything I know about wearing provocative clothing. At a very young age, she would embarrass me by wearing see-through tops and shorts that revealed her butt cheeks. I guess at some point I took after her.

My mom was so happy I called. She regretted how we ended the last call. I didn't remind her that she'd hung up on me. I tried my best not to be snotty. Both of us shed tears and choruses of "I love you." Cheryl can always get me to feel sorry for her. She makes poor decisions in the moment. But she's instinctively manipulative.

Cheryl and her new live-in boyfriend, Leon, invited Tyler and me over to their home for a visit when we returned. Cheryl couldn't go five minutes without a man. This one, she claimed, like the rest, was The One. I was well aware of her codependency. All I knew about this guy was that he used to have a parrot named Shit-head. He was also fresh out of prison. Not jail, but prison. He did ten years of hard time for selling cocaine. He was supposedly clean now, or else he would be in violation of his parole.

Cheryl certainly was not clean. She still took a fair share of sedatives and methadone. She also smoked pot all the time because of its medicinal value. Her body was a wreck from various ailments. As a kid, it used to frighten me that she was such a mess. It didn't matter to me what she was taking anymore. I had my own drug issues.

Leon was overly friendly. Tyler and I had met him a few brief times before, but now that Leon knew about us doing porn, he was extra delighted to have us over. With relish, he asked about our involvement in the porn business. How much money did we make? How many scenes did we do? Who did we work for? What were the people really like? Was it easy for us to get started?

Hesitantly, we answered all of his questions. My mom didn't get into the conversation at all. She just sat there, quietly, letting Leon do all the talking. I wondered why she quietly accepted her boyfriend virtually getting off on talking about porn with me. I just tried to be polite and not look offended.

Leon led us all into his office. He had saved everything he could find about me and Tyler in a folder on the desktop of his computer. Images of me naked, sucking cock, and Tyler fucking my ass popped up on the screen. It was too bizarre to be real, yet was all too real. Leon was all jacked up about showing us. He was so proud of his collection of my porn clips. My mom never looked me in the eye the entire time. I ducked out of the room and walked down the hall.

"Ori, hey," Leon called out. He came down the hall after me. "I just wanted to ask you and Tyler if you could put in a good word for me, you know, in the porn business. I was wondering if they need any guys who are in their forties, like me? I think I can measure up. Ask you, mom."

I looked at Cheryl. She looked back at me, smiling. She nodded and said, "Do you think you could help him get in? He really wants to try doing porno movies. I don't mind."

They both hung on me for an answer. I turned to Tyler, who had a hopeful look on his face. I was the only one who thought this was wrong.

The corners of my mouth turned down as I spoke. "I don't know." It made me sick to even open my mouth.

"You two don't have to tell anyone I'm with your mom. Just say I'm a friend."

I wanted to kick his teeth in.

Tyler stepped in, but instead of siding with me, he sided with Leon. "Well, maybe, Ori. There's always Jim. He hires anyone. You don't have to do a scene with him. Let's just see."

I looked at Tyler with fractured eyes. The discussion was over. I was ready to puke. I didn't even want a stepdaughter's relationship with Leon, let alone a professional one. "We have to go home. I'm really uncomfortable that you guys asked me this. I don't know what to say."

Leon's feathers got ruffled. He stiffened up and acted put out. My mom acted like nothing was wrong. Tyler and I hugged her and said goodbye. None of the other men she'd been involved with over the years ever acted perverted toward me.

In the car, Tyler wanted to continue the discussion. "It would help them out with money. Your mom said she didn't care if he did scenes. I think he's disappointed that you said no, just like that."

"We are not going to do anything to help that man. This is unthinkable. It's almost incest. I don't care if his feelings are hurt."

If we would have gotten Leon into porn, directors would have worked the incest angle to no end—or at least marketed him and me in the same films—and that was downright disgusting, even for me. How my mother could sit there blankly smiling, a doped-up specter, I could barely fathom.

I shouldn't have expected much from a woman who basically never had a chance to learn how to be a mother. Her own mother gave her and her twin up for adoption when they were newborns. Life had dealt Cheryl a sad hand from the start. At fifteen, she got pregnant by a guy named Chuckie, my sister's dad. When my mother got to the hospital to deliver, one of the nurses called out, "Here comes another baby havin' a baby!"

Cheryl was wild too. She started smoking cigarettes and pot in elementary school. She repeatedly got into fights in junior high and high school, resulting in expulsion. As a teen mother, she was already married and divorced by the age of eighteen. Chuckie taught my sister a nursery rhyme that went something like, "Two Englishmen, two Englishmen digging a ditch / One called the other a son of a bitch / And if you ever get hit with a bucket of shit, be sure and shut your eyes."

Cheryl and I once had a close relationship. She called me her best friend. When I was a child, she would let me get out of bed late at night and play gin rummy. At thirteen, I was old enough to smoke cigarettes with her. I admired the way she could blow enormous smoke rings. I don't remember an age that she didn't allow me to drink alcohol. There was always a bottle of vodka in the freezer. Cheryl never cared if I drank from it, just so long as I left some in there for her. She would even order margaritas and kamikazes for me at restaurants when I was underage. She was into really good, racy literature. Of course, I thought she was cool at the time. Being a cool mom was the top priority for her. Never mind that she forgot to pay electricity bills and spent all the grocery money on perfume and boots.

I learned the difference between being drunk and buzzed by watching my mother. A few drinks meant she was buzzed. Her complexion would get a little flushed. Laughter would come easily and loudly. She'd start singing and dancing, full of joy. Drunk Cheryl, on the other hand, was nasty. Fights would break out. She always fell to the ground in some way, usually on her ass. Once, she was severely drunk at my cousin's tenth birthday party.

Our extended family went to Roller Gardens. The Wagon Wheel Bowling Alley was next door. My mom and her brothers got shitfaced at the bowling alley before joining the kids for some skating. Cheryl laced up her roller skates and barreled out into the rink. Halfway around the lap, she fell on her ass. She was just lying on her back, in the middle of the polished floor, kicking her legs in the air while sprawled out, slurring and unable to get up.

Still, there was more love than hate most of the time, at least when I was young—just enough. And I admired Cheryl's brash fuck-off attitude, although her unpredictable and out-of-control behavior caused me to develop into a worrier. She might crash her car on the way home, drunk. My dad, Gary, might catch her in a lie about where she'd been. She could lose her job because of her bad temper. The cops might come and take her to jail for smoking pot or fighting with my dad. On and on.

When she had self-esteem, she was lively and unstoppable. She was the life of the party. My mom was the funniest person on Earth, always cussing and making me laugh. Her sense of humor was mean. The outgoing message on our answering machine said, "Leave a message, and fuck you." My friends all thought it was hilarious and envied me.

I don't remember her ever telling me not to do drugs. Throughout my childhood, both of my parents smoked pot. Cheryl openly admitted that she smoked weed while pregnant with me. I think she was proud of it. My parents sniffed speed too. I think their drug use is the reason why my parents split up. All the fighting and lying was amplified on drugs. They stayed out all night sometimes, doing speed and drinking. All I could think about was them ending up in jail, until I became an adolescent and began to think about exercising all the freedom their behavior provided me. At age thirteen, I got picked up by the police while I was riding around in my neighbor's van. I was drunk with some other thirteen-year-old girls, high on oregano. The cops dropped us back at my house and we never got into trouble for it because my mom and dad weren't home.

Cheryl constantly cheated on Gary. It began when I was a toddler. She abandoned my sister and me with my dad while she ran off to Nebraska with her lover. Gary took her back a few months later, but she never stopped screwing around with other men. She brought me out on her dates sometimes, while my dad was at work. One of her boyfriends took us to Catalina Island for the day when I was seven years old. She told me never to tell my dad who we were with or where we went. I followed her instructions carefully. I was her little sidekick, her accomplice.

My parents started abusing speed when I was around eleven or twelve. By my fourteenth birthday, they were out of their minds on it. I'd become bulimic and started having sex. Then my dad and I left my mom. We moved to Texas.

Cheryl went to live with some other guy. She started using heroin with this other guy, so he became her boyfriend. She went from using speed with my dad to shooting heroin and speed with her new boyfriend. I loathed this man. I came to live with them when I returned to California. I couldn't stand Texas for very long. My father made it clear that I was choosing my mom over him. He was hurt. It ended our relationship. Gary no longer wanted to be my dad after I returned to Cheryl.

The plumbing at her and her boyfriend's house was a mess. The only thing that worked in that house was sadness. I wanted to run away, but I didn't want to be a loser. I needed to finish high school. I made the best of this gloomy life. My mom was always passed out from drugs. She could barely speak half of the time. She would go crazy and fight with her loser boyfriend every few days. She had a gun and would threaten to end her life with it. She held the gun in her mouth and to her head, in front of me, many times. I would cry and tell her not to do it.

I wanted to kill myself too. A few times, I came close. I wanted to electrocute myself by tossing my radio into the bathtub with me. Thankfully, the thought of dying in the presence of my junky mother and her equally despicable boyfriend prevented me from trying. I lived through my depressing teen years. I smoked a little pot and tried speed, but I didn't want to be like my mom and dad.

As much as my real parents fought and did drugs, it was nothing compared to how much worse things became after they separated.

Both my mom and her boyfriend contracted hepatitis C. They got it from used heroin needles. It didn't stop their drug abuse. They would often pass out with lit cigarettes dangling from their mouths. As early as six or seven in the evening, they would be smacked out of consciousness. I would peek into their bedroom and glare at the two lifeless bodies on the waterbed. My heart would fill with darkness. The ash would fall and smolder on the blanket, never turning into flame.

At fourteen, my sister, who lived with her father and stepmother, took me to live with her for six months. The living conditions in our home had become unsuitable. There were needles lying around the entire house and two other junkies living there. The house was full of cigarette smoke and ashes. The carpet had too many burn holes to count. There were broken windows with tape on them. Until Cheryl could provide me a real bedroom and clean up the rest of the house, I would live with my sister.

My mom was in and out of mental health facilities as well. She had to find ways to get prescriptions for downers. Because she was so fucked-up all the time, my mom couldn't work. Her job became a full-time effort to find ways *not* to work. She compelled countless doctors and psychologists to deem her crazy and disabled. Her liver and thyroid were legitimately shot. The Valium, Vicodin, Percocet, methadone, and codeine pills she was taking made her incoherent enough to be viewed as mentally incapable. She collected worker's compensation and disability. She qualified for welfare until I turned eighteen. After she could no longer claim benefits in the name of her child, she began making a case for social security.

The fact that I returned to and graduated high school (not on "independent study") was miraculous. My mom never made me go to school. I ditched all the time. She was so out of it she never even knew when I was in the house. She let me get tattooed at fifteen. I got picked up by the cops pretty regularly for alcohol and curfew violations. I chain-smoked and drank hard alcohol until I was sick. I came and went with my friends as I pleased. It wasn't a real home for me, just a place I had to live.

My mother always had an excuse, a reason, for poisoning herself in all of these ways: to deal with the pain of being alive.

No matter how much I tried to assert my individuality, I ended up being like her. I was a rebel like her. I started to take drugs. They started out as something fun, just like they probably had for Cheryl. Then I turned to them when everything was going wrong. My mother ruined her life because she never stopped using.

Now, Cheryl lives just down the street from my sister. When we talk about it all, my sister with an even, noble tone, suggests, "Just wait until you have kids, Ori. You will understand how much it hurts when a child turns their shoulder to their mother."

Each day I get older and closer to understanding my own mortality, I think of my mother's life. She was a vibrant person once.

When I was a child I often wondered, if I am unable to take care of myself when I grow up, will all I need to do is shack up with some asshole and get wasted to survive? But I never fully fed into the legacy. Tyler had his faults, and we had our chemical fun, but the reciprocity of love was more than maybe even I give it credit. I do, however, think my mom definitely contributed to my drug addiction. She and I did drugs together until I stopped.

But only her good characteristics influenced me—gave me the balls, so to speak—to get into porn. She showed me D. H. Lawrence, Henry Miller, and Anaïs Nin when I was a kid, and my sexual life, for pleasure and for work, has been its own poetry. My mother was open about sex, positively. And she was the life of the party. In her better days, she taught me a fun way of being, by example. Her *fuck you, don't tell me what to do* attitude built me to be bold enough to start doing porn, and I thank her for that.

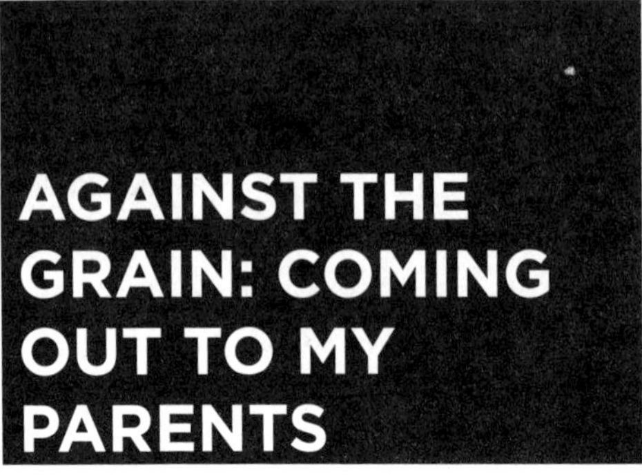

AGAINST THE GRAIN: COMING OUT TO MY PARENTS

Phoenix Askani

Phoenix Askani is a writer and former adult performer from Chicago, Illinois. She has been featured in adult movies from studios such as BurningAngel, Kink.com, Evil Angel, Naughty America, Brazzers, Devil's Films, Filly Films, Dungeon Corp, and more between 2009 and 2014. You can find more of her writing at ThoughtCatalog.com. She currently resides in Los Angeles.

As long as I can remember, I've always been the member of my immediate family to make decisions that one might consider to be against the grain. I was brought up Catholic and attended public school in our residential neighborhood just outside of Chicago, Illinois. I have two brothers, one about two years my senior and one born four years after I was. We all attended church together every Sunday and my mother also played piano for mass regularly; in fact, I believe she still does every so often. We played piano recitals. We were in the choir. My older brother and I served as altar attendants. I attended religious education classes and went on to confess to my parents that I didn't wish to be confirmed on the day of the confirmation. My name was in the pamphlet and I didn't go. I told my mother that I didn't want to lie. I continued to swim against the stream on through my adolescence.

In high school, I started listening to more punk rock and heavy metal, and quickly decided wearing mostly black was the most comfortable option for me. My parents and brothers questioned the loud music that sounded "like a screaming monkey playing garbage cans" and my dark styling options. I frequented concerts and basement shows and got picked up from a metal band's hotel after-party at 4:00 a.m. by a very frustrated father who had no idea that was his sixteen-year-old girl's first time drinking a beer.

I lost my virginity at the age of eighteen to my first serious boyfriend, a long-distance relationship that lasted just shy of a year and fizzled out the winter after I graduated from high school. I recall expressing to him on the phone that I wanted to pose nude for an "alternative" website of some sort, and he expressed his discomfort. Truthfully, I was not entirely comfortable with the idea myself yet and still beginning to explore my sexuality, but I let the idea of getting naked on the Internet swim around in my mind for two years before it actually happened. I joined an adult website as a member to make sure I knew what I was up for before I eventually clicked the page that said "Model Application." That website was BurningAngel.com.

If there's one thing I could change, it's not the fact that I started doing porn, but the fact that I wasn't honest to my parents about my intentions when I got on a plane to Los Angeles at age twenty to "model." I confided in my mother that I would be posing nude for photo sets only but I was hiding a lot of information. She knew I had an interest in modeling and had posed for friends studying photography in college, but what she did not know was that I had been posting scantily-clad photos of myself on the Internet since age nineteen on message boards and submitting them to a blog that now no longer exists. That year, I began booking more photo shoots through sites like ModelMayhem.com and posing topless or nude in photos. Through other modeling work and networking websites, I chatted with adult performers and models with varying experience. Some of those people I befriended by chance as they inspired me to do whatever I wanted with my body and just own it, and they gave me well-intentioned advice. When you have at least one person you can talk to about deciding to work in the adult industry, it makes you feel a little more at ease.

By the time I was on the phone with BurningAngel.com CEO, performer, and director, Joanna Angel (whom I now consider a good friend), discussing wardrobe options and the next day's flight, I had already told my mother that I was working for a woman and that I felt safe doing the shoot and she needn't worry, I'd be back in just a couple of days. I even showed her the website and repeated I'd only be doing photos as she scrolled over Google results that highlighted potential risks of the porn industry and stalkers. She questioned my safety, stated once the photos were up, "creeps" and the like would be able to see them, and asked if I was sure about my decision. Knowing that I'd secretly been considering it for nearly two years, I got on the plane with the intention of telling the truth after I shot my first few scenes that weekend and could speak some truth about the industry, or at least what I had experienced of it in that brief amount of time. I wasn't really given that option, but you could certainly say I set myself up for that.

I filmed my first hardcore pornographic scene in July 2009 in Los Angeles. I had a fun weekend shooting and felt amazing after shaking off my nerves and embracing my visceral side and inner exhibitionist. After shooting a few enjoyable scenes, I boarded my connecting flight ready to head back to Chicago with a new sense of confidence, as if I had truly let the beast out of its cage. It was so incredibly freeing to be naked in front of a crew and do something that felt so exhilarating and natural to me while knowing it would later be distributed and on the Internet, available to even more eyeballs. During a short layover, I charged my phone and turned it on to text my mom and let her know I was soon to board the last leg and arrive home safely. She has always been the safety first, worrywart type (I don't blame her), so I made an effort to check in with her often in an effort to ease her worries some. The glow and thrill depleted some when I received an unpleasant text message from her that read, "I know what you did."

The truth came out and it wasn't on my own terms. A member of a hardcore message board I posted on frequently knew about my interest in shooting porn and took it upon himself to find my mother on Facebook and send her my Twitter link, where my public feed included tweets that mentioned which performers I was working with that day. There was no way to dig myself out of this one except to come completely clean and face the music. I knew I was going to walk into a very uncomfortable home situation now that I was caught red-handed. Hell, I was not disowned or kicked out, but words were thrown around and my blurred memory offers up a vision of my father raising his voice—but saddened—exclaiming "You're not my daughter anymore. Why would you do this?" It pained me to know that I wasn't really prepared to talk to my father about what all of this meant to me or for my life. Our perspectives and opinions were very far apart as emotions flew through the air like torpedoes, rational or calm conversation unable to take place under these conditions until the smoke had cleared.

After less than two weeks of disagreements with my parents and continuously trying to explain to them that I was very sorry that I didn't tell the truth but I was going to make my own decisions as an adult, I decided to move in with my then-boyfriend of about a year. I had never moved out of my childhood home before then. I knew it was about time that I made a big step toward independence from the nest. I recall passing my mother in the hallway when I was home a few weeks after moving out to collect some additional things I had left behind, and she dropped the previously catty attitude that clearly came from hurt and admitted that she missed me. We embraced and I knew it would get better with time. I was certain of her unconditional love. She has a deep warmth and compassion, especially for other women, and I knew that she would eventually have to let go. Her only daughter and little girl became an adult and continued to make decisions that felt right to her. I didn't want to hurt her, although my gut reactions or opinions often differed from hers, and being myself is one thing I've always been the best at.

My friends were mostly supportive and asked a lot of questions out of excited curiosity. Some didn't expect it at all, and others knew how in-tune with my sexuality I was and had heard me speak of my desire to express it on a grander scale. I lived with my now ex-boyfriend for about a year during the time immediately after I started filming porn. He eventually begged me not to film more and was not keen on it to begin with, but initially offered me the support to try something new, possibly figuring I wouldn't continue after the first trip to Los Angeles to film. I didn't for a little while, but after about two and a half years together, we slowly grew apart and I moved out. I started making more trips to Los Angeles and eventually signed with an adult agency. I approached potential dates with the truth when questioned because I didn't want to waste my time with potential lovers that were not understanding, open-minded, and sex-positive. Two years later, I made the leap and moved to Los Angeles, knowing I would have friends, warmer weather, and job opportunities waiting for me on the West Coast.

In retrospect, I would've liked to be upfront with my parents on my own terms, but I was scared of how they'd react, of course, and worried they'd try to prevent me from leaving town. The "informer" forced me to face the reality of my decisions head on, so in a strange way I am thankful for his actions, despite how rude and intrusive they were. I've certainly moved on since that relationship, but what I'm most thankful for is the fact that I still have a relationship with my family. It wasn't all sunshine and rainbows overnight, but I've had many sit-downs with them to explain my intentions; it seems my parents gradually have come to understand that I'm an adult and I'm going to do what I wish with my body and life. I talk to my parents on the phone regularly, and when we visit with each other, we have a great time. They may never fully understand the reasons behind many of my decisions, but they show unconditional love and support with the hope that I'm happy and healthy with all I do. At a hockey game with my dad before I moved out to Los Angeles, I considered how grateful I was to have those bonding experiences with him, despite how uncomfortable things felt just a couple years before.

The more time I spent on set and at various adult conventions and related functions, the more educated I became and confident I felt talking to others about my profession. If I'm ever asked by a stranger, acquaintance, or friend about porn, I'm usually pretty transparent, but there have been times when I have omitted some details in regards to the line of work I was involved in to spare myself the interrogation. I once met a lovely woman on a short flight back to Los Angeles from shooting at Kink.com in San Francisco. She told me she was a motivational speaker and life coach and asked what I did for a living. She seemed sweet and likely wouldn't have been rude or passed judgment, but it just seemed easier to tell her

I was a model/actress than a porn starlet on her way home from a BDSM shoot, especially on such a short flight next to a complete stranger in a confined space. I wasn't entirely lying, but leaving out the part about having sex on film for money certainly paved the way to avoid awkward reactions or uncomfortable silence for the remainder of the flight.

I would recommend to any person new to the adult industry or sex work to go with their gut, but to be honest with those that they love because it's likely to save you headache or heartache later. You can become informed by asking people in the industry who work in your respective field tips and tricks for talking to others about what you do and maintaining some level of privacy in your life. It's no one's business unless you want it to be, but if you're a performer, with increased shoots and involvement in the business, your name and picture will pop up more often, and you shouldn't be surprised if someone you know confirms that they came across your work. I've been contacted by people I went to high school with that recognized me, and I've also been recognized in public at metal concerts or even driving in Los Angeles. Friends have seen thumbnails of me on tube sites. It happens. Fortunately, most people are mature enough to brush it off and ignore it.

As of April 2014, I'm now a former adult performer and decided to step away from shooting on a positive note in order to focus on other goals. The fact that I no longer film does not mean I will try to cover up my past or act like it never happened. It did, and it changed my life. I've learned so much, met so many wonderful people, and I've had the pleasure of experiencing many different fantasies in the comfort of a safe and controlled environment while fulfilling my exhibitionist desires. In an interview with the *Chicago Reader* in 2012, I stated, "I did it because I wanted to and I could." And I would do it all over again.

HARDCORE DYKECORE

Shar Rednour

Shar Rednour and wife Jackie Strano founded S.I.R. Productions that created best-selling, award-winning, and critically acclaimed movies including Bend Over Boyfriend *(with coproducer Fatale Media),* Hard Love & How to Fuck in High Heels *and* Healing Sex: A Mind-Body Approach to Healing Sexual Trauma with Staci Haines. *They've been featured in award-winner Ken Swartz's historical documentary* San Francisco: Sex and The City *among many others. Her books include* The Femme's Guide to the Universe, Virgin Territory, Starf*ckr, *and in 2015 coauthored* THE Sex & Pleasure Book: Good Vibrations Guide to Great Sex for Everyone with Dr. Carol Queen.

My dad was notorious for picking up the phone and interrupting conversations. A big, loud, macho guy who collected guns as well as Barbie dolls, he grilled steak daily but insisted he delighted in his only child's veggie burgers. He didn't let me cut my hair and his voice when angry could shake the Richter scale more than the San Andreas Fault. With a clunk and possibly a tonal beep, he picked up a handset and interrupted my mom and me on the phone. "Hey, Sharlene!"

"Yeah, Daddy?"

"Tell her, Mavis. Your mother has something to ask you."

My mom: "Well, now, did, were you on HBO?"

"Yeah, Mom, I thought I told you that. We were on—"

"Sharlene."

"Yes, Daddy?"

"You won awards, right?"

"Yeah, Dad, we did."

"Now, Mark, I read to you the email she sent," Mom began, but he interjected with that tone saying there is a right and wrong answer—maybe for some moral reason but more likely to settle a wager. "Hey, Sharlene."

"Yes," I said. No matter how old I get, I can still cop the attitudinal and impatient voice of a teenager. "Yes, Daddy."

"You hardcore?"

"Mark!"

"Yes, Daddy, I am."

"Ha! I told you, Mavis." I could hear his smile 3,000 miles away. "If Sharlene does something, she does it hardcore. Bye." He hung up.

From Dictionary.com:

<ex>hard-core
[hahrd-kawr, -kohr]
adjective

1. unswervingly committed; uncompromising; dedicated:
   a hard-core segregationist.
2. relating to or containing sexually arousing depictions
   that are very graphic or explicit:
   hard-core pornography.
   Compare soft-core.
3. being so without apparent change or remedy; chronic:
   hard-core inflation; hard-core unemployment.
4. very intense or extreme:
   hard-core workouts at the gym.
5. Usually, hardcore, noting or relating to the music
   genre hardcore, or the subculture, clothing style, etc.,
   associated with it: hardcore T-shirts and jeans.
6. Being brazen, in your face, authentic and challenging.

As in, Sharlene Rednour.

While Dad laughed at his victory and went back to his TV show, Mom had some concerns.

"Sharlene." When your mom says your name a certain way, no words are needed.

"You know, Mom, my movies are really fun and authentic. People thank me and Jackie for representing them [unsaid: dyke porn] on screen. No one gets to see lesbian sex made by lesbians instead of some Playboy version. It's a big deal. I am proud of my work."

She said, "Well, I know you are—"

I wasn't defensive, but I did think fast on my feet, and I am a truthful person, so I simply told one of my truths: "You and Dad helped make me this way. You could be a little proud too, you know. You influenced me. I am good at my job, Mom. Healthy sexuality is important. It can even save lives, and you and Dad were always so honest and open about sexuality. You raised me knowing you loved each other and that you weren't ashamed of sex." I let that sink in.

"Oh. Hm." She thought about it. "Well, Sharlene, I never thought about it that way. I guess we did, didn't we. Okay." She sounded like she was smiling too now.

My parents bought one of the first satellite dishes produced for consumers. It was huge, nothing like the little dishes that sit on rooftops today. This gigantic, white disc looked like it had fallen from the sky via a 007 spy movie and sat in the backyard of our five-acre field so we could watch more than four TV channels. We were going beyond ABC, NBC, CBS, and public television. MTV was brand new, created for me and my generation. And yet, what did we watch as a family? The Playboy Channel's *Great American Strip-Off*, hosted by Lyle Wagner, the costar of Linda Carter's *Wonder Woman*! My best friends, my parents, and I chimed in with our opinions on who should win each week as six men and six women from all across America stripped and teased and danced in competition against each other.

My parents were not educated academics or hippies or taboo-breaking swingers of the 1970s. They were relatively average blue-collar, working-class, working-for-the-weekend people. On these weekends they had fun barbequeing with family and friends, boating and water-skiing, waxing Daddy's fast cars, tinkering on motorcycles, playing loud country music on my daddy's six speakers. Mom was usually in a halter or bikini top with shorts, her long red hair teased up on top and hanging long in back; she couldn't let go of the '60s beehive, yet relished the long soft drapes of the new decade.

They were open and not shameful about sex and sexuality. I was raised knowing they had sex, that they liked feeling attractive and sexy, and that they valued sex in a relationship. That value was instilled in me. I was almost grown before I realized that other people's parents didn't go to bed and have sex after the weather segment on the 10:00 news. I presumed that marriage went hand in hand with a healthy and happy sex life. My parents weren't gross or sleazy about it. It was just like anything else that was part of what we valued in our family. As a matter of fact, their lack of mystery and openness made me feel very safe and protected. I didn't really think about what sex was. I didn't care much; it was for grown-ups and obviously made them very happy and easygoing.

A good parallel example to their sexual attitudes and how they were conveyed to me is driving: My parents also valued driving—not being merely a good driver, but a highly skilled driver. My mother was an excellent driver; my father should have been a racecar driver. When I was young, I loved riding around with him, letting him be the grown-up expert on all things automotive while I simply enjoyed the fun rides. Driving was clearly for the adults and not me, but I could tell it was important. When I got to a certain age, my dad started teaching—narrating—what he was doing as he drove, and after a few more years this narration expanded into flat-out orders: "Sharlene, don't you ever do a U-turn from the shoulder. That's how teenagers die." Or: "Sharlene, here's how to lose someone. Watch the stoplight, wait until it's yellow . . ." Eventually the day came for me to be a great, skilled driver.

My dad, and mom too, felt that my being a good driver would save me from more than car crashes. Without telling me directly, they felt that a girl with her own car would be safe from date rape or any other deplorable teenage boy antics. A woman needs her own wheels—that is, her own power. My dad would bellow, "Sharlene, you drive. You are the driver. No other assholes are the driver, and you don't ride with anyone else. Do you understand me?" I think that example parallels learning about sex: safety, protection, and skill.

Ever since I was a child, I thought, when I'm a mom I will do this or that thing like my parents. For instance, I knew I would say "I love you" all the time; my parents say "I love you" daily. I also, of course, had a list of things that I would not do. I would not put peas in soup. And when it came to sex, I knew that (1) I would have a great sex life and not be like the sad parents of some of my friends; and (2) I would be a parent that a growing child could say anything to. I'd been able to ask my parents about anything from birth control to what popping a cherry meant, and my kid would be able to do that too.

I've always been out there. I wonder what phrase was used to describe me when I was six or eight or ten. Most of my teachers loved me, except for those who didn't question the status quo. Most adults, from relatives to teachers, thought I was fun, very kind, and unique. Unique. Walks to the beat of my own drummer. I was and am gay. Sappho spoke to me loudly. Lesbos was my landing page. I was born with an upside-down pink triangle on my forehead as a birthmark. My Barbies lived in love communes where they dated and married each other, although the one with a permanent ponytail coming out of the top of her head was named Linda and she had a dominant relationship with Ken, keeping him topless as a dog-boy. In my whole life, only two men have ever piqued my interest. On the Kinsey scale of 0 to 6, I am a 5.75 without even trying. I am the first person to love a bisexual—most of my best friends are bi. Side note: I argue that since I like butch women and femmes of any stripe it makes me more bi than femmes who like cis or trans men and butch women.

When you're a super out queer person, there is no turning back. I moved to San Francisco and let my girlfriend, who didn't want to hold my hand in public, dump me.

I never stuck my nose up at people who have sex or strip or are sexy for money. I know it's a perfectly good way to make a living, and I have always supported friends, relatives, and strangers in the business. If there were an alternative world where I could have stripped or masturbated for women for money, I would have. Jackie and I helped start that alternative-world option with our work. But I have never liked money enough, or to be precise, been motivated enough by money to do anything that's on a high level of fakery. When I worked at a bakery for minimum wage, I loved serving sugared goods to people. I got lots of compliments and had customers who came specifically to see me on my shift. On the other hand, I was fired from McDonald's.

All this is to say that I couldn't have been in the closet with my family even if I wanted to. I fretted over being gay, figuring out that I really was and admitting it to myself. I fretted over my fundamental religious fanaticism (which was not from my parents; my mother is a moderate Methodist) and left formal Christianity in order to be myself. I did all this and more, and came out to my parents. It wasn't easy, but to my mind, there was no choice. I couldn't have not done it. I don't mean to come off as amazingly strong and cool. I did fret. I cried, worried, argued with myself, hated myself, and more. But all that diffused once I was out during the short time before I came out to my parents; at the time it seemed lengthy, but it wasn't. Eventually I moved an hour away to college, then five hours away to another college, and finally cross-country. All so I could be myself and find others like me.

What does this have to do with porn? Everything. Highly valuing honesty affects all my decisions. My personal experience of being queer in relation to the intersection (more like overpass) of sex and money. Having a big personality affects them as well. Once a friend gave me a sit-down about how I overwhelm her and others at times, and I retorted, "How in the hell do you think I feel?" Years later, I realized that she thought I was referring to our friendship or the interaction, but what I meant was, "If you think I overwhelm others some of the time with our relatively few exchanges in the course of a friendship, then imagine how often I overwhelm myself with all these dialogues running through my head 24/7 of never-resting morals, motives, agendas, visions, brainstorms, and ideas?"

I may sound carefree or tough, but actually, I set things up so I did what I wanted but in a way that no one could disappoint me. I couldn't get kicked out because I supported myself. I couldn't lose my cousins' friendships because I didn't live in their town and talk with them daily. I couldn't get kicked out of church by my God because I decided my God lived somewhere else.

Also note that all these reflections are of my childless years. Now that I'm a mom, do I tell porn stories on the playground to other parents? Of course not. Before kids I wouldn't have scrutinized each person before discussing work, "I am who I am!" being my battle cry. Now strangers are sized up before I decide someone could be a real friend and then we might talk about it. Part of this is everyday life with kids; you're thrown together with parents because your kids have something in common, not you. And part of it is specific to my background. Did I quit video production and open a cupcake business so that we could adopt? Yes. And when someone working in the adult industry asks my advice about becoming a parent or someone who is a parent asks me about going into the industry, I don't have pat answers but instead listen to their situation. Many factors can affect your life's decisions, including prejudiced exes, adoption, and the state or county you live in, among others.

Recently, my mother moved in with us. Cleaning out boxes in the rafters of her barn I found files of all my correspondence to her. First letters, then emails that she'd printed and saved. I wrote so earnestly to her and Dad about every step of our company S.I.R. (Sex, Indulgence, and Rock-n-Roll) Productions.

When I was going to perform live on stage and would get a set of nerves, I'd call Mom. Sometimes I timidly, barely gave the perimeters of the event (it's a benefit for AIDS, or at a dive bar or at a fancy university). Without knowing any details of what I was about to do, she would say, "Well, Darlin', I hate to hear you get yourself so worked up and I just wish you wouldn't. You always get up there and do just fine, and that's exactly what's going to happen tonight." Her confidence was immediate comfort, like ice on a burn. If my mommy says it's so then, yeah, it's so. I'm so big, I'm so much, I'm so overwhelming—but not to her. Her honesty and knowledge of me is my humility. And humility is safety. The comfort of the truth.

Now I am a mom with my own kids. I recognize that I have that same power to provide immediate comfort. I sometimes do a Mavis play-by-play. I repeat the mantra: In our family, we talk. In our family, honesty is important. In our family, we can tell each other anything. In our family, we aren't scared of love.

Our oldest child is grown now and he never really thought or cared about our hard-core work. He is gay, he was a dancer for years and has a sensitive artistic nature, so maybe that influenced him. I don't know. He just never cared. Our two younger children don't know anything about the adult industry. What they do know is that in our family, we believe in education, doing the right-for-you thing, individuality, standing up for anyone being bullied, standing against racism and homophobia, and being a support system for trans people (in the language of that age, a kind friend or having their back on the playground). We make a point to show we don't slut shame, and when someone makes a derogatory remark about strippers or working women, I openly state my opinion in a fun and neutral tone. I take questions on all these topics and more. We've had conversations around twerking, Beyoncé, and lap dancing. We've discussed economics, personal joy, personal job satisfaction, and not having shame about our bodies. We talk about how it's complicated to talk about certain names that are derogatory to many people, yet others might use them as reclamation. I think and hope that our attitudes prepare them for when they know about our past work so that, like our oldest child, it won't be a big deal.

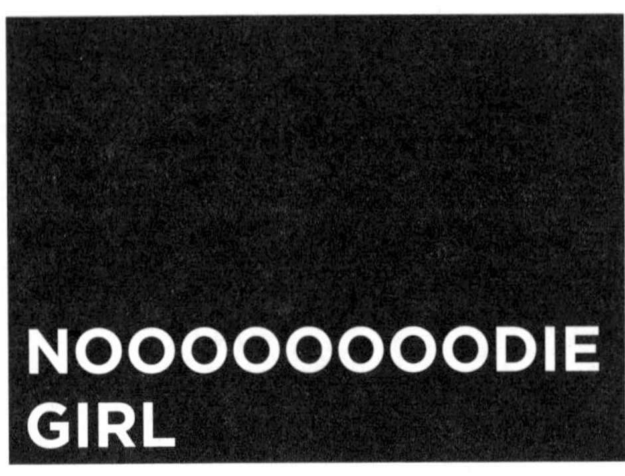

NOOOOOOOODIE GIRL

Stoya

Stoya is an adult performer, writer, and master of avoiding pants. Her writing has been published by the Guardian, *the* New York Times, *and the* New Inquiry. *She maintains a blog at GraphicDescriptions.com and recommends you refrain from Googling her at work.*

Murphy's Law of Inappropriate Behavior states that if you make a habit of taking your clothes off in public, eventually everyone in your family (including members so distant they share less DNA with you than a chimpanzee does with a cuttlefish) will somehow stumble upon documentation of what you're up to.

My grandmother is a very smart woman, and I'd been dodging the question of what I did for a living for at least three professionally naked years. I really had been meaning to tell her about my job before she found out from the television or a newspaper, but I thought I'd do it when I was ready. "Ready" consistently being defined as any time except for right now.

So I was completely unprepared when she called and said, "Your mother says that you're sort of like a model. I don't know what that means because if you were a model she would just say you're a model, and you're a bit short for that anyway. No offense, dear. What do you do with your days?"

I wished I'd discussed this inevitability with my mom or had some legitimate reason to get off the phone. My usually dodgy cell service was clear as a bell. I worried: What if I failed at easing her into the whole idea of my career in pornography and she had a heart attack, leaving me accidentally guilty of grand-matricide?

What if she decided to just cut me out of her life? More pressing—how was I supposed to explain what a modern pornographic actress was to a woman who doesn't know how to work a cell phone and still had typesetting tools laying around from her days in advertising?

"Well, um, do you remember Bettie Page and pinup? What I do is kind of like pinup but more explicit. Like, with no clothes on."

"Oh! So you're a nooooooodie girl!"

Either I was hallucinating or that statement had been delivered in a positive tone.

"Yes, ma'am. But, uh, pop culture is a bit more edgy now than things were in the '50s, so I have actual sex with people and it goes on video or DVD."

"In the mooooving pic-tures! Do you enjoy it?"

"I have fun. It's always interesting. I only do things that I want to do, with people that I want to do them with. It's good."

"Well then, that's all very nice and I'm glad to hear you're doing something you like."

Since the conversation was going so well, I figured we might as well get everything over with at once.

"There's something else I should probably tell you while we're on this subject."

"Ohhh?"

In addition to being smart, my grandmother is an incredibly expressive woman. You know that Mehrabian's rule thing about how communication is 93 percent nonverbal? In my grandma's case, 99 percent of communication is pure vocal inflection. There's something in the way she draws out the vowels. They become a whole adventure.

This particular "ohhh" had started out some distance into curiosity land, passed over the gosh-what-else-could-top-the-last-thing mountains, and settled on the patiently-waiting-to-hear-more plains.

"I'm using your name as my stage name. Well, I'm using the Americanized diminutive. The point is, I'm using part of your name as my stage name."

"Vera? That's not very sexy."

"No, ma'am. I mean, I think Vera could actually be quite marketable with the current neoburlesque scene, but I'm using Stoya."

"Oh? Oh."

The first oh was surprised, and the second oh sounded less than enthused. In my head, I stared into the largest imaginable pit of uh-oh. I wondered if she could hear my heart pounding over the phone. My left hand frantically picked at the stitches on the hem of my shirt. I became concerned that I might be the one to have the heart attack, and I wasn't going to die without one last cigarette. I lit up, inhaled and exhaled, inhaled and exhaled again. Finally, I couldn't take the extended silence any longer.

"Gramma?"

"I was just thinking. I hope none of the men at the nursing home get us confused and try to put my feet behind my head. I don't bend that way anymore."

Apparently, since the death of her last husband, she'd acquired three boyfriends. Because it takes that many of them to keep up with her. My stressful and dramatic coming-out-to-Grandma moment turned into a farce because although the promiscuity gene may have skipped a generation, it most definitely runs in my family.

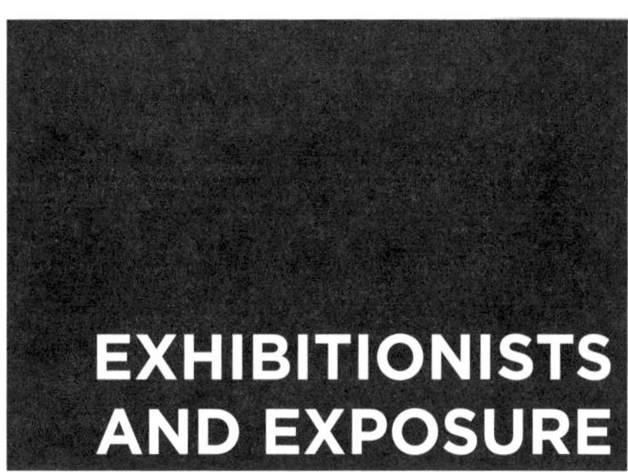

EXHIBITIONISTS AND EXPOSURE

Tina Horn

Tina Horn is a writer, teacher, and media maker. She produces and hosts the sexuality podcast Why Are People Into That?! Her first book, Love Not Given Lightly, *is a collection of nonfiction stories about sex workers; she is currently writing a book about sexting etiquette for Quiver Press. Her writing appears in* Vice, Nerve, *and* Best Sex Writing 2015, *and she was the cocreator/director of the Feminist Porn award–winning Queer-Porn.tv. Tina once sold a golden dildo to Beyoncé. Find her on Twitter @TinaHornsAss and at TinaHorn.net.*

In 2013, at the very first Feminist Porn Conference, I curated and moderated a panel called "Being Out Now: How Performers Navigate Sexual Morality and Media Representation." For two hours, five other queer porn performers and I discussed the stigma we face when disclosing to our families, dates, friends, and communities that we had been paid to have sex on camera. Some of our experiences were constructive, but many were dispiriting. We shared stories of excommunication, stalking, slut shaming, ridicule, nonconsensual outing, and being fired, all in response to our honesty about our jobs.

Afterward, many professional academics and other conference attendees approached us to say how impressed they were that we had shared our intimate selves in the interest of truth and understanding. We all looked at one another nonplussed. Of course we bared ourselves in public! We're porn stars. That's what we do!

Frankly, I am not the world's most prolific porn performer. You could count the scenes I've done on two (fapping) hands. At this point, I'd rather be moderating academic panels about porn than making it. I have, however, spent nearly a decade devoting myself to numerous jobs that employ my naked body and wicked mind: professional BDSM with private clients, explicit kink education workshops, producing and directing explicit art. I'm very proud of that work, and I'm very lucky to have had safe, lucrative platforms for my shamelessness.

Yet every time I submit a resume, CV, and cover letter to an editorial or educational job listing for which I am qualified, I have to figure out how to spin the story of the work I did for most of my twenties.

The reason it can be challenging to come out as a sex worker is that in order to be a sex worker in the first place, you have to put aside the neurotic voice in your head that says:

You'll regret this.
Your father will be disappointed in you.
Your mother will be scared of you.
Your dates will be disgusted by you.
You will be forced out of the jobs you want.
No one will let you near children again.
You have to decide that the adventure and the money are worth it.

About a year into being a professional dominatrix, when I knew it wasn't a lark but rather the best paid improv gig in town, I decided to come out to my parents. I figured I'd get up the nerve and get it out of the way.

My mom and dad are very different people. Dad's face got all twisted, and he said something about remembering one woman he'd known at one point whom he thinks did sex work kinda and she had issues then so I shouldn't do it now (#daditude).

Mom asked, "What's a dominatrix?"

It didn't go horribly, but it didn't exactly go well. So I've retreated back into the closet somewhat. It has become a "don't ask, don't tell" subject in my family.

When I started doing sex work on camera in the Bay Area queer and kinky porn scenes, I knew I wasn't going to bother telling my parents. I justified this to myself. They knew I was supporting myself being a sexual extrovert; they didn't need to know the details. It may be appropriate to tell your parents that you're sexually active, but it's not all that necessary to tell them specifically that you really, really love it up the butt.

I'm not ashamed of what I do. But I am terrified to my core that the people I love will be ashamed of me for doing it.

The saddest part about this is that my parents raised me to be honest with them. For the most part, I have been, and suffered very little judgment. Nothing makes me happier than making them proud. Yet I couldn't call my mom when I won Feminist Porn Awards, and I couldn't tell my dad I was saving more money than I had ever before in my life.

Coming out to your family as a sex worker isn't all that different from coming out to your family as queer. We've all heard someone proclaim, "Oh, I'm okay with it, as long as *my* child isn't gay." Even people who are politically and socially comfortable with sex work have emotionally complicated reactions to someone in their family identifying with that work. Sex work sets off insidious moral panic that is validated everywhere. For this reason, many people feel that their aversion is justified; instead of what it actually is, which is a big conflated tangle of misogyny, homophobia, moral imperialism, and most likely also hypocritical envy.

Many incredible people are studying the rise of feminist porn. However, a fact that isn't being discussed enough by well-meaning fans, academics, and journalists is that the production of feminist porn requires feminist sexual labor. It must be a key tenet of the feminist porn movement to dismantle the whorephobia that oppresses sexual laborers.

The thing to remember about being a feminist porn star is that the stigma is exactly the same as being a nonfeminist porn star.

Here is something that will never happen: The administration is going to fire you because they have discovered you are naked on the Internet (and not, like, socially sanctioned "wearing nothing but a heteronormative bikini basically advertising Bacardi on Myspace" naked—more like, "you had the nerve to get paid to be naked" naked).

You're in the office getting the pink slip, and you protest, "Why, Sir or Madame! You don't understand. It was Feminist Porn!"

And they say, "Oh! Well, why didn't you say so? How embarrassing for us. How about we give you a raise and just forget this little misunderstanding ever happened?"

People claim all of this is evidence that people shouldn't do sex work. On the contrary, social microaggressions about whores are more traumatizing than anything that has ever happened to me in the sex industry. When I perform in porn, I make myself vulnerable in ways that I have negotiated, that I have control over. The judgments that people make when they find out are beyond my control.

We need to keep fighting for ethical porn production and sex worker rights. In the meantime, we need to accept that media representations and social conceptions of sex workers are not changing. The big red "W" that goes on your forehead when you out yourself, or are nonconsensually outed, still closes the same doors it always has.

I chose "Being Out Now" as the session I wanted to lead at the Feminist Porn Conference because it has been one of the most difficult things in my life to figure out. I wanted help and support but I also wanted to raise awareness. I want to be bold, but I don't want to be stupid. I want to be honest, but I'm terrified of not being taken seriously.

Like many sex workers, I'm a professional exhibitionist who is terrified of being exposed.

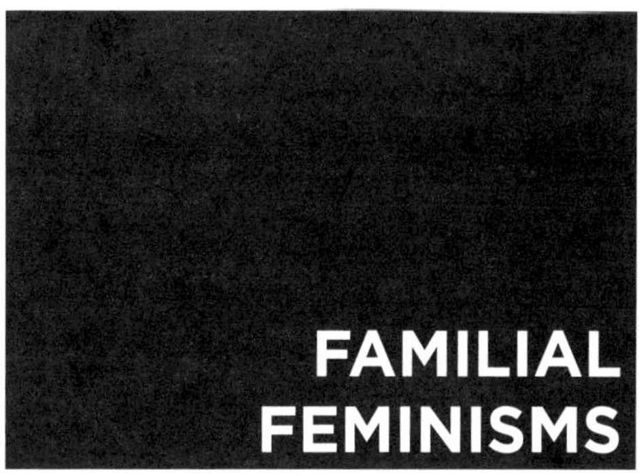

Tobi Hill-Meyer

Tobi Hill-Meyer made her filmmaking debut with Doing It Ourselves: The Trans Women Porn Project, *winning a Feminist Porn award for Emerging Filmmaker and being named #3 in Velvet Park Media's list of the 25 Most Significant Queer Women in 2010. She is a multiracial trans woman with over a decade of experience working with feminist and LGBTQ organizations on a local, state, and federal level, having served on several boards and offering support as a strategic consultant, currently serving on the board of the Gender Justice League. With her background in activism, she uses her media production company, Handbasket Productions, to create stories and entertainment that reflect community needs and values. Most of her work can be found at HandbasketProductions.com or DoingItOnline.com*

One day when we were out shopping, my mom casually asked, "So what are you going to San Francisco for?" once we got back to the car.

The question hung in the air for two, three, maybe four seconds as I searched my mind for an appropriate answer. Previously, I had always avoided outright lies by going with half-truths—mentioning some other thing I was going to do on the trip without bringing up porn. But it wasn't pride season, my annual board meeting for LGBT advocacy organization COLAGE wasn't for another couple months, I didn't have a performance, and I was only going to be there for a day or two to wrap up the final shoot of *Doing It Ourselves: The Trans Women Porn Project*. It was a shoot I'd been trying to schedule for almost a year, and due to the timing, there wasn't any chance to visit friends or family.

So after a long pause, I finally said, "I'm, um, making a feminist porn film."

I must have been eleven or twelve when my moms first caught me with porn. It was a floppy disc containing 1.3 megabytes of grainy downloaded photos along with a ten- or twenty-page printout of sci-fi BDSM stories in small text that I had hidden in my closet. They then sat me down for a rather mortifying discussion about how unrealistic porn is, how it sets up unfair expectations of women, and how it depicts a life where sex is all that matters. They told me stories of protesting porn in the '70s and told me about the infamous *Hustler* cover with a woman being run through a meat grinder.

I understood exactly what they were saying, but their arguments felt off, like a reflex that didn't quite match the situation. Of course the sex stories I was reading were unrealistic; it was set in space ships and on extraterrestrial planets. I wasn't going to start believing that women ought to work for interstellar spy agencies interrogating captured space marines.

All jokes aside, I knew my parents were right that there was sexism in those stories and pictures—even the women in positions of power were playing out sexist assumptions and stereotypes of femininity—but I already knew that. Especially in the photographs, it wasn't hard for me to spot the influences of sexism. My parents had raised me in a feminist household. They raised me to think critically about media. This was nothing new. I was used to seeing the influence of sexism in TV shows like *Seinfeld* and *Friends*, in my video game magazines, and even in my textbooks for school. Yet my parents never sat me down for a talk like this over the sexism in any of those other forms of media. They had singled porn out as special, different than other kinds of media.

Of course, at the time I didn't say any of this. I was just grateful they had only read far enough to realize it was about sex and then put it down. I didn't want to have a whole other conversation about the power dynamics in my chosen sex stories. However, the discrepancy between how my parents treated porn compared to other forms of media stuck with me throughout my teenage years.

In high school, as a part of being on the competitive speech and debate team, I had a chance to choose my own topic for an informative speech. I chose feminist perspectives on porn. I dove into the research, reading Dworkin and MacKinnon, Califia and Queen, Women Against Pornography, Annie Sprinkle, and more. I created a presentation that was part theater, putting excerpts from their work in conversation with each other as I did my best to embody each one of them, their values and concerns. I even placed in two tournaments, winning a sixth-place and first-place trophy.

The process of researching, writing, practicing, adjusting, and competing with this piece took almost a whole year. During that time, I'd often discuss the issues with my parents. For them, talking about theories on pornography was very different than discussing my own sexuality. They encouraged the discussion of theory. So, over the dinner table we'd discuss the difference between pornography and erotica, the value of banning porn and the value of creating your own, the harm of using state power for censorship, and the harm of freely distributed depictions of eroticized violence, racism, and misogyny.

I'm sure you wouldn't be surprised to find out that arguments that concluded the solution to bad porn isn't no porn but to try and make better porn resonated with me. But my parents were always skeptical of that idea. So seven years later, when I finally told them I was making porn, I was apprehensive about their response.

However, as soon as the discussion shifted from an ongoing academic debate to the reality of my life, things changed. I saw none of the judgment I feared in their eyes. Encouraged, I explained to them the problems of mainstream trans porn and that my film was an attempt to allow trans women the opportunity to represent their sexuality the way they wanted to have it represented.

"Well, we trust that whatever you're doing is good," they said. And for them, it was just that simple.

They didn't ask me if I was performing in my film or just directing. I also chose not to tell them that what I knew about problems in mainstream trans porn came in part from my own personal experiences as a porn performer. I would tell them eventually, but in that moment I was happy with taking smaller steps toward that conversation.

A little over a year later, my film was finished and was being considered for a Feminist Porn award. When I mentioned it to my parents, they excitedly told me that I should text them to let them know if I win. When the moment came and I walked off the stage, elated, I made my way to the back of the crowd, stepped into the stairwell, and sent them both a text.

I didn't find out until after I got home that one of my moms was off visiting family at the time. Apparently, my cousins, aunt, uncle, and my grandfather were all around when she got my text, and she had been so excited for me that, without stopping to think about it, she announced my award to everyone around her.

I wish I could have been there to see their reactions. My mom tells me that they were all supportive and proud of me. I suppose being told, "Your granddaughter/niece/cousin just won Emerging Filmmaker of the Year from the Feminist Porn Awards" might be a little easier to take than, "She is a porn star." They don't have to imagine me fucking on film or think of all of the stereotypes and assumptions associated with that. Still, knowing that they are proud of me and what I do means a great deal.

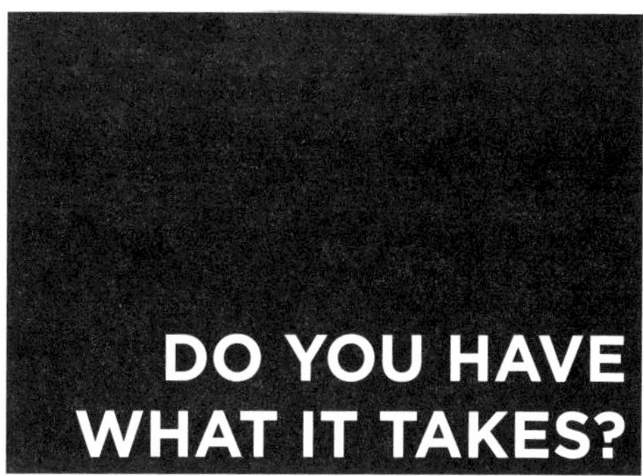
DO YOU HAVE
WHAT IT TAKES?

Verta

Art school reject/college dropout/aspiring adult entertainer, Verta is all compulsive energy searching for an outlet. No amount of previous shark wrestling experience or hydraulic rescue equipment can pry her teeth out of the flesh of her aspirations. She can be found on Twitter @ perVerta_. Best when wild caught. Do not attempt to domesticate.

Names have been changed to protect the identity of the people and shows within.

I remember when I realized I was bisexual. I was excited. I was young enough to know that it was unusual; I was too young to know that it might be illicit. I went to my mother.

"Mom," I loudly proclaimed, "I like girls."

She didn't look up. She didn't hesitate or reflect. "No, you don't," she immediately replied.

That is how I came out as bisexual, the entire conversation. It was all so very inconsequential; my mother doesn't remember it happening. I will never forget it.

I spent a year obsessively researching the adult entertainment industry. I started using a Twitter account that previously sat virtually dormant and ignored for years. I followed my favorite porn stars. I paid close attention to the production moratoriums. I watched videos on YouTube of porn stars explaining the industry. I read interviews from people who had left the industry. I wanted to know everything. I spoke with my friends and significant other about my findings. I had lengthy and heated conversations with my significant other about the porn industry. He didn't care and he didn't understand why I cared. It is obvious, as it usually is in hindsight; I was on the threshold of chasing another dream.

My significant other and I broke up. It was inevitable. I packed up everything I owned, rented a minivan with his help, and drove, alone, from White Bear Lake, Minnesota, to Yuba City, California. Several people asked what I planned to do once I got to California, and I jokingly responded, "Porn." The answer was met with chuckles and, "That's so Verta." We all knew I wasn't joking.

None of the research I'd done on pornography taught me anything about actually entering the adult entertainment field. The closest I'd come to adult entertainment was a stripping gig I held for three weeks, which ended in a rock-bottom nightmare I'm still clawing my way out of. Fun fact: An ex I lived with at the time had a rather large and unnecessary fit once I started stripping; he tried to throw me out in the middle of winter, called the police when I refused to leave, and told them I was a prostitute. Although my phone is filled with pictures of me in various states of undress and sexual positions, I had no professional photos to send out. My imagined savior came in the form of a Twitter page for a reality show promising to make a porn star of the winner. I applied via their website and, at their request, posted nude photos and taunts and tagged their page. I didn't start a separate account for my "persona," as they suggested. It seemed, in a word, antithetical to what I was looking for. I didn't expect to be able to hide pursuing a porn career from anyone, and I absolutely did not want to. My mother follows me on Twitter. I don't care. I played along and, when the time came, I made the eight-hour drive from Northern California to the Palm Springs area.

Shooting for the show began the morning following my arrival. As we lined up single-file to enter the house, I thought, "I don't want to do this." I'd met most of the people who were also auditioning, and they were the type of people you'd expect to audition for a reality show. I am not saying this as a negative; they were all very nice, fun people to be around. I simply do not view myself as reality television material. I wanted to do porn. This was not that.

When I got around to reading the contract for shooting, I told myself, "I'm not doing this." I didn't see any of the other contestants actually read the contract, but it seemed pretty standard for what you'd expect for shooting reality TV. I'm fairly certain I am not allowed to disclose the contents, but it induced an eye roll and solidified my position. I spoke with Steve Stone* (an agent present during shooting) and told him I would gladly finish out the day, but I had no interest in continuing with the competition. He told me not to tell anyone I intended to leave. Exhausted, I could not stop drinking coffee. I had coffee jitters through all of my interviews. I cannot accurately count how many times I was asked, "Do you have [what it takes]?" But I can say I got very sick of hearing it.

The audition for the show, where you reveal your sexual superpower, what makes you deserving of being a contestant, went rather well for me. I confessed to a lot of things, and I'm interested to see how the people involved respond, if they ever see the show. I honestly don't know that I would encourage them to, not out of embarrassment, simply because nothing was what I thought it to be. Steve appeared enthusiastic about the audition, and I finally told the producers and director I was not staying. They told me I was incredible, and the judges discussed my audition for ten minutes. I was flattered. I am still flattered. They filmed me asking one of the judges, a well-known porn star, for advice. Her advice was, "Be yourself." If that's the only guidance you need going into porn, I certainly didn't need to be told. After my exit interview, Steve assured me he would have a contract for me. I celebrated, with banners and confetti, in my mind. I thought, "*Finally*. I'm in." I will spend my entire life writing odes and sonnets to how avidly wrong I can be.

My friends were very supportive. They congratulated me on getting out of being on a reality television show and getting into the porn industry because they knew that was what I wanted. I called the woman I was a nanny for and we laughed about things that happened at the auditions. Many of my friends shared concerns and nearly all of them told me to be careful, but no one questioned what I was doing. I don't surround myself with yes-men. My friends have their own opinions, and I'm sure none of them share my enthusiasm about entering the adult entertainment industry. I am very lucky to have friends who know that when I want something, I will stop at nothing to get it, and they would be suicidal to stand in my way.

Before I continue, I need to make this very clear: I do not wish to bad-mouth Steve. The agency he represents is a respected agency. Steve is a very nice gentleman. I hold no ill-will against anyone involved. At the time of my writing this, I am still being told I could have a future with this agency. Although I do not necessarily believe it to be true, I wish to be as respectful as possible while also being completely honest.

Steve Stone was nearly impossible to contact. I am equally, if not more, impossible to discourage. I sent emails and photos (not professional) to other agencies. I applied to sites such as Hustler. I received nothing but denials, with no explanations, even when I asked for explanations or to be told what I was doing wrong so that I may improve my approach. I'm sure this is normal. When Steve finally contacted me, he told me he had shoots for me, but I would have to wait until after the holidays. My relief was palpable. I only needed to employ some patience.

The holidays passed and I tried, once again, to contact Steve. I called. I texted. I emailed. I raged to any of my friends who would listen that this industry was shockingly unprofessional. I sent Steve an email pleading to be told anything, including whether or not he thought I could actually make it.

I got my answer. It was, substantially, "You're beautiful, but you're not white enough."

Verbatim, he intimated, "Take a look at all the major porn tube sites. That's a great indication of what's hot/selling in the industry. Count how many exotic (black/Asian/etc.) models you see. Unfortunately, not a lot because that's not what people are buying." That comes directly from the email. After so many assurances he'd have work for me, after being told he had two shoots lined up, after being ignored, this was what it came to. I cried. I was sitting next to my best friend/roommate in an urgent care waiting room. I handed her my phone so she could read the email. I covered my face with my jacket and I silently sobbed. I'm not ashamed to admit how much that hurt.

What I loved so much about the idea of doing porn is there

is no typical porn star. They're all humans, from different backgrounds, whose common denominator is exhibitionism. To me, having sex for money was not at the top of my list of reasons for going into this industry. All I wanted was to enter a community of people who Get It.

"Why don't you fix up your resume and get a real job? Apply at the Backroom Boutique," my best friend suggested. All I heard was, "Now that your dream has been crushed, why don't you face your worst nightmare and work retail?" No, thanks.

"God is trying to steer you away from porn, B," my former significant other joked in a text message, after I sent him a screenshot of the email. I still don't find that funny.

My friends have withdrawn their support as they've seen the reality of my aspirations crumble in racial defeat. I am a stunning mixture of African American, French, Irish, and Mexican. I am neither proud nor ashamed of that; I simply am. I won't be told that's something people don't want to see.

I went into this industry. I opened the door and I shouted, "I'm here to do porn!" No one looked up. And the collective response was, "No, you aren't."

Once I've realized myself, I am there: graffitied in Sharpie and blood as a bold declaration. It cannot be erased. It cannot be painted over. No one tells me who I am or what I'm going to do. I still love girls, and yes: I'm going to be a porn star.

COMING HARD, COMING OUT: PRIVACY, EXHIBITIONISM, & RUNNING FOR PARLIAMENT

Zahra Stardust

Zahra Stardust is the 2014 Feminist Porn Awards Heartthrob of the year, 2014 Adult Industry Awards Best Porn Actress, and 2012 Eros Shine Awards Best Adult Star. She is an Australian Penthouse Pet and PhD candidate, writing her dissertation on the legal regulation of pornography. Her films combine art, porn, and politics, and have screened at festivals around the world. She loves fisting, body fluids, and intimate encounters with strangers.

"Porn Star Runs for Lord Mayor," the headlines said, alongside a photograph of me in full fuchsia and black latex with hot pink PVC flogger. If I was going to come out, I may as well do it in style.

I'm quite sure my parents knew all along.

I started taking my clothes off in the supermarket when I was three years old.

My mom found my first pair of six-inch stripper heels in my bedroom when I was twenty.

At the time, I tried hard to convince her they were for a fancy dress party. In hindsight, I don't know why I bothered. I was completely transparent and a bad liar. My parents kept wanting to come visit me at this twenty-four-hour café where I supposedly worked.

I never actually sat down and had that conversation with them. I didn't need do. Being a shameless exhibitionist, my family eventually found out through newspaper articles, magazines, and next-door neighbors. Besides, there was always my unexplained suitcases, my garish makeup, DD cups fresh from Thailand.

What can I say? I am a lifer in the sex industry. I can't keep my mouth shut about how much I love my work.

In 2009, I abandoned a legal career to run for Parliament with the Australian Sex Party. At the time, it caused somewhat of a scandal. My employer issued a formal media statement, appearing in *Lawyers Weekly*—presumably they felt the need to explain how a person of such disrepute ended up working for a top-tier firm.

Hot on the heels of my escape from the legal profession, I spent my time wisely. I walked on people in stilettos. I undressed upside down on trapeze. I pulled pearls out of my vagina. I used cucumbers and Barbie dolls as dildos. We did X-rated double tricks in people's garages that audiences described as "adult Cirque du Soleil." I dressed in latex and learned anal fisting and cock-and-ball torture. I rode in limousines and hummers. I ejaculated liters of fluid and screened it at film festivals. I trained to hold my entire body out sideways on a pole.

And I wanted to tell everybody how fabulous it was! It was obvious: I needed to share the love!

We began our electoral campaign against compulsory Internet censorship, to decriminalize the sale of X-rated films, to enact legislation to protect sex workers from discrimination and to establish a national comprehensive sex education curriculum. We pole danced at bus stops, handed out How To Vote condoms, and launched campaigns from backstage at Miss Centrefold Oceania.

As it turns out, we were far from alone. I saw a senior associate of my former firm while on the husting; he later told me he "Voted for Sex!" I received emails from a barrister in Western Australia with his support and from a social worker in South Australia asking for advice on how to tell her colleagues she was a pole dancer. Turns out there were plenty of pole-dancing lawyers around me. My friend Shimmy joked that she paid her way through pole school by working as a lawyer—and later left the corporate world to open her own studio.

I won't lie. I love the fast-paced, whirlwind opportunities to advocate, but it is a love-hate relationship. It wasn't all golden showers and giggles.

I have now run for Parliament three times—for House of Representatives, Senate, and Lord Mayor of Sydney. When the Sex Party announced me on Facebook as their mayoral candidate in 2012, seventy-five online comments appeared, including:

> "Feminist striptease. Give me a fucking break."
> "It's an oxymoron, stripping is not a feminist act."
> "I can't vote for a rep who is a proud 'feminist stripper' and dresses up like this."
> "Zahra is against women being considered 'objects.' Poses for front cover of Penthouse magazine anyway."
> "Feminism, to me, is about developing higher-order abilities so one doesn't have to rely on materialism/sexuality to survive."
> "How can you be a feminist and a stripper at the same time?"

When you are out as a sex worker, your voice is regularly distorted; your body is considered expendable; your life is treated as public property; your behavior is misinterpreted; and your mind is dismissed as ill informed. Your body bears the brunt of scrutiny as a place where social fears about consumer culture, objectification, and sex acutely intersect.

Journalists demonstrate disregard for the effect of their articles on your personal life and career and, especially when they misquote you or pan down to your diamante stilettos while you are speaking about human rights, reinforce discourses of fetishization, titillation, pathologization, and victimization.

The favorable media I have received is no doubt because I am white, middle class, cisgender, and tertiary educated—my agency is not disputed.

There are opportunities to "sanitize" how I talk about my job. If I am concerned for my safety, unwilling to respond to probing questions, or uncomfortable with strangers accessing my life, I could refer to my work as a dance instructor, a policy officer, trapeze artist. All these things are true. But I also stick lollipops in my cunt, put electrical devices on stranger's genitals, and pose nude in magazines. And I'm proud of it!

Hierarchy comes with the language we use—and our work doesn't need to be "cleaned up" to make it palatable. If you have a problem with sex work, that's your problem. Our movement should not defend certain kinds of sex work whilst stigmatizing others.

This question of reconciling feminism with the sex industry used to interest me. I am grateful I was able to ask sex work 101 questions to peers, mentors, and role models in the industry. They critically informed my politics, challenged my internalized stigma, and gave me a historical, theoretical, and legal context to situate my own practice.

Ten years later, having answered this question repeatedly, it has become a little jading. To put it politely.

Anti-sex work feminist focus on 'raunch culture', 'sexualization' and 'pornification' have been used to call for increased criminalization of our workplaces, clients, and colleagues. They are echoed uncritically throughout popular culture, media, universities, and parliamentary inquiries.

We are luring girls into a triple-X-rated world, perpetuating antifeminist stereotypes, hijacking sexuality, complicit in violence against women. We should wake up. We are traitors, victims, objects, commodities, pornified, sexualized, sexist, postfeminist, low-brow, degraded, clichéd, brainwashed.

These accusations—and their implicit assumptions about what is natural, normal, and feminist—are employed without reference to sex workers' own individual sexualities, identities, politics, strategies, or feminist practices.

They are debilitating. They are depressing. They are relentless.

Of course, I take it personally.

It grates down on me like a war of attrition slowly scraping away the layers of glitter from my skin. I have a physically sick reaction to news reports. The ferocity and violence of abolitionist tactics make me cry. My heart sinks. I have become closed, private, protective of a part of my life that for me has been a refuge.

Nowadays, here is what goes through my head whenever I am

asked this question: Do I have the emotional stability to facilitate a vicious Internet debate? Do I have the time to outline a history of sex-work feminism, queer theory, and the global sex worker rights movement? Do I have the inclination to recount the methodological flaws in nonpeer studies of the sex industry? Why is it my responsibility to defend my profession instead of their job to challenge their prejudice? Will I be further attacked if I even engage in this dialogue? What is the cost?

Managing this stigma on a daily level means that I have become a jaded, resentful, walking encyclopedia. I have a photographic database—bibliography, footnotes, policy messages, statistics—burnt into my brain that I can never afford to switch off.

Stigma forces us to be reactive. And more—it drains vital energy that could actually be invested in creating, dreaming, producing new sexual material, new theoretical paradigms and new kinds of ethical intimacies. This is the worst.

This in turn feeds into ammunition for abolitionist feminists to argue that our industry is narrow, stereotyped, and predictable.

It's not just that these assumptions are offensive. They are dangerous.

Law reform is occurring in every Australian jurisdiction with proposals to criminalize clients/workers/workplaces, remove anti-discrimination protections for sex workers, impose mandatory STI/HIV testing, and require permanent registration on police and government databases. Parts of our community are marginalized by criminal laws, racial profiling, barriers to service provision, lack of funding for peer projects, and excessive policing. Submissions processes are being fuelled by readings of objectification, degradation, rescue, and rehabilitation, rather than informed by sex worker voices, epidemiology, human rights, or United Nations recommended best practices.

Over time, any solid line that ever divided my work and personal identities has slowly eroded. I think, feel, dream, and breathe sex and politics. My house is a library of queer, feminist, and sex worker literature. My work name is now my legal name. I wear Sluts Unite and Feminist Stripper singlets. In porn, I fuck real-life lovers.

I give strangers unsolicited lap dances. I take my work home and I take home to work. I take my ten-inch cocks, pink gloves, and organic lube through X-ray at airport security. For now.

Because being out does not mean that you are invited to dissect our lives to satisfy your own curiosity.

Sex workers are not on call for your university assignment. Our bodies are not open slabs for you to project your opinions, voice your concerns, open up and extract information: Certainly, this has been the hobby of the medical profession, rescue NGOs, and governments.

We are not a walking research project to appease the voyeurism and sexual tourism of middle-class careerist professionals who want access to our sexual communities while avoiding stigma and protecting their reputation.

We are human. We breathe, we bleed, we break.

Being out and proud is a strategy of visibility and activism; it fosters community and belonging, but it is also, for me, a necessity. I am too tired to hide my "lifestyle" because it makes you feel more comfortable. Why should I?

Besides, being out can be such a pleasure. I get to be a queer stripper auntie and buy pole-dancing baby jumpsuits. I am surrounded by a sex worker family who I know are always there for support, advice, and tears. Cute dyke daddies have helped me build stage props, film porn, and been my bouncer at Buck's parties—not that I need one with my killer stilettos! In supportive relationships, I come home and share stories of work to my lovers. Because of my job, I have learned to think critically, love generously, and speak loudly.

Being out is a privilege, sometimes a burden, but also a blessing.

"Porn Star Runs for Parliament" again.

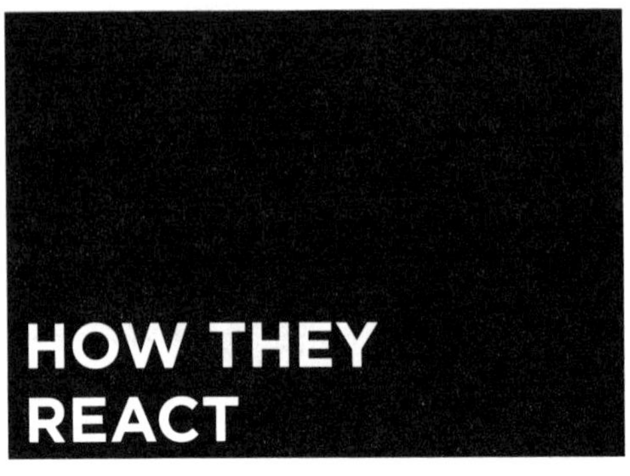

HOW THEY REACT

Zak Sabbath

Zak Sabbath is the porn name of an artist named Zak Smith. They wrote a book called We Did Porn, *which has true stories and pictures in it. His paintings and drawings are held in worldwide major public and private collections, including the Museum of Modern Art and the Whitney Museum of American Art. His other books include* Pictures of Girls *and* Pictures of What Happens on Each Page of Thomas Pynchon's Novel Gravity's Rainbow.

How Your Friends Act

"What's up, Craig?"

"Hey."

"So, what's the score, are you . . . uh . . . coming to samurai night?"

"Am I coming? I don't know, what are we doing?"

"We're gonna . . . uh . . . go to BBQ's and then go watch *Goyokin*."

"'Guy Oakin'? What the fuck is 'Guy Oakin'? Is it, like, gay Finnish porn?"

"Yes, Craig, it is gay Finnish porn, that's what I really want to watch. I want to go to BBQ's and then see mad Finnish loads. All over. Creamy."

"Is there, like, reach-arounds where they're, like, Finnish-ing each other off?"

"That was so stupid."

"Well, what the fuck is it? I don't want to watch Finn fucking."

"Oh, y'know, it's like a fucking samurai movie! You know, there's like vengeance and honor and stuff."

"Is it gonna be like that last one with people rolling around in barrels?"

"I don't fucking know. I haven't seen it. It's a fucking samurai classic or some shit, there's like some fighting in the snow or some shit and a kabuki face."

"A 'kabuki face'?"

"I don't know, I saw a still somewhere. Okay, I got the box. 'A young samurai returns to his home and discovers a higher calling . . . revenge.' Okay? 'Directed by . . . ' Okay? 'Tells the story of a haunted samurai . . . past massacre, revenge . . . . soul.' Another massacre, there's a woman and 'Mango-bei absorbs a truly phenomenal amount of punishment as a way for atoning for the sins of his clan.' See, good, right?"

"And what's it called?"

"*Goyokin*."

"Why is it called *Goyokin*?"

"I have no idea."

"And where are we eating?"

"BBQ's."

"Do I have to wear one of those greasy bibs?"

"I don't know, you wear whatever you want."

"No, but I mean, I'm just saying—"

"What the fuck is wrong with you?"

"No, I'm just saying, if I wear something nice, then are you gonna, like, drool barbecue sauce all over me?"

"I don't know. I have not yet come to a decision about that. Are you coming?"

"I guess. What time is it at?"

"6:30."

"Okay, but if it's fucking Finn porn, I'm not watching you jerk off."

"Get off my phone, you freak."

How Drunk People in Berlin Act

[Eight college guys come into the kebab place where I'm eating a chicken filet and cheese with a side of fries. They all sit around me at my table. They are German and drunk. One Drunk German College Guy grabs the two men on either side of him and explains about how he wants to suck their cocks.]

ZS: "Y'know, when I saw you walk in that's exactly what I thought. I thought: Now, that guy wants to suck some cock."

DGCG: "Yah! Right now! Both of their cocks!"

DGCG2: "Yah! He loves cocks!"

DGCG3: "His cock is also the biggest cock!"

ZS: "Really? I didn't know that."

DGCG: "It is!"

DGCG2: "Yah! You have seen the tower of Alexanderplatz? It is bigger than this size!"

ZS: "That's a large cock."

DGCG: "All of the women, they know about it!"

DGCG3: "It is legend!"

ZS: "That's so strange—it's not in my guidebook . . . "

DGCG2: "It is underground phenomenon! Not for tourists!"

ZS: "His cock? So, if it's so big, how do they know it's his? I mean, they must see it long before they see him. Um, I'm very hungry and if you keep eating my fries, I'll be very upset."

DGCG: "They all know it because I am a porno star!" (He isn't.)

ZS: "Really? I've fucked some porn stars."

All of them stop their drunk munching and look very gravely at me.

DGCG2: "Really?"

DGCG3: "The porrrrrn stars?"

ZS: "Yeah."

DGCG (suddenly friendly): "I am Thomas. I don't know your name!"

How Suzanne's Parents Act

One morning—before shooting starts—around 5:00 a.m., Suzannne calls from her car crying and tells me that "the worst thing" has just happened.

"The worst thing?" I ask.

"They found out," she says.

"Your family? About the porn?"

"They said that . . . "

The theology involved was more complex than the threat, but it involved the staining of the family honor, and murder being acceptable in God's eyes under certain circumstances, and Suzanne being defective from birth. All of these ideas she seems to believe or not believe or repeat or question, like a true sub, depending on who is talking to her. The basic idea is that she would come to live with her family again and not talk to any of her friends again, and then eventually the whole family would move back to Japan, and so she should go out in the car and think, but if she drove away she was disowned, and that, most important, no one else was ever to know about this.

"You should come home, Suzanne."

"He said he saw something, he saw me in something, a clip, I don't know what it could've been—like, he said it was something with cum in it—but I don't think I have any creampies online but—and—and he saw God when he saw it."

"Okay. That's crazy and you should drive away and come back to Los Angeles," I tell her.

"But don't you think that's kind of a scary thing to see God in?" she asks.

"Listen to me, Suzanne, this is important. Are you listening?"

"Uh-huh."

"I think it's very important that you drive home now."

But she stays on the phone, crying and sifting through meaningless arguments, unnoticed, on a street somewhere in Orange County.

"I think my battery's dying," she says.

"Are you sure you don't want us to come get you?"

"No, I'll be okay. I'll just talk to them in the morning."

"Do you think you'll be okay?"

"I think I'll be okay . . . as long as that scarecrow doesn't come any closer."

"Scarecrow?"

"There's a scarecrow on the hill. When I look, it moves closer."

"Suzanne. You're hallucinating and that isn't real."

"It's not real?"

"No, and I think you must be really tired."

"Yeah."

"You think so?"

"Yeah, I'm going to sleep."

"Okay, you sleep, but call again in the morning when you wake up so we know you're okay?"

"Okay."

The opinions expressed here are those of the individual authors and do not necessarily reflect the beliefs of every porn performer or pornographer.

COMING OUT LIKE A PORN STAR *is by no means a comprehensive collection, but the tip of the iceberg on conversations about pornography from the people who have had experienced it first-hand. For more information about the book and its contributors, or to share your own story, please visit ComingOutLikeAPornStar.com.*

Jiz Lee
San Francisco, California
June 2015